CONFRONTING ANIMAL ABUSE

CONFRONTING ANIMAL ABUSE

Law, Criminology, and Human–Animal Relationships

PIERS BEIRNE

ROWMAN & LITTLEFIELD PUBLISHERS, INC.
Lanham • Boulder • New York • Toronto • Plymouth, UK

ROWMAN & LITTLEFIELD PUBLISHERS, INC.

Published in the United States of America
by Rowman & Littlefield Publishers, Inc.
A wholly owned subsidiary of The Rowman & Littlefield Publishing Group, Inc.
4501 Forbes Boulevard, Suite 200, Lanham, Maryland 20706
www.rowmanlittlefield.com

Estover Road
Plymouth PL6 7PY
United Kingdom

British Library Cataloguing in Publication Information Available

Library of Congress Cataloging-in-Publication Data

Confronting animal abuse : law, criminology, and human-animal relationships / Piers
  Beirne.
    p. cm.
  Includes bibliographical references and index.
  ISBN 978-0-7425-4743-8 (cloth : alk. paper) — ISBN 978-0-7425-4744-5 (pbk. : alk.
paper) — ISBN 978-0-7425-9974-1 (electronic)
  1. Animal welfare—Law and legislation. 2. Animal welfare—Law and legislation—
History. 3. Animal welfare—Psychological aspects. 4. Bestiality (Law)
K3620.L39 2009
344.04'9—dc22   2009004788

Printed in the United States of America

⊗ ™ The paper used in this publication meets the minimum requirements of American
National Standard for Information Sciences—Permanence of Paper for Printed Library
Materials, ANSI/NISO Z39.48-1992.

SFI

For Geraldine

CONTENTS

Acknowledgments

THIS BOOK HAS BEEN A LONG WHILE in the making. Its debts are legion, though several deserve special mention here. My first acknowledgment must be to Sibyl Burls, my beloved great-aunt and for four decades a headmistress at a school in London's East End. As a white-attired and broad-hatted suffragette who was once arrested in London for having chained herself in protest to the railings of a government building, Aunt Sibyl was the first person to kindle my interest in rights talk. She did this with a heady brew of anti-Establishment invective, Darjeeling tea, chocolate biscuits, the occasional cigarette, and anecdotes about the respective and sometimes intersecting histories of feminism, human rights, and trade unionism. I regret that I had no opportunity to introduce my aunt Sibyl to those animal beings who have helped sustain me over the years: Lola, Widdle, Max, Bozz, Livvy, Daisy-the-Good-Listener, and Lydia.

I must also mention Professor Alasdair MacIntyre, my tutor in sociology and moral philosophy at Essex University. I especially wish to thank him for a comment he made during a sunny afternoon's walk together on the shores of Merrymeeting Bay in Maine. In the midst of a conversation about the local flora and fauna, I confided to him, a tad nervously, that if I were to continue to use animals as food, then it behooved me to catch and to kill them myself, which I was at that time trying to do with a Boer War–vintage Lee Enfield 303 and a graphite fly rod. Alasdair replied that he thought my new outdoors-to-table practices might be ethically sound, but only on the condition that the deer and the salmon and the trout had exactly the same opportunity to shoot and to hook me as I had with them. At the time, I thought he was pulling a fast one on me. But he wasn't, of course. I hope he will not think that his wise advice has been altogether wasted, even from the relative safety of afar.

Ken Shapiro and Ray Michalowski have nourished me through thick and thin with their old-fashioned and unselfish comradeship. I wish to record that with his organizational skills and depth of commitment to animal rights, Ken Shapiro has been a cornerstone of the emerging movement in human–animal studies. It has been a privilege to witness his marvelous behind-the-scenes encouragement of younger scholars and his founding and editing of new animal-centered journals—all undertaken with great patience and good humor. I must place roughly the same sort of accolade at Ray Michalowski's doorstep, though this would be in testament to his development of critical criminologies rather than human–animal studies. Like Ken Shapiro, Ray has over the years become a cherished colleague and a dear friend. Thanks to both of you for giving me your advice on different aspects of this book and for helping me avoid many a rocky hazard.

Many other colleagues have generously commented on chapters or parts of chapters and at different stages in the book's lengthy period of gestation. Over the years, in this regard, I am indebted to Carol Adams, Virginia DeJohn Anderson, John Archer, Frank Ascione, Simon Beirne, Bonnie Berry, Geertrui Cazaux, Nicholas Canny, Chris Curtin, Amy Fitzgerald, Erica Fudge, Ray Gillespie, Willem de Haan, Jim Messerschmidt, Ian O'Donnell, Nial Osborough, Chris Powell, Tom Regan, Nigel South, Sydney Thomas, and Roger Yates. Because I'm quietly confident that there is someone who is not on this lengthy list who should be, please forgive me if I have forgotten you, gentle reader, and kindly put it down either to my aging memory or to a better excuse if I can come up with it. For whatever other errors remain in this book, it should go without saying that I am their sole author.

Without some measure of relief from the day-to-day or semester-to-semester obligations, however fulfilling and rewarding they may be, of college teaching, it is difficult to write any book. I am therefore most grateful to the College of Arts and Sciences at the University of Southern Maine (my home institution), which has been most generous with the provision of research monies and, especially, with that most precious of resources, time. My colleagues in the Department of Criminology have graciously suffered my absences of late with goodwill and encouragement. I must say, too, that without the energy and sound advice of administrative assistant Rosemary Miller, who is our resident expert on the *Guardian*'s Notes and Queries, I would have routinely floundered quite badly. Two of my students, Rebecca Grotton and Wally Brown, were kind enough to lend me their considerable bibliographic skills just when I needed them.

I am also most grateful for grants and awards, both small and large, and at quite different stages of this project, from the National Endowment for the Humanities, the Clark Foundation for Animal Welfare, and the Humane Society of the United States. In the fall of 2007, a Liberal Arts Fellowship in Sociology and Political Science at the National University of Ireland, Galway (NUIG), helped me research and write the first chapter of this book. I am indebted to Galway's Chris Curtin and Kay Donohue, in particular, for their many courtesies and for the provision of such a wonderful environment in which to work. My task in Galway would have been more onerous had I not enjoyed the superb skills of staff in the NUIG Hardiman Library, especially Marie Boran, Margaret Hughes, and Fergus Fahey in Special Collections.

I must mention with gratitude, too, other library staff who have welcomed me over the years with their hospitality and expertise. Among them are librarians at the Hawthorne-Longfellow Library, Bowdoin College; the British Library of Economic and Political Sciences, LSE; and the Bodleian Library, Oxford University.

Various institutions kindly invited me to give early versions of the chapters in *Confronting Animal Abuse* as seminars and lectures. Among them were University College Cork; Edinburgh University; University of Ghent; University of Iceland; University of Maine; National University of Ireland, Galway; University of New Hampshire; Princeton University; St. Thomas University; Tufts University; and the University of Wales-Bangor. Thanks to all the seminarians, discussants, and other participants there for their good fellowship, constructive criticism, refreshment, and lodging.

I also thank the staff at Rowman & Littlefield, Alex Masulis, Sarah Stanton, and Lynn Weber.

Chapters 3 to 5 first saw the light of day as journal articles. Parts of chapter 3 appeared in *Theoretical Criminology* 1, no. 3 (1997): 317–40, and in the *Journal of Critical Criminology* 10, no. 1 (2001): 43–55; of chapter 4 (originally written with Chris Powell and Roger Yates) in *Society and Animals* 9, no. 1 (2001): 1–23; and of chapter 5 in *Society and Animals* 12, no. 1 (2004): 39–65. I am grateful to their respective journal editors for permission to revise and update these articles for publication here.

The dedication to my wife Geraldine speaks for itself. She is my joy and my sine qua non.

List of Illustrations

Introduction

THIS BOOK REFLECTS A COINCIDENCE in the domain concerns of three movements, namely, animal rights, human–animal studies, and green criminology. Since the mid-1960s, support for animal rights has grown into a large-scale, well-publicized, and theoretically informed social movement. In some parts of the more developed world, the movement's gains seem to have been extraordinary. Among its achievements might be counted its contribution to regulation of the production, transport, and slaughter of cattle and poultry; a gradual decline in the consumption of meat and a concomitant rise in consumption of grains, fruit, and vegetables; stricter controls on animal shelters, zoos, circuses, and aquaria; greater restrictions on the use of vivisection in scientific and commercial laboratories and in schools; a drastic reduction in sales of animal skin and fur; and the protection of endangered species, especially exotica such as whales, wolves, and raptors.

The animal rights movement actually has little by way of an agreed-on theoretical core. Rather, it comprises numerous and often internally conflicting theoretical assumptions and tendencies. Depending on how these are characterized, by whom, and with what intent, they are variously known as animal rights, animal liberation, animal welfare, animal defense, and animal protection. Behind these several pro-animal labels lie very real political, ethical, and moral differences. They include disagreements about the obligations of humans toward animals, about the latter's rights, and about whether and under what circumstances those rights may be overridden.

The key theoretical perspectives within the animal rights movement have emerged from the writings of a small group of moral and legal philosophers.[1] Their chief goals have been, first, to end the practices and ideologies of speciesism and, second, largely through the vehicles of utilitarianism and rights theory, to create a nonspeciesist discourse for the just governance of our relationships with animals. Alongside these founding statements from moral philosophy must be placed pioneering contributions from feminism and from the philosophy of science.[2]

Much of this literature is impaled on a debate that begins with the common rejection of the Cartesian view that animals are machines but that then fractures, sometimes bitterly so, into several camps whose answers to a number of difficult questions are informed by utilitarianism, liberal-rights theory, and feminism. Differences among these pro-animal perspectives are motivated as much by genuine concern for animals as by perennial puzzles about the nature of the good society and of a responsible citizenry. How do animals and humans differ? Are animals' interests in avoiding pain of the same sort as those of humans? Are the grounds for not abusing animals the same as those for not abusing humans?

In the past decade, sometimes in parallel to the animal rights movement and at others from within it, there has emerged a new animal-centered field of human–animal studies. The disciplinary antecedents of this field are moral philosophy, feminism, law, and biology, though the proponents of human–animal studies are also drawn from animal sciences, anthropology, economics, environmental studies, geography, cultural history, literary studies, political science, psychology, sociology, and criminology. Accompanying the intellectual development of the field has been a small flurry of ongoing institutional activity, including dedicated book series; revised reading lists for animal-centered journals, such as *Society & Animals* and *Anthrozoös* and the online journals *Between the Species* and the *Journal for Critical Animal Studies*; and new or repackaged undergraduate courses, a few postgraduate dissertations, and even a small handful of new interdisciplinary degree programs.[3] Evidence of this apparent shift in scholarly attention can be found in small pockets in the United States, the United Kingdom, Belgium, Ireland, Australia, Canada, and New Zealand.

Sociology, nervously abandoning Durkheim's imperialistic dictum in *The Rules of Sociological Method* that the social and cultural realms are autonomous from the biological, has played an at-first precarious but now increasingly prominent role in the development and maintenance of human–animal studies. Beginning with the application of sociological theory to the history and aims of the animal rights movement, these perspectives now include but are by no means limited to social constructivism, intellectual history, social problems, sociolegal theory, ethnography, and ethnomethodology.[4]

Criminology has been slow to respond to these recent developments. Although the several objects of animal rights theory lie squarely within its intellectual and moral compass, criminology as a discipline has generally seemed in a state of denial about animal rights issues or else indifferent to them or even unaware of them.[5] The few apparent exceptions have been marginalized either by the esoteric nature of their subject matter or by their historical specificity or radical political viewpoint.

When animals do appear in criminology, they are almost always passive, insentient objects acted on by humans. Discursively, as objects of human agency, animals reflect or are drawn into some aspect of the complex web of human relationships that is deemed problematic or undesirable. In research on family violence, for example, investigators admit the discursive relevance of animal abuse but tend not to perceive the physical, psychological, or emotional abuse of animals as objects of study in their own right. In the literature on rapists and serial murderers, as another example, animals acquire significance only as preassaultive or prehomicidal signs of interhuman conflict. Animal abuse has little or no significance, presumably, because it is seen not as "real" crime but rather as a minor offense against property.

Animals' role as the property of humans tends to be their master status in criminology. In part, this reflects their status in anticruelty statutes, for example, and in other dividing practices where a human community's moral standards are invoked to support legalistic norms about acceptable and unacceptable treatment of animals. Animals typically enter criminology as objects whose property identity has been stolen, poached, damaged, held as ransom, rustled, or otherwise misappropriated or spoiled. It is in such cases, when the primary attribute of animals is their status as property or commodities, that the harms that are inflicted on them are the least visible. Nowhere is this more striking than in the Federal Bureau of Investigation's annual *Uniform Crime Reports*, which, though they include no data at all on crimes against animals, do refer—next to "office equipment" and "televisions"—to the proprietary items of "livestock" and "clothing and furs" within the category "Type and Value of Property Stolen and Recovered."[6]

As property, animals enter criminological discourse in diverse ways. They do so, for example, as momentary stage props in historical treatises on crime and criminal justice. Deer, for example, have appeared as written evidence ("the taking of deer") in a search for the authentic Robin Hood in fourteenth-century England, horses as sheriffs' transport harnessed for purposes of policing in early colonial America, and steers as an occupational definer ("cattlemen") in the denomination of conflict between white settlers in Wyoming. Horses, again, have entered criminology as the objects of deviant practices by owners, trainers, jockeys, and punters at racetracks, where they are the source of profits, purses, wages, and winnings. In some cases horses as objects occupy quite prominent places in the history of criminology, as in uses made of criminal biographies by Edwin Sutherland and others from the 1930s onward. As property, too, animals appear at different points in the food chain of carnivorous societies. In this guise, they appear in studies of aristocratic hunting and poaching, where their deaths serve for young males as adolescent rites of passage and as substitutes for war; of gamekeepers and of ecological law enforcement; of deterrence, when their survival or death is used to test the effect of hunting laws on the poaching of game; of gun ownership, when rural gun owners are distinguished from urban gun owners because many of the former are hunters who own rifles; and of the meat and poultry industries, when their quantity or quality as commodities may signify theft, fraud, or deceptive advertising. Animals also appear in studies of class, gender, cultural, and other practices to do with the appropriation of animals from the "wild"; and of the utility of law, of gamekeepers, and of ecological police set against the desired health and size of animal populations.

Marshall Clinard's *The Black Market* is a classic example of just this. Clinard's focus was white-collar crimes associated with the slaughter and distribution of meat in the context of the system of meat rationing that existed in the United States during World War II. Yet the animals in his analysis appear only as commodities that arrive in supermarkets and butchers as neatly wrapped packages of flesh and that can be had for tickets in coupon books. Nowhere did Clinard consider whether, before the rationed carcasses of these animals were distributed, white-collar executives or slaughterhouse workers had participated in cruel practices against them (or what those practices might be). This said, it is thus the ideational pressures around meat consumption in a time of national emergency that also need to be investigated. As Carol Adams argues in her book *The Sexual Politics of Meat*, in a society where meat consumption has always been very much a masculine activity, government rationing policies reserved a consistent supply of meat for U.S. soldiers, who were the epitome of masculine men during World War II.[7]

Other examples of the positing of animals as property are found in the voluminous research on game laws and the crime of poaching in eighteenth-century England. Analytically, animals enter this social history as they existed in the eyes of English society itself, namely, as the private property of the landed gentry and the monied classes and, therefore, as coveted and contested objects of law. The function and position of animals in this can be illustrated by Douglas Hay's history of the enforcement of the English game laws against poachers on Cannock Chase, an area of heath and woodland between Stoke and Birmingham in the English midlands.[8] Hay shows that game were enmeshed in a complex web of attitudes in rural society that reflected a variety of social conflicts and alliances among the rural gentry, justices of the peace, servants, gamekeepers, warreners, poachers, black marketers, and the poverty-stricken masses. This rich cast of characters interacted with animals only in the sense that the latter existed as objects and prizes of class struggles. Thus, the fact that rabbits, hare, deer, pheasants, and partridges ("game") were netted, snared, attacked with razors, and shot is not regarded as significant. For eighteenth-century English society and so too for Hay, the peculiar significance of objects, such as sides of venison, is that they represented in rural society no more than tokens of social position. As Hay records,

> Game was a special currency of class based on the solid standard of landed wealth, untainted by the commerce of the metropolis. It could be spent lavishly at dinners in order to command esteem, or given to others to mark important relationships: to inferiors as an indulgence, to superiors as a mark of respect. The significance attached to it could create long, rancorous disputes over apparent trivialities.[9]

Only rarely have animals been understood in criminology other than in terms of their legal status as the property of human masters. One exception that merits attention is John Archer's study of animal maiming in nineteenth-century Norfolk, Suffolk, and parts of Cambridgeshire. In that its explicit focus is animal suffering, Archer's study is a self-conscious corrective to the standard works on rural protest that acknowledge the existence of a crime that was forbidden by the Act to Prevent the Cruel and Improper Treatment of Cattle (1822) but that at the same time do so perfunctorily and in misleading ways. As Archer points out, social historians have been reticent to deal with the crime of animal maiming because they assume that nothing further could be said about an isolated crime largely involving the hamstringing and the hocking of the forelegs of cattle.[10]

Contrary to the traditional view that animal maiming was simply a vicious form of rebellion by rural laborers against the landed gentry, Archer shows how in practice it was a peculiar, complex, and quite varied activity. It was sometimes undoubtedly a form of social rebellion, as in the maiming of their masters' horses by horsekeepers. Typically, however, animal maiming was a form of psychological terror, of symbolic murder, that resulted from personal feuds between members of the same social class. Thus, the maiming of donkeys and asses tended to indicate a dispute between one craftsperson and another—such as blacksmiths, cordwainers, butchers, and laborers—since they were the chief owners of such animals. But the poisoning of cats and dogs suggests a conflict between farmers and gamekeepers over the rearing of game birds.[11] Moreover, Archer shows that there was great variety in the method of maiming, in the choice of target, and in the ownership of the maimed animals. Referring to "those acts of mutilation that outraged people's sensibilities more than any other form of maiming," Archer describes cases where two-foot knotted sticks were thrust into mares' wombs, which were then vigorously rented ("a nine-year-old boy found guilty of such a crime at Nayland in 1842"); where the penises of cart horses and donkeys were cut off; or that of "labourer Robert Key of Reydon, Suffolk, who tore out a sheep's entrails with his bare hands from the hind parts of the animal."[12]

Archer's study of animal maiming represents one of the all-too-rare analyses that challenge the notion that animals are simply commodities of human owners. Besides showing how complex a crime animal maiming can be, Archer's sensitive investigation diverts attention from the social relations between maimers and owners and directs it, instead, toward the plight of the suffering animals themselves.

There have been signs of late that the lengthy scholarly neglect of animal abuse in sociology and criminology may be ending. For example, in 2004, a chapter titled "The Greening of Criminology" appeared in a popular British criminology text.[13] Although green criminology is defined there as the study of "crimes against the environment,"[14] there is much discussion of crimes and other harms to animals, including the poisoning of cattle during the 1984 Bhopal disaster in India, the illegal trawling for salmon and other fish in seas off Alaska, crimes of species decline, and the resurgence of animal spectacles for entertainment purposes, including dog-fights and badger baiting.

In 2007, Nigel South and I edited a collection of thirteen original essays—*Issues in Green Criminology*—that addressed such diverse topics as animal rights and animal abuse; the techniques used to identify or label

animals, such as branding, tattooing, ear tagging, radio collaring, the ampu-
tation of toes and radio transponders; the case for the abolition of vivisection; the competing images of human–animal relationships in the online
public marketplace; food crime; and conflicts over fisheries. Other essays
in *Issues in Green Criminology* were concerned less with animals, as such,
than with various aspects of ecology and the environment. But these envi-
ronmentalist essays frequently touched on animals and animal abuse, too,
because animals also live in environments and because their environments
are sometimes degraded by environmental disasters. Sometimes, environmental disasters occur naturally, as is the case with earthquakes, tsunamis,
and hurricanes. At other times, though, animals' environments are harmed
and destroyed through human-made actions, including global warming,
agribusiness, toxic dumping, and road construction.

A green criminology has a valuable role to play in the development
of human–animal studies.[15] As a harm-based discourse, green criminology
seeks to uncover the sources and forms of power and social inequality and
their ill effects. As such, it examines the whys, the hows, and the whens of
the generation and control of the many aspects of social harm—including
abuse, exclusion, pain, injury, and suffering. Its natural contribution to
human–animal studies is therefore the study of harms committed by humans against animals. By way of shorthand, for the moment, these harms
can be termed "animal abuse."

Law, Cruelty, and Animal Abuse

What counts as animal abuse varies enormously both between cultures and
within any given culture over time. This variation also naturally applies
to the understanding of related practices like "cruelty" and "neglect" and
the much visited notion of "rights." With respect to its cross-cultural and
historical variation, animal abuse is no different than child abuse, woman
abuse, or bias and hate crimes.

What counts as "animal" in the concept of animal abuse? The answers
that have been given to this question are many and varied. Omitting some
of the more outrageous religious claims, we can begin by admitting the
obvious if rather unhelpful fact that animals are not humans. That said,
among the characteristics that have been said to distinguish animalness
from humanness are the inability of animals to feel pain, at least at the
lower levels of the phylogenetic scale; animals' lower levels of sentience
and consciousness; their inability to use tools; their unawareness of their
own impending deaths; their inability to sing, to speak in language, or

to engage with their fellows in musical harmony; animals' faces and skin differing from those of humans; animals' inability to feel shame or embarrassment when they are naked in front of others or when they urinate or defecate in public; and their inability to inherit property or to bequeath it. Yet most of the alleged differences between animals and humans have no basis in fact. Most are altogether false.

In the United States today, the content of animal abuse is specified in a mass of federal and state legislation, according to which animals can be personal or public property, hazards, nuisances, and victims of ecological crimes and cruelty. Current legislation includes the Federal Meat Inspection Act (1958), the Humane Slaughter Act (1958), the Animal Welfare Act (1966 [as amended, 1970, 1976, 1985, 1990]), the Endangered Species Act (1969), the Horse Protection Act (1970), the Wild Horses and Burros Act (1971), the Marine Mammal Protection Act (1972), the Toxic Substances Control Act (1976), the Food Security Act (1985), the Health Research Extension Act (1985), the Improved Standards for Laboratory Animals Act (1985), and the Pet Protection Act (1990). In addition to this legislation, all fifty states have now enacted anticruelty statutes. While these latter vary considerably in how they define crucial terms like "animal" and "cruelty," they generally recognize that animals ought to be protected from cruelty, from abandonment, and from poisoning and that they must be provided with necessary sustenance, including food, water, and shelter. However, a majority of state anticruelty statutes still define the acts of commission and omission that constitute cruelty to animals as misdemeanors rather than felonies.[16]

Can criminal law provide an objective basis for the study of animal abuse? How are animals constituted in this legislation? How are their interests secured by it? If it is proper to regard the intentional infliction of pain on animals as a form of abuse, then consider the status of the two chief legislative controls in this regard, namely, the U.S. Animal Welfare Act (1966, as amended) and individual state anticruelty statutes. The U.S. Animal Welfare Act, first, was enacted "to ensure that animals intended for use in research facilities . . . are provided humane care and treatment" (s.1, b.3). Although long-standing controversy exists both about the morality of using animals in scientific research and about the number of animals involved,[17] the fact remains that a large number—perhaps many millions—of animals are used in experiments in which they are burned, scalded, probed, and injected with substances, blinded, and otherwise mutilated, often without anesthesia. Although under the terms of the act some of this pain is excusable because it is deemed necessary for advancing knowledge of cures and treatment for diseases and injuries that affect both humans and animals, no such anthropocentric utilitarianism should be uncritically appropriated as the basis for determining what, for objective scholarly purposes, constitutes animal abuse.

In regard to animal abuse and cruelty, consider for a moment the great diversity of how "animal" is defined in the animal abuse statutes of several states in the United States:

A vertebrate living creature not a human being, but does not include fish. (Alaska)

Animal includes every "dumb creature." (California)

Cruelty to Animals in the First Degree, specifically limited to causing animals "to fight for pleasure or profit" protects four-legged animals; Cruelty to animals in the second degree protects any animal. (Kentucky)

Animal means every living, sentient creature not a human being. (Maine)

For purposes of this section, animal shall be defined as a mammal. (Missouri)

Animal means a domesticated living creature and wild creature previously captured. Animal does not include an uncaptured living creature. (Texas)

According to these definitions of animal cruelty, the most generous to animals is found in Maine, though even there no formal guidance is offered about the meaning of "sentient creature." The worst is Texas, which protects only domesticated animals. In between are Missouri, which protects mammals only; Alaska, which covers vertebrates but not fish; California, which borrows a page from seventeenth-century Nonconformism by covering "all dumb creatures"; and Kentucky, which bars animals from being forced to fight (if two legged) and any animal (undefined) from cruelty. It is obviously preferable not to be a cock in Kentucky, a reptile in Missouri, or a nondomesticated animal in Texas.

Rather than rehearse the language of each of the fifty state anticruelty statutes one by one, one can instead refer to the practices criminalized by the American Law Institute's Model Penal Code of 1980. The code provides that a misdemeanor is committed if any person purposely or recklessly

(1) subjects any animal to cruel mistreatment;
(2) or subjects any animal in his custody to cruel neglect;
(3) or kills or injures any animal belonging to another without legal privilege or consent of the owner' (§250.11).

The code's anticruelty provisions harbor several difficulties. First, its language and terms of reference are most vague. Thus, §250.11 of the code altogether fails to define such crucial terms as "animal," "cruel," "mistreatment," "neglect," and "injury." While imprecision in the term "animal" creates no overwhelming definitional problem except for those unfortunate creatures at the lower end of the phylogenetic scale,[18] the vague character of the other language is a serious practical and analytical problem if the study of animal abuse is to be approached through the lens of criminal law. What, exactly, constitutes "cruel mistreatment" and "cruel neglect," for example? Why is the term "injury" exclusively confined to physiological harm rather than expanded to embrace other harmful conditions undoubtedly experienced by nonhuman animals—mammals, most obviously—such as prolonged suffering and psychological distress?

Moreover, while the code (and most other anticruelty statutes) excludes from its scope accepted veterinary practices and activities carried on for scientific research, it implicitly licenses any abusive treatment of animals that is not perceived as cruel by community sensibilities. To the code's drafters, the purpose of anticruelty statutes has never been to create a direct duty to exercise care toward animals as such but rather to prevent outrage to the sensibilities of the community. Also exempt from the code, therefore, are the branding, castration, and killing of animals for food—practices that, in the United States alone, are applied to 9 billion farm animals annually.[19] Again, cruelty may be inflicted on animals in the course of training, governing, and disciplining them, provided that it is not "excessive"; deadly physical force may also be used both against one's own animal, even if the death is unnecessary, provided that the killing is done "humanely," and against the animals of others if they threaten property, however trivial. Moreover, even if particular acts of animal abuse are defined as cruel or otherwise illegal, detection of them is quite rare, and prosecution and conviction are very difficult.

None of the deaths or painful practices inflicted on animals by humans and listed here violates anticruelty statutes. None of them therefore necessarily involves a crime as such. But precisely because so many human practices that are harmful to animals lie outside the scope of existing criminal law, the latter is far too narrow a basis for the study of animal abuse. In other words, animals remain without standing in a sort of legal and moral wilderness.

So far from being a useful device for the study of animal abuse, criminal law is a major impediment to this endeavor.

The Contents of This Book

Both chapter 1 and chapter 2 began as part of an enthusiastic if rather naive quest on my part to respond to the question, When, where, and under what circumstances was the first legislation enacted to protect animals from cruelty? Quite different answers to this question have been given by the small handful of historians who have responded to it. Some have said that the first such law was the Ill-Treatment of Cattle Act (Britain, 1822), otherwise known as the Martin Act, so named for its crusading champion Richard "Humanity Dick" Martin, the Irish Member of Parliament for Galway. The Ill-Treatment of Cattle Act penalized with a fine or imprisonment anyone who cruelly beat cattle. Its enactment was accompanied in 1824 by the introduction of a policing machinery, the Society (later, Royal) for the Prevention of Cruelty to Animals, though its effectiveness, however understood, in enforcing the 1822 act, has yet to be properly documented.

The 1822 act was preceded by three other legislative devices, each of which seems to have addressed animal cruelty. One was a little-known state law enacted in the United States in Maine in 1821. A section within Maine's code of that year forbade intentional cruelty to the horses, sheep, or cattle of another; on conviction, first-time offenders were to be punished either with a fine or with up to six months' imprisonment. In addition, at least two seventeenth-century laws explicitly expressed their opposition to animal cruelty as one of their stated justifications. One was enacted in 1635 in English-dominated Ireland and the other in 1641 in the Massachusetts Bay Colony. Chapter 1 ("Against Cruelty? Understanding the Act Against Plowing by the Tayle") and chapter 2 ("The Prosecution of Animal Cruelty in Puritan Massachusetts, 1636–1683") examine the emergence and the meaning of these two latter, premodern laws, enacted, respectively, in Ireland and in colonial America. To date, very little indeed is known about either law. As such, I believe that both individually and together, these opening historical chapters have something to contribute to our understanding of the variety of conjunctures and trajectories— pro-animal or otherwise—into which notions of cruelty and abuse can emerge and be formalized in law.

Chapter 1 examines the emergence in 1635 of the Act Against Plowing by the Tayle and Pulling the Wooll Off Living Sheep (to give the act its official title). By way of introduction, stripped of all subtleties and complexities, it can be said that in the midst of a situation of great military, economic, and cultural oppression, the English conquerors used the 1635 Act to criminalize the actions of those poor Irish farmers who used horses' tails to plow. However, did the act criminalize this practice because it was seen as cruel? If so, then by whom? Whose interests did criminalization serve? Were the act's provisions enforced? What were its consequences for the lives of animals?

Chapter 2 examines what was intended by the Massachusetts Puritans when in 1641 the colony formally enacted "Of the Bruite Creature" (Liberties 92 and 93 of *The Body of Liberties of 1641*). "Of the Bruite Creature" stated, "No man shall exercise any Tirranny or Crueltie towards any bruite Creature which are usuallie kept for man's use." What can we learn from "Of the Bruite Creature" about attitudes toward human–animal boundaries? Did its moral horizons herald a genuinely progressive, pro-animal trajectory? How was it enforced, if at all?

It is not only their chronological proximity that makes examination of these two legislative devices so compelling. Both the 1635 Irish act and the 1641 "Of the Bruite Creature" share the same intriguing difficulty of trying to understand the intentions of those who drafted their respective provisions. One possible if inevitably limited solution to this difficulty is to uncover how strictly each law was enforced (if, indeed, they were enforced at all). Were offenders prosecuted and punished for their misdeeds? With what consequences for humans and for animals? Regrettably, there are no available judicial records of violations of the provisions of the 1635 Act. This means that it is nearly impossible to assess its framers' intentions and seriousness if, in principle, these would have in practice been reflected in their bearers' willingness to seek out, prosecute, and punish offenders. But it just so happens that what one law lacks altogether, the other does seem to have, if in rather limited supply; that is, there is a potentially very useful set of judicial records with which we may be able to assess the enforcement of "Of the Bruite Creature," namely, the *Records and Files of the Quarterly Courts of Essex County Massachusetts, 1636–1683*.

In some respects, the historical tone of the first two chapters is continued in chapter 3 ("Toward a Sociology of Animal Sexual Assault"). It, too, asks why it is that certain human–animal relationships (I use the term "relationship" here quite loosely, at least for the moment) and not others have been criminalized and decriminalized and even recriminalized.

The chapter can best be introduced by confiding that almost a decade ago, at the end of a lecture on the sociology of bestiality that I had just delivered to an audience of veterinarians and graduate students at Tufts University, a somewhat agitated middle-aged woman who, identifying herself as a farmer who was in the business of breeding cattle, demanded to know my opinion of her practice of extracting semen from bulls by electronic stimulation. Was her animal husbandry "bestiality"? Almost needless to say, I had never imagined such a scenario before and had no idea whatsoever of how to respond to the question. I therefore mumbled something about what a good question this was and that, if she did not mind, I would get back to her later when I had had more time to compose an appropriate answer. This chapter contains my belated response to her question, unsatisfying though she still may find it.

Chapter 3 introduces a view of bestiality that differs radically from both the anthropocentrism enshrined in the dogma of Judeo-Christianity and also the pseudoliberal tolerance fashionable today. I argue, in part against Peter Singer, the renowned author of the book *Animal Liberation*, that bestiality should best not be tolerated at all. This is so because it is actually a form of sexual assault. Animal sexual assault should not be tolerated because human–animal sexual relations almost always involve coercion, because such practices often cause animals pain and even death, and because animals are unable either to communicate consent to us in a form that we can readily understand or to speak out about their abuse.

The chapter also assesses the fragmented claims of psychiatry, sexology, and sociolegal studies about the prevalence of animal sexual assault and how it is structured by relations of age, gender, social class, and geographical location. In so doing, it offers a tentative typology of the forms of animal sexual assault, including commodification, adolescent sexual experimentation, aggravated cruelty, and zoophilia.

To a certain extent, each of the first three chapters uncovers the politics of selectivity that is always at the heart of any given criminalization process. Which species are positively valued? Which are deemed worthy of legal protection? Which species are excluded from the circle of moral consideration? Chapter 4 ("Horse Maiming and the Sport of Kings") continues this line of inquiry. It is a revised version of an essay originally written with my colleagues Roger Yates and Chris Powell. It considers the public and media indifference toward the numerous harms inflicted on horses used in racing who have their tendons "fired," the hundreds of horses who are quietly and without protest annually "put down" after having "fallen" on racetracks, often breaking their legs, and then shipped to abattoirs. This indifference is juxtaposed with the focus of the chapter, namely, the noisy, well-publicized moral panic in 1990s rural Hampshire about gentry- and middle-class-owned horses who were hideously maimed by unknown assailants. The societal reaction to these continuing horse assaults is a rare example of a moral panic about crime and deviance in which animals other than humans occupy—or seemed to occupy—the central role of victim.

The nature of the relationships between humans and animals is revealed through authoritative utterances about offenders and victims by the mass media, by the police, and by the concerned citizens who felt they had a stake in the horses' well-being. Analysis of how and when victimhood is ascribed to animals helps uncover the invisible assaults routinely inflicted on them—in the name of business or pleasure, for example—and against whose human perpetrators the categories of criminalization are almost never applied.

Chapter 5 ("Is There a Progression from Animal Abuse to Interhuman Violence?") offers a largely sympathetic examination of what is currently known about a central aspect of the claimed-for link between animal abuse and interhuman violence. Specifically, it reviews evidence of a progression from one to the other. The progression thesis depends on the successful combination of two quite separate causal propositions: that those who abuse animals are more likely subsequently to act violently toward humans and that those who act violently toward humans are more likely previously to have abused animals. How robust and persistent is the association in each of these propositions? If the associations are indeed strong ones and if there is a progression from one to the other, then how is this link to be explained?

The chapter is set in the context of a widespread reluctance to debate the theoretical adequacy of concepts like animal abuse and animal cruelty. As such, in a way that sits well with the rest of the book, the chapter concludes that a properly well-rounded account of the progression thesis should be sought not only in the personal biographies of those individuals who abuse animals but also in those institutionalized social practices where animal abuse is routine, widespread, and socially acceptable.

In an epilogue, finally, I draw together and make explicit some of the several threads that run through the previous chapters. At the same time, I take the opportunity to revisit the contribution of animal rights to some of the concerns of the developing field of green criminology.

A Note on Speciesist Language

As a form of animal abuse, speciesist language is an ubiquitous institution-alized social practice that much merits an introductory comment. The dictum that we are all prisoners of our language is not generally recognized as inhering in descriptions of animals and of human–animal interaction. In the same way that we are today attuned to use language that is neutral with respect to gender, race, age, and physical and mental disability, for example, so we also need to develop an awareness of speciesist language. However, as will soon become clear, my intentions in this regard have met with only limited success: it is one thing to identify speciesist language and quite another successfully to escape its clutches.

The somewhat clumsy term "speciesist language" may be defined as utterances that express a prejudice or attitude of bias in favor of one's own species and against those of members of other species. In this definition, I follow the general though not altogether unproblematic direction of its popularizer Peter Singer, who has written that the term refers to the view that "species membership is, *in itself*, a reason for giving more weight to the interests of one being than to those of another."[20]

Historically, the distinction between *Homo sapiens* and animals carries with it a cumbersome cultural baggage. Implicitly, it tends to be voiced as if humans were somehow not animals and as if all nonhuman animals were *insapient* ("dumb animals"). At root, the distinction is based on the prejudice that nonhuman animals are necessarily the Other. At times, this Other is viewed as the embodiment of virtue. Thus, at least since classical antiquity, humans have anthropomorphized their deities, among whose numerous emblems are the eagle of Jupiter, the owl of Minerva, and the serpent of Aesculapius. At other times, the animal Other is assigned to the nether regions since it is of course not only to gods that theriomorphic symbols have been attached but also to devils. Indeed, the earliest known usage of the word "animal" referred to diabolical or inferior traits typically associated with the Devil, with the Antichrist, and with feral animals.

These traits of the animal Other included—and in many respects still do—uncleanliness, irrationality, untrustworthiness, lust, greed, and the potential for sudden violence. According to the *Oxford English Dictionary*, the Latin words *anima* ("spirit" or "breath") and *animal* probably entered old English as *beste* or *beast* from the French *bête*, which in turn likely derived from the Sanskrit "that which is to be feared."[21] The Devil's earthly manifestations have been held to include animals such as snakes, cats, toads, goats, and, more imaginatively, dragons and vampires. These occur not only in the Homeric myths and in the Icelandic sagas but also in our own fairy tales and morality plays. To mention but one example from this list of satanic animals, cats have traditionally been invested with a cultural repertoire of deep symbolic significance. They have been held to be in league with the Devil, and their occult powers were to be feared by sensible folk. At medieval carnivals, cats were thrown onto bonfires in the belief that this would bring good luck. In an episode recounted by the Enlightenment historian Robert Darnton, one night in Paris in the late 1730s, a group of young male printer's apprentices administered the last rites to several offending cats owned and adored by their master's wife, strung them up on an improvised gallows, hanged them, and then erupted into gales of joyful laughter.[22] To understand their merriment, we need to know that the vengeful apprentices suffered appalling working conditions, including being fed far less well than Madame's cats. The cat massacre was a low-risk method of causing great emotional distress to Madame and to her husband. Because cats have long represented female genitalia and so too have been associated with the cuck-olding of men, to the apprentices the killing of her cats was thus to take exquisite revenge on Madame and on her as her husband's property. The occasion was thus worthy of joyous celebration.

Modern societies, too, continue to be saturated with speciesist social practices, among them words and phrases that derive from dubious animal images and metaphors. In this regard, the English language is richly en-dowed with attributions to animals of deviant and criminal characteristics. Indeed, in the dog-eat-dog world of our rat race, we fret about bats out of hell and deride those who are as crazy as cuckoos, loons, or coots and who are as mad as March hares. We refer to sly or cunning foxes (especially when they "steal" chickens or "fleece" their prey) and to rogue elephants, black sheep, dirty or traitorous rats, murderous hyenas, and thieving mon-keys and jackdaws. Moreover, speciesist terms of derogation are increas-ingly lodged in the discourse of descriptions of violent criminals, such as serial murderers, mass murderers, rapists, and child molesters ("animals" one and all). In June 2007, the outgoing British prime minister, Tony Blair, blamed the media for having contributed to his political downfall, complaining aggressively about the media's declining standards, stating that they hunted in packs and acted like feral beasts.[23]

The often-violent images and metaphors of speciesist language are saturated with implicit declarations about how worthwhile lives differ from lives with little or no intrinsic value. For example, we refer without hesitation to humans as human "beings"—a symbolic term of personhood denoting volitional and sentient forms of life with self-consciousness and with bundles of rights and obligations that are worthy of respect. But we rarely if ever refer to nonhuman animals as "animal beings." Rather, they are named simply as "animals"—the Other—an implicitly derogatory term synonymous with the notion that they are altogether different from hu-mans and, as such, necessarily less important than humans and less worthy of consideration and respect.

Humans, instead, tend to be understood as complex creatures whose gender is an important item in forms of address. For example, we refer to Jane Smith as "*Ms*. Smith," to Jack Jones as "*Mr*. Jones," and to "*she* who . . ." or "*he* who . . ." Except for animals appointed as companions ("pets"), however, nonhuman animals are seen as undifferentiated objects each of whom is normally identified not as a "she" or a "he" but as an "it" ("*it* which . . ."). Speciesism and sexism clearly often operate together and in tandem, with women and nonhuman animals depicted as objects to be controlled, manipulated, and exploited. Thus, when men describe women as "cows," "bitches," "(dumb) bunnies," "birds," "chicks," "foxes," and "fresh meat" and their genitalia as other species, they use derogatory language essentially to relegate both women and animals to the inferior statuses of "less than male" and, even, "less than human."

Some forms of speciesist language are seemingly more subtle. These often hinge on animals' master status as the property of humans. "Fisheries," for example, refers not to an objective ontological reality but to diverse species that are acted on as objects of commodification by humans and, as such, trapped or otherwise "harvested," killed, and consumed. The same sort of egregious misdescription appears in many other categories as well, including "laboratory animals" (instead of "animals used in laboratories"), "pets," "circus animals," and "racehorses." The last of these, to offer another example, misdescribes as "racehorses" those horses who are used by humans to race against each over tracks and on courses (a misdescription that is specifically explored in chapter 4). In fact, they are horses *used* as racehorses. Clearly, radical revision of speciesist language is long overdue. In some cases, new descriptions altogether are needed— for example, misothery for hatred of and contempt for animals,[24] animal sexual assault for bestiality, and theriocide for the killing of nonhuman animals by humans.

But the central juxtaposition, namely, that between humans and all other animals, seems quite a hard one to avoid. Several attempts have been made to overcome it, including "nonhuman animals," a term that has been in vogue among many members of the animal protection community. Other candidates include the rather cumbersome "animals other than humans" (the preferred usage in the journal *Society & Animals*) and, derivative of this, Geertrui Cazaux's clever if obscure acronym "aothas" (animals other than human animals).[25]

However, set against the obvious errors embedded in the dichotomous phrase "human/animal," neither of its two erstwhile alternatives manages quite to escape the clutches of speciesism either. In a sort of Wittgensteinian vicious circle, both fail for precisely the same reason. Thus, while the term "nonhuman animals" is a welcome reminder that the terrain of human–animal relationships is marked by speciesist language, to speak of "*nonhuman* animals" is ironically to privilege humans, for it defines all animals other than *Homo sapiens* as lacking in certain qualities that allegedly inhere only in humans. Put another way, the phrase "nonhuman animals" involves rather the same sort of error as if we were to speak of (human) women as nonmale humans. For the very same reason, the acronym "aotha" also fails to avoid the embrace of speciesism.

So, what is to be done? Unsatisfactory though it might be, my own practice is initially to juxtapose "humans" with "nonhuman animals" and then, at a suitably proximate point, to attach "(hereinafter, 'animals')" after the term "nonhuman animals." This might look like a lot of effort to arrive at a point no further than the one of departure. But the jarring effects of the journey are well worth it, especially if our fellow creatures are thereby accorded more respect.

Notes

1. Somewhat invidiously, I should mention as among the most influential texts Stanley Godlovich, Roslind Godlovitch, and John Harris, eds. (1974), *Animals, Men and Morals*; Peter Singer (1975), *Animal Liberation*; Stephen Clark (1977), *The Moral Status of Animals*; Tom Regan (1983), *The Case for Animal Rights*; Gary Francione (2004), *Animals, Property and the Law*; and Gary Francione (2008), *Animals as Persons*.

2. See Josephine Donovan (1990), "Animal Rights and Feminist Theory"; Josephine Donovan and Carol J. Adams (1996), *Beyond Animal Rights: A Feminist Caring Ethic for the Treatment of Animals*; Carol J. Adams (1994), *Neither Man nor Beast: Feminism and the Defense of Animals*; Carol J. Adams (2003), *The Sexual Politics of Meat: A Feminist-Vegetarian Critical Theory*; Carol J. Adams and Josephine Donovan, eds. (1995), *Animals and Women: Feminist Theoretical Explorations*; Barbara Noske (1997), *Beyond Boundaries: Humans and Other Animals*; Joan Dunayer (2004), *Speciesism*; Donna Haraway (2004), *The Haraway Reader*; Robert Garner (2005), "Feminism and Animals"; and Josephine Donovan (2006), "Feminism and the Treatment of Animals: From Care to Dialogue."

3. By one estimate, there are more than 110 university and college courses in the United States with "Animals and Society" as one of their themes, representing more than twenty academic disciplines (Alagappan [2003], "Expanding Humane Education: The Development of 'Animals and Society' Courses in Liberal Arts Colleges").

4. Moreover, exceeding the requisite minimum of 300 signatories, "Animals and Society" has recently achieved full section status within the American Sociological Association. Sociologists have also contributed frequently to the journal *Society & Animals*, which celebrated its fifteenth anniversary in 2007.

5. See especially Robert Agnew (1997), "The Causes of Animal Abuse: A Social-Psychological Analysis," and Stanley Cohen (2001), *States of Denial: Knowing about Atrocities and Suffering*, pp. 205, 289.

6. Federal Bureau of Investigation (2008), *Uniform Crime Reports: Crime in America*. Available at http://www.fbi.gov/ucr/07cius.

7. Adams, *The Sexual Politics of Meat*, p. 32.

8. Douglas Hay (1975), "Poaching and the Game Laws on Cannock Chase."

9. Hay, "Poaching and the Game Laws on Cannock Chase," p. 246.

10. John Archer (1990), *By a Flash and a Scare: Incendiarism, Animal Maiming and Poaching in East Anglia 1815–1870*. Archer argues about social historians that "they feel little sympathy with, let alone understand, the perpetrators of such 'abominable acts.' The maimers were and are seen as perverted and inexplicably cruel. It takes little imagination on the reader's part to re-enact, let us say, the stabbing of a carthorse with a dung fork. . . . While it is difficult to conceal a sense of outrage when reading of the many and varied tortures the animals had to suffer, moral outrage on the historian's part does not add to our understanding of this crime" (p. 198).

11. Archer, *By a Flash and a Scare*, pp. 209–10.

12. Archer, *By a Flash and a Scare*, p. 210. Archer concludes by invoking greater sympathy for the maimers than for the maimed animals. "Before historians shudder at these violent deaths of animals and pass moral value judgements on the maimers," he writes, "they should remember that the maimers often had grievances and that the death of an animal was, perhaps, preferable to the murder of a human being" (p. 221).

13. E. Carrabine, P. Iganski, M. Lee, K. Plummer, and N. South (2004), *Criminology: A Sociological Introduction*.

14. Carrabine et al., *Criminology*, p. 313.

15. Accounts of the history and content of green criminology can be found in Nigel South and Piers Beirne (2006), "Introduction to Green Criminology," and Piers Beirne and Nigel South (2007), "Introduction: Approaching Green Criminology." Differing accounts of criminology's several environmentalisms are given by Mark Halsey (2004), "Against 'Green' Criminology"; Ted Benton (2007), "Ecology, Community and Justice: The Meaning of Green"; Michael J. Lynch and Paul Stretesky, "Green Criminology in the United States"; Rob White (2007), "Green Criminology and the Pursuit of Social and Ecological Justice"; and Rob White (2008), *Crimes against Nature: Environmental Criminology and Ecological Justice*. The placement of animals in green criminology is discussed in Piers Beirne (2007), "Animal Rights, Animal Abuse and Green Criminology."

16. Francione, *Animals, Property and the Law*, pp. 121–23. Among the states that define the offense as a felony, penalties for violations vary considerably. For example, while the maximum fine for cruelty to animals is $5,000 in Alaska and Pennsylvania and $10,000 in Wisconsin, it is only $50 in Missouri. Prison sentences, too, span a wide range: from nothing at all in Ohio and Virginia to a

maximum of six months in Alabama and California, three years in Maine, and five years in Oklahoma.

17. See, for example, Tom Regan (2007), "Vivisection: The Case for Abolition," and A. N. Rowan, F. M. Loew, and J. C. Weer (1995), *The Animal Research Controversy*, pp. i–vii. According to these authors, in the United States, 1.2 million dogs, cats, primates, rabbits, hamsters, and guinea pigs are used annually in laboratories; including rats and mice, total annual animal usage is 20 million.

18. Older statutes defined "animal" variously as "all brute creatures" (Michigan); "any animal in subjugation or captivity, whether wild or tame" (Oklahoma); "every living creature" (Arkansas); and "any useful beast, fowl or animal" (North Carolina). In the code, as its drafters point out (p. 426), the division is between humans and all other living creatures. But should fish, birds, spiders, and worms, for example, not also be considered animals?

19. U.S. Department of Agriculture, National Agricultural Statistics Service (2008), "Livestock Slaughter: 2005 Summary,", pp. 2–3, and U.S. Department of Agriculture, National Agricultural Statistics Service (2008), "Poultry Slaughter: 2007 Annual Summary," pp. 2–3.

20. Peter Singer (1990a), *Animal Liberation*, p. 6, and Peter Singer (1990b), "The Significance of Animal Suffering," p. 10. See also Richard Ryder (1979), "The Struggle against Speciesism," and, especially, Joan Dunayer (2004), *Speciesism*.

21. Andrée Collard (1989), *Rape of the Wild*, p. 24.

22. Robert Darnton (1999), *The Great Cat Massacre and Other Episodes in French Cultural History*.

23. For an outline of Blair's feral beasts comments, see, for example, Owen Gibson (2007), "Interview with Christopher," p. 5.

24. Jim Mason (1993), *An Unnatural Order: Uncovering the Roots of Our Domination of Nature and Each Other*, pp. 163–68.

25. Geertrui Cazaux (2007), "Labelling Animals: Non-Speciesist Criminology and Techniques to Identify Other Animals."

Against Cruelty? Understanding the Act Against Plowing by the Tayle (Ireland, 1635)

1

O F THE NUMEROUS ISSUES THAT LIE at the intersection of animal protection and criminalization practices, one of the most intriguing is the emergence and history of the concept of cruelty. This chapter examines the emergence of the Act Against Plowing by the Tayle and Pulling the Wooll Off Living Sheep, which was enacted in the Irish Parliament in 1635. For brevity's sake and because I am not concerned here with the outlawing of "pulling the wool off living sheep," I will refer to the act either as the "Act Against Plowing by the Tayle" or, more often, simply as the "1635 Act."

The 1635 Act criminalized, in particular, the "barbarous custome of ploughing, harrowing, drawing and working with horses, mares, geldings, garrans and colts, by the taile" (see Appendix 1). The act's stated justifications were that plowing by tail involved, first, "cruelty used to the beasts" and, second, impairment of the "breed" of horses in Ireland.[1] Although the circumstances of its emergence have never been examined in any depth, the 1635 Act was among the first formally to criminalize a given practice because it was cruel. Or so it would seem.

Organizing Questions

In collecting the primary materials relating to the 1635 Act, I was guided by several questions. What is the meaning of cruelty in the 1635 Act? What were the intentions of the act's framers? Was the act enforced and, if so, how and to what extent? What, if any, were the respective effects of the act on the lives of horses and of those convicted of the crime of plowing by tail?

Considerable hardship confronts the construction of a narrative of almost any aspect of the legal and social history of Ireland in the first half of the seventeenth century. This problem applies especially to the emergence of the 1635 Act and to its self-stated opposition to cruelty. The quality of the evidentiary material that bears on the 1635 Act does not inspire a great deal of confidence. From the outset, several caveats must be expressed about their poor quality. First, as I eventually discovered, there are apparently very few judicial records that have survived from seventeenth-century Ireland. Among the missing records are those of the day-to-day business of the ecclesiastical courts, the central law courts, the assize courts, quarter sessions. and the manorial courts. This means that there are apparently no available judicial records of violations of the 1635 Act. For the crime of plowing by tail, specifically, there are no records of legal argument, testimony, dispositions, sentences, or appeals. This regrettable absence of court records derives partly from the generally poor quality of record keeping in early modern Ireland and partly from the ravages of time. Among these latter must be counted the wholesale destruction in 1922 of documents stored in the Public Record Office in Dublin.

This void in the judicial record of the 1635 Act can perhaps be overcome, to a certain extent, with the aid of two sorts of other seventeenth-century text. One is the various documents of the colonial administrators produced and preserved by English government officials in the *Calendar of State Papers, Ireland* and elsewhere. The other is the diaries of those who observed aspects of the towns and countryside in early modern Ireland. However, each of their respective views of the 1635 Act is in its own way malformed and tainted, and it is possible that they succeed only in aggravating the task of understanding the 1635 Act.

In regard to the former, it must be cautioned that orders from the Privy Council and the published findings of state commissions and other London-appointed official bodies are not the most reliable of sources for uncovering a history of practices outlawed by the British in seventeenth-century Ireland. Such sources represent, rather, the bureaucratic and political indices of English hegemony in a period dominated by the conqueror's raw cultural prejudice and military power, even if neither of these were ever altogether unchallenged or uncomplicated.

The other main textual source for understanding the passage of the 1635 Act is provided by the diaries and other written descriptions of men with money and inclination who traveled in Ireland and who recorded their observations. Their authors were mostly peripatetic gentlemen of leisure, retired army officers, and religious zealots. Not a few of their written observations, it must be said, appear half baked and highly prejudiced. Among these, for example, is the *Itinerary* of 1617 written by Fynes Moryson, secretary to the Lord Deputy of Ireland, General Blount. Others, however, seem more or less plausible, among them the descriptions of life in rural Ireland by Barnabe Rich, a Puritan pamphleteer (Rich's *A New Description of Ireland* of 1610 will be referred to toward the end of this chapter).

Investigation of the 1635 Act is made even more hazardous because there is no extant word or phrase for plowing by tail in the Irish language. Perhaps "plowing by tail" was rendered as either *treabhadh an leath deiridh* ("*leath deiridh*" being the horse's hindquarters) or *treabhadh céachta dromluise* ("*céachta*" being the plow and "*dromlus*" being a derivative of either "*dromlach/dromluí*" or "*dromach*," meaning either the back band of the harness or a particular rope for tying the plow to the tail).[2] But no dictionary has an entry for it. This is probably because those poor Gaelic Irish who practiced plowing by tail were mostly illiterate, and their traditions in this regard, even if not entirely expunged, were passed down not in script but by word of mouth and doubtless less and less so after the practice was criminalized in 1635. It would of course be helpful if descriptions of plowing by tail survive in Gaelic poetry. But even this avenue is not especially promising, in part because, from about 1600 onward, the Gaelic bardic tradition was subject to increasing English influence.[3]

Cumulatively, these several silences amount to a great disappointment. They mean that there is only scarce empirical referent for the use of horses' tails to plow. They also imply that there is no clear idea of how the notion of cruelty might have been constructed by Irish farmers. If the notion of cruelty in the 1635 Act was not *their* concept but one forcefully imposed on them by their English conquerors, then how in their practices—physical, cultural, and mental—did they resist English law if they were both willing and able to do so?

In what follows, I detail and explore four of the most likely explanations of the emergence of the 1635 Act. These are as follows:

1. That, as specified under the provisions of the act, fines for the crime of plowing by tail amounted to a much-needed source of revenue for the English administration in Ireland.
2. That criminalization of plowing by tail was a continuing act in a deadly cultural drama set within the overriding importance of the power of the English conquerors to impose their will on the Irish.
3. That the act reflected changing, pro-animal sentiments toward the welfare of animals.

4. That the act was a consequence or an aspect of the relationship between early modern state formation and the motivations that English Puritans might have had for outlawing animal baitings.

The order and presentation of these explanatory perspectives on the emergence of the 1635 Act is not meant to imply that one of them necessarily has more logical or explanatory power than the other two.

To begin with, however, it would be useful briefly to describe both the practice of using horses' tails to plow and the legislation that outlawed it.

Using Horses' Tails to Plow

Not a great deal is known about agricultural practices in early modern Ireland. This is especially true for the habits and customs of the lower levels of Gaelic society, including the small tenantry and agricultural laborers. Indeed, Gaelic Irish texts are completely lacking in detailed descriptions of plowing methods.[4]

The practice of using horses' tails to plow almost certainly did not originate in Ireland, and it was never a peculiarly Irish custom. Whether in Ireland or elsewhere, it is likely that it was during the Neolithic period that plowing by tail originated in Europe. Early petroglyphs in caves at Tegneby, Sweden, for example, suggest that the practice of plowing by tail existed there—or, rather differently, that it was recorded there—some 3,000 to 4,000 years ago.[5] The historian W. Pinkerton has claimed that plowing by tail existed "from time immemorial" and that it might well have existed wherever there were short plows (i.e., plows akin to a digging stick or *ard* with a lightweight beam in front for connection with rope directly to the draft animal).[6] He indicates that the ancient Egyptians used short plows and that an exactly similar plow is represented by a large, Romano–British bronze found at Piercefield in Yorkshire. But if Pinkerton is mistaken and plowing by tail was not practiced in England, then strong evidence suggests that the use of horses' tails to plow occurred in medieval Scotland, possibly as early as the fourteenth century[7] and continuing there as late as the 1790s.[8] It is likely that the practice occurred in many other early and early modern European societies. This is so not least because, as a means of plowing that used neither trace rope nor harness, it was relatively inexpensive.[9]

A necessary condition of the emergence of plowing by horses' tails, almost needless to say, was the introduction of the notion of horse draft. In Ireland and elsewhere in Western Europe, horse-draft plowing began to

Figure 1.1.   "Ploughing by the Tail" (appended to E. E. Evans, 1976).
The purpose of such illustrations was chiefly satirical and designed for an English audience already prejudiced against most things Irish. In the scene, the two horses' tails are
attached with the help of "wooden" ropes (*gads*) to a short transverse draw-bar at the end
of the beam. Perhaps the plough depicted is more cumbersome than necessary.

Source: Appended to E. E. Evans (1976), "Some Problems of Irish Ethnography: The Example of Ploughing
by the Tail," p. 37, is a scene of ploughing by tail. (Originally published by Hood in *My Pocket Book; or
Hints for a Ryghte Merrie and Conceited Tour* [1805, An improved edition, London, 1808].)

displace ox draft at the end of the thirteenth century, when a heavy breed
of horse was first introduced. By the fifteenth century, horse draft was the
normal practice among Irish farmers, ox draft still continuing to be used
only on the estates of Irish and Anglo-Irish large landholders and by the
English army in Ireland.[10]

There is no agreement on when the use of horses' tails to plow actually began in Ireland. Nor has it been established when its use became
widespread. Ireland does, however, boast a case of plowing by *camel*'s
tail in 1472, a curiosity that nevertheless points to the likelihood that the
idea of plowing by tail was a familiar one in Ireland by or in the fifteenth
century.[11] Some have said that when and if it made its first appearance, it
might have been a ritual.[12] However, what sort of ritual and what purpose
it might have served have not yet been determined. Others have expressed
doubt that it ever existed at all and—probably motivated by a sense of Irish

patriotism—even that its existence was fabricated by English colonialists in an attempt to portray Irish farmers as barbarous and uncivilized.[13] However, the use of horses' tails to plow was probably widespread in Ireland before 1600. This is so not least because on several occasions, beginning in 1606, the English went to the trouble of criminalizing the practice.

The first written description in English of plowing by tail—or "drawing by tail," as it was also sometimes termed—was probably the one provided in 1610 by the pamphleteer Barnabe Rich. In *A New Description of Ireland*, Rich observed as follows:

> The Irish will not . . . imitate our English manner, in divers pointes of husbandry, but especially in the ploughing of their land; in the performing whereof, they used the labour of five severall persons to every plough, and their Teem of Cattle, which commonly consisted of five or sixe horses, were placed all in front, having neither cordes, chaines, nor lines, whereby to draw, but every horse by his owne taile; and this was the manner of ploughing when I knew *Ireland* first, and is used still at this day in manie places of the Countrey.[14]

Plowing by tail was often undertaken with short plows in shallow stony ground. The horse most commonly used was the small, strong *"gerrán"*, which would also have been used to transport peat, turf, agricultural produce, and manure.[15] Another description of plowing by tail was given in 1622 by the Scotsman William Lithgow: "I remember I saw in Ireland's North-parts, two remarkable sights: the one was their manner of Tillage, Ploughes drawne by Horse-Tayles, wanting garnishing [harnessing], they are only fashioned with straw or wooden Ropes to their bare Rumps."[16] Thomas Dineley gave another account of plowing by tail, penned in his diary kept while traveling in Ireland in the 1670s:

> Here four horses abreast draw the plough by the tails, which was a custom all over Ireland till a statute prevented it; yet they are tolerated this custom here because they cannot manage their land otherwise, their plough gears, tackle and traces being . . . of gads or withes of twigs twisted, which here would break to pieces by the ploughshare so often jibbing against the rock, which the gears being fastened by wattles or wisps to the horses' tails, the horses, being sensible, stop until the ploughman lifts over it.[17]

And again, plowing by tail involved

> the hitching of six or eight garrons to a rough and cumbersome swing plough. In addition to the ploughman himself there was a man or youth to lead each horse; and it is not hard to imagine the shouting and swearing

and the constant stops and restarts which marked the slow progress of the plough as it turned its uneven furrows.[18]

Plowing by tail would often have been followed by harrowing by tail, that is, loosening up the soil and then compacting it. The two practices are announced together on at least three occasions—once in the *Annals of Ulster*,[19] once when they were both outlawed by the 1635 Act, and once by Arthur Young, who claimed in 1780 that young colts were used to harrow by the tail.[20] For both plowing and harrowing by tail, Young recounted that

> the fellow who leads the horses . . . walks backward before them the whole day long, and in order to make them advance, strikes them in the face; their heads, I trow, are not apt to turn.[21]

Making English Law in Ireland: The Criminalization of Plowing by Tail

From the 1580s, the ties between Britain and Ireland increasingly displayed all the classic characteristics of colonialism. These included territorial conquest through overwhelming military power, to which the conquerors attached a variety of ideological justifications in order to champion English hegemony; the appropriation of raw materials for private profit and export; and the implantation of colonists, both old and new, to control the indigenous population and to organize and maximize economic efficiency. To these typical characteristics might usefully be added an eventual recognition by the colonists, sooner or later, of the importance of wielding their power less through naked military force and more through the cultivation of a reliable group of indigenous officials who would participate in the labors of administrative, juridical, and, sometimes, religious officialdom.

Prior to recounting how plowing by tail was criminalized in Ireland, it is worth rehearsing how statutes were enacted in seventeenth-century Ireland. Some statutes originated in the English Parliament, others in the irregularly convened Irish Parliament. Those laws that originated in Ireland often had greater practical effect there, though under the provisions of Poynings' Law (1495) no law pertaining to Ireland could be passed or enforced without the prior consent of the Privy Council in London. Besides statutes, a bewildering variety of other laws held sway in Ireland, including ordinances, writs, acts of state, orders in council, royal proclamations, and proclamations from the Privy Council. To this lengthy list must be added the system of assizes, quarter sessions, and other courts introduced by the English. This judicial system operated most effectively inside the Pale (i.e., in Dublin and in parts of Kildare, Louth, and Meath); outside the Pale their jurisdiction and determinations were more precarious and existed in parallel with the ancient Brehon law and the decrees and customs of Gaelic Irish clans.

It is a mystery whether the creation and maintenance of so many complex and overlapping legal forms was designed to rule through the principle of divide and conquer or to bewilder those whom the English attempted to govern. In all probability, they were simply the legislative expression of the anomalies associated with the haphazard development of expanding English imperialism in the early modern era. In any event, between 1495 and 1782, usually supported by just enough military power and on occasion by crushing military force, the Crown and the English Privy Council exercised an immense political and cultural hegemony over the Irish legislature and over the freedom of action of the English-appointed Lord (or Deputy Lord) Governor of Ireland.[22]

From the very beginning of the Anglo-Norman occupation of Ireland, mutual hostility and contempt were aroused by the differing farming practices of the occupiers and the Irish. Among the practices that generated the most hostility—and the most legislation—were the practices of plowing by tail, pulling wool off sheep instead of shearing it, and the custom of producing cereals like corn and wheat by separating grains from the stalks by burning them. Of these practices, plowing by tail was mentioned by far the most often in official documents.

Correspondence among government officials compiled in the Irish *Calendar of State Papers* clearly indicates that from the early seventeenth century, legislation to outlaw plowing by tail was strongly supported both by the governments in London and in Dublin and by English and Scottish settlers. Plowing by tail was first prohibited by Order in Council in 1606. Under this order, the penalty for the first offense was forfeiture of one horse, for the second two horses, and for the third the whole team. However, not until 1611 was any formal attempt made to enforce this order.[23] In that year, as payment for his military support during O'Dogherty's rebellion of 1608, Captain Paul Gore was granted the right for one year to collect in one or two counties a fine of ten shillings for each illegal plow. This income must have padded Gore's purse quite well because the next year James I granted the right to levy the fine to the government official Sir William Uvedall for a fee of 100 pounds.

The first mention of a possible statutory prohibition against plowing by tail is in 1611. In that year, an order from Lord Deputy Arthur Chichester proposed an Act for the abolishing of barbarous and rude customs: as howling and crying at the burial of the dead, drawing their plough-cattle only fastened at the tails, and blowing their milch-cattle to make them give milk, &c, and pulling of sheep.[24]

No act ensued. However, ten years later, in 1621, prompted by a number of factors, including the resumption of Protestant–Catholic hostilities on the Continent, widespread financial corruption in Ireland, and the desire of the English, in order to finance many other colonial adventures, to extract as much revenue as possible from a stable Ireland, James I demanded an investigation of various administrative disorders in Ireland.[25] In early 1622, the commissioners were briefed on "questions touching the planting of civility and removing of certain barbarous customs, long continued in Ireland." Among these customs were the existence of "large numbers of masterless men and idle persons . . . [who were] apt to steal, to revolt and to commit many mischiefs," including promiscuous living, adultery, and incest.[26]

The commissioners also inquired into whether "the drawing of plough horses by the tails till they pull off the rumps" was not a "barbarous and hurtful usage and whether the king should ordain sharp penalties for [its] users and maintainers." Elsewhere, the Irish Commission of 1622 (hereinafter the 1622 commission) variously condemned the use of short plows as "barbarism," "an abuse," "hurtful," "ploughing after the Irish fashion," and "one of the defects of the natives . . . [for which] we require a speedy reformation."[27] The commissioners once again proposed that Parliament itself should outlaw plowing by tail and that, this time, the fine should be raised from ten shillings to ten pounds.[28] Reinforcing English stereotypes of the Irish poor and of their barbarous customs, the recommendations of the 1622 commission were not the subject of sustained or serious parliamentary debate in England. At one point, it was proposed, also without effect, that fines for plowing by horses' tails be extended to "horses or other beasts"[29] ("horses" no doubt referring to mares, geldings, garrans, and colts and "beasts" to bulls, bullocks, oxen, and donkeys).

The recommendations of the 1622 commission did not prefigure as markers of new English policies in Ireland until the watershed moment, a decade later, in January 1632, when Sir Thomas Wentworth (later, Earl of Strafford) was appointed Lord Deputy of Ireland.[30] One of Governor Wentworth's first actions was to ponder the 1622 commission's recommendations for increasing English and, in his and in his monarch's eyes, royal power in Ireland and, indirectly, for enhancing his own considerable financial and political fortunes.[31]

In early 1634, Wentworth summoned the first Parliament to be held in Ireland since 1614–1615. Amidst rumor and high drama but with little yet settled, it soon became clear in outline that Wentworth's policies toward the Anglicization of Irish society were intended to operate at a whole panoply of levels. These included far-reaching constitutional reforms, the forceful simple seizure of land through enforced English settlement, the establishment of formal plantations,[32] the easing out of the Gaelic Irish from the most fertile farmland, and the portrayal of their methods of agriculture as primitive and barbaric.

In July 1634, after negotiations between Wentworth and the Irish parliament, there emerged a package of fifty-one legislative reforms (the "Graces"). The Graces included bills that forbade such behavior as "idle wandering" and swearing; another for "the erection of houses of correction for the punishment of rogues, vagabonds, sturdy beggars, fortune tellers, jugglers, and other lewd and idle persons;"[33] and yet another for altering the penalty for "the barbarous abuse of the short ploughs."[34]

Despite the enactment of most of the Graces in 1635, it is unclear how Wentworth actually secured the enactment of his favored legislative package in the 1634–1635 Parliament. The language and intent of all the legislative reforms must have passed Wentworth's scrutiny and more or less met with his approval. But it is hard to determine his precise role in the passage of the 1635 Act. Perhaps this is largely because, as Stephen Merritt has argued, from the very beginning of his rule in Ireland, Wentworth greatly restricted access to the one type of information that he possessed and of which others knew nothing, namely, his intentions.[35] No private diaries have survived, and there are no division lists in either the House of Commons or the House of Lords. What remains is official and therefore highly contentious correspondence either emanating from Wentworth himself or else sent to him by government officials and other men of property and influence. It is known, however, that in 1634 Wentworth was assisted, in his push to enact the various Graces, by his alliance with a parliamentary group called the Old English and that it was this group's detailed commentary on the Graces that gained Wentworth's support and that led to the statutory changes effected in 1635.[36] As for the proposed statutory ban on plowing by tail, it is likely, as Hugh Kearney has suggested, that this was one of ten Graces that were of minor importance and that, accordingly, it met with no parliamentary opposition.[37]

Punishment, Profit, and Plowing by Tail:
The "Economic in the First Instance"?

With a rough outline in hand of how the 1635 Act was enacted in the Irish Parliament, I now want to suggest that the emergence of the 1635 Act can initially be explained by some of the consequences of the punishment that the English had reserved for the crime of plowing by tail. This seemingly roundabout explanation derives from English administrators' own reckoning that the system of fines was failing to reduce the prevalence of plowing by tail: "[fines have] failed to curb the practice."[38] Perhaps some English comptroller had known of this difficulty as early as 1606, the first year that an order in Council had banned plowing by tail. But we cannot be sure. Perhaps failure was compounded by ineptitude in accounting practices.

It must be said that this failure is variously alluded to in English state documents of the time, even if it is not mentioned in the plainest of terms. But whenever plowing by tail is mentioned there, it is accompanied by an implicit tension. In these documents, on the one hand, the custom of plowing by tail tends to be laced with pejoratives like "backward," "unproductive," and "disprofitable." It is also several times explicitly stated, on the other hand, that the fines for plowing by tail were a considerable source of revenue that was much appreciated by the English in Ireland. For example, in 1612 in Ulster alone, fines for those convicted of plowing by tail produced a gross income of 870 pounds for the licensee Sir William Uvedale.[39] In 1613, according to Arthur Chichester, then Lord Deputy of Ireland, the fine of ten shillings per year for plowing by tail produced a revenue in the northern counties "of very great value . . . to the great grief and impoverishment of that people, who have neither the means nor the skill to use other ploughs."[40] For each of the years from 1615 to 1621, the king sold the license to collect monies for plowing by the tail, the revenue amounting to "a considerable sum" for the grantee.[41] Elsewhere, the "considerable sum" has been described as "an exact revenue of extraordinary great value."[42]

In effect, therefore, the fines for plowing by tail were not so much a fine extracted from Irish farmers as a use tax for giving them permission to engage in the practice. Indeed, fines for plowing by tail were on occasion actually referred to as "plough-money" or even "short plough rents."[43] Clearly, licensees or grantees were actually fining Irish farmers caught or convicted of plowing by tail less than ten shillings—the standard fine—and then not reporting this income to the Crown, with the result that "the use of this patent tends more to be private gain than reformation."[44] The king himself complained that the agents employed under his patent had "contracted with the offenders, and reduced the fine to be taken of every plough to two shillings and sixpence, and so by lessening the punishment opened the way for that rude and hurtful custom to spread."[45]

That economic considerations were perhaps uppermost in the minds of the English is partly confirmed in a letter of 1627 from Governor Lord Falkland to the Privy Council.[46] Falkland was of the opinion that because fines for using short plows were likely to fall below 425 pounds per year, he would therefore recommend that they be leased to Lord Caulfield for one year at a rent of 500 pounds. In making this recommendation, Falkland had identified a simple if delicate problem with the fines–revenue balance sheet. This problem must have been grasped immediately by the wily Wentworth: if trying to end the practice of plowing by tail by fining unreformed violators resulted in both the further impoverishment of already poor Irish farmers and a failure to reduce its prevalence, then an increase in the fine from ten shillings to ten pounds would have had a catastrophic effect. To wit, through criminalization and the imposition of fines for plowing by tail, the English were in danger of killing the goose with the golden egg.

The solution to this delicacy was proposed in a bill in 1634 and then formalized in the 1635 Act itself. The 1634 bill had stated that

> for reforming the barbarous abuse of the short ploughs, we are pleased that the penalty now imposed thereon shall be presently taken away, and that hereafter an Act of Parliament shall pass for the restraining of the said abuse upon such a penalty as shall be thought fit.[47]

The 1635 Act, though symbolically raising the punishment for plowing by tail to a fine or imprisonment, nevertheless postponed a decision on what punishment "shall be thought fit" by intentionally leaving the precise punishment vague and at the discretion of justices of the peace.[48]

It is not difficult to suppose that the reaction of poor Irish farmers to the English-imposed 1635 Act would have amounted to some combination of exasperation, resentment, and anger. First and foremost, the fines for plowing by tail must have threatened the very existence of a peasantry that was among the very poorest in the whole of Europe. The English-appointed 1622 commission blandly reported "fines [for plowing by tail] had in many places hurt and impoverished the country."[49] Moreover, a bemused English official with a weak and misplaced sense of humor, Sir Charles Cornwaleys, noted "what great sums of money have been drawn out of the supposed commiseration of the hinder parts of these poor Irish garrons."[50]

In a backhanded swipe at otherwise unrecorded Irish complaints about the criminalization of plowing by tail, the jocular Cornwaleys mused that "the garrans, though strained (perhaps beyond ordinary existence) in those parts, complain not."[51] Formal complaints by Irish farmers about the fines for plowing by tail met with little or no success, their considerable grievances tending to be dismissed out of hand by the English administration.[52] However, the roughshod manner of collection of the fines for illegal plowing would have been a strong additional source of complaint. Indeed, in dealing with Irish complaints that they had been abused by soldiers, a commission of 1613 cited grievances of "particular instances of oppression and exactions by soldiers, provosts-martial, and some others," which included extortions of money, meat, drink, cattle, and household goods.[53] According to the commission, there were very few complaints about this; "the reasons given by the people for forbearing to complain is the fear that had to be worse used by the soldiers complained of."[54]

The desire of the English colonists for revenue from fines for plowing by tail is an explanatory piece in the puzzle of the emergence of the 1635 Act. If plow fines provided the economic incentive for the imposition of punishment for plowing by tail, then the act's older and much broader context was the extraordinary denigration of Irish culture by the English. We now turn, therefore, to how opposition to plowing by tail was used as a vehicle for the promotion of Englishness—reinforced by the ability of the conquerors to impose their cultural prejudices on much of Ireland.

Contested Cultural Practices: Plows, Horses, and Plowing by Tail

Thou husbandman that faine would know
Some remedies to finde,
How far to help thy sickly beast,
To satisfy thy minde:
When thou wouldst faine callet keepe,
For to maintain the stocke:
Thou must then learne as well the helpe
As to encrease thy stocke.[55]

—Leonard Mascal, "To the Husbandman," 1620

Any narrative of plowing by tail, including whether it was seen as cruel and, if so, what was meant by the term "cruelty" and to whom, should begin with the recognition that using horses' tails to plow was probably not, for the most part, an unduly complicated affair for those who engaged in it. Most regrettably in this regard, contemporary Irish voices are largely absent from the historical record, especially their speech and actions of resistance.

To its Gaelic Irish practitioners, however, plowing by tail would doubt-less have recommended itself on several counts. Those Irish who plowed by tail were not freeholders but overwhelmingly poor farmers who rented their land from Anglo-Irish landlords, from plantation farmers, and from small English farmers.[56] Plowing by tail could not have been efficient enough or profitable enough to produce a surplus cash crop, and so, if they were at all to eke out a living, however precarious, then Irish farmers would have had to plow with an apparatus that required as little monetary investment as pos-sible. Plowing by tail was thus likely to have been used only with a cheap and lightweight plow. The use of this plow—attached to horses' tails—was the only method of plowing available to poor Irish farmers who had not the capital needed to invest either in a long or heavy plow or in harnessing apparatuses for any sort of plow.[57] It was not, in short, the sort of method "by which the wilderness could be made to blossom like a rose."[58]

Historians have not been able to uncover the prevalence of plowing by tail with much precision except in the plantations in East Ulster and in [London]derry.[59] However, it was probably most common in northern and western Ireland, around the Cavan and Fermanagh regions, where by far the predominant crop in the seventeenth century was shallow-rooted oats rather than wheat and where the preparation of the soil by the use of horses' tails attached to short plows would have recommended itself most to poor farmers.[60]

In addition, plowing by tail would likely have been used mainly to scratch the surface of the soil—to break through the top thin layer or skin on the land that had already been turned over for many years. When the plow hit a stone or a rock or something solid or heavy, it would jerk the horses' tails, thereby forcing them to stop. Moreover, horses would be less sensitive when plowing with a harness and collar than without, thus even-tually causing serious damage to the plow:

> This usage . . . can be explained . . . by a fact overlooked by those who most vehemently condemn it. This was the nature of the land which had to be ploughed. Apart from the numerous large stones, which in course of time have since been removed from arable land, there were then innumer-able stumps and roots of trees still below the surface of the ground, relics of the woods which had but recently covered a great part of the country and against these the ploughshare was liable to strike at any moment.[61]

In order to add to add to the understanding of why the English were so keen to outlaw plowing by tail, one must begin by acknowledging their long-standing and vehement animosity toward Irish culture. Much of this animosity can be traced to the polemical observations of Giraldus Cambrensis ("Gerald of Wales"), whose twelfth-century texts *Topographica Hibernica* and *Expugnatio Hibernica* are laden with his pontifications on the barbarity of the Irish and on their peculiar and extremely uncivilized customs. Cambrensis's texts established against the Irish a lengthy English prejudice based on a combination of ridicule, contempt, fantasy, and national chauvinism—a dreadful demonization of the wild Irish Other that continued into the 1630s and far beyond.

Chief among the exponents of this anti-Irish prejudice was Edmund Spenser, the English poet, soldier, Munster settler, and author of the celebrated Elizabethan paean *Fairie Queene*. It is not known with certainty if Spenser had actually read Cambrensis, but it is very likely that he had done so because the latter's views were widely known among the Old English in Ireland.[62] Of Spenser's texts, the most influential was the quasi-Machiavellian political tract *A View of the Present State of Ireland*, which was written in 1596 and first published in 1633, two years before the passage of the 1635 Act. In this text, Spenser condemned as barbarous and backward Irish customs such as the wearing of hooded cloaks ("mantles") and long hair ("glibbes"), both of which, he claimed, hampered proper recognition of those with "thiefish appearances."[63]

Among Spenser's vigorous and sometimes contradictory recommendations for solving the "Irish problem(s)" were the extension of English law beyond the Pale to the whole of Ireland (an imposition that, he also thought, because of the continuing power of the old Brehon law, would not achieve its purpose) and the wholesale slaughter of those less than enthusiastic about his proposals. At the same time, he vigorously advocated the employment by reformed Irish farmers of the new principles of English husbandry. "Husbandry," waxed Spenser, was "the nurse of thrift and the daughter of industrie and labour."[64]

Mention might also be made of the opinions of diarist Fynes Moryson, secretary to General ("Scorched Earth") Blount, Lord Mountjoy, the Lord Deputy of Ireland. In true Spenserian fashion, Moryson wrote in his *Itinerary* of 1617 that the Irish

> are by nature superstitious and given to use witchcrafts. . . . Their opinions, that some one shall dye if they fynde a blacke spott vpon a bared Mutton bone; and their horses shall lieu long if they giue no fyer out of the howse, and that some ill lucke will fall to their horses if the ryder hauing

eaten eges doe not washe his handes after them, or be not carefull to chuse the eggs of equall bignes.[65]

Concluding that "they abhor from all things that agree with English civility," Moryson complained that "our cheefe husbandry is in Tillage, they dispise the Plough, and where they are forced to use it for necessity, doe all things about it cleane contrary to us."[66] Added William Lithgow about husbandry in Ireland, "It is bad a Husbandry I say, as ever I found in any the wildest savages alive."[67]

In various ways, plows and horses clearly mattered very much to those who staffed the English occupation of Ireland around 1600. Sometimes, plows were seen as symbols of wisdom or abstinence; at others, they were associated with mortification. In his book *God Speed the Plough*, Andrew McRae documents that in the century after 1560, the plow became an embattled sign of contesting views of agrarian England. Thus, the plow was severally constructed as an emblem of the traditional structures of rural society, as a flag for farmers dispossessed by the enclosure movement of large landowners, and as a godly and gentlemanly tool in enlightened husbandry practices.[68] Secretary of State Robert Cecil is even said to have declared, during a debate in the House of Commons in London in 1601, on the possible repeal of the *Statutes of Tillage*:

> I do not dwell in the Country, nor am I acquainted with the Plough. But I think that whosoever doth not maintain the Plough, destroys the Kingdome.[69]

For improving the kingdom and for making it prosperous, a crucial medium was the new discourse of husbandry. Husbandry manuals by John Fitzherbert, Leonard Mascall, Gervase Markham, and others disseminated information about beekeeping, fishing, animal husbandry, fruit and vegetable cultivation, livestock production, the rearing of game animals, the use and maintenance of tools and implements, soil improvement, the destruction of vermin, and a great deal more besides. The intended audience of the purveyors of husbandry was anyone connected to the land but especially "every man of discretion and judgement" who was desirous of self-improvement.[70] The goal of the husbandry movement was nothing short of the transformation of local communities into precapitalist, profit-seeking individuals who worked the land with proper knowledge, thrift, hard work, and ambition. These very qualities were, of course, perfectly consistent with early seventeenth-century Calvinist teachings on individual responsibility, thrift, and hard work.

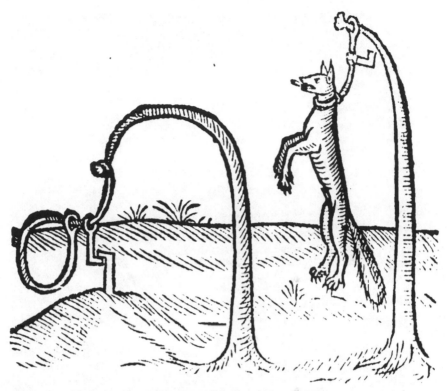

Figure 1.2.   "The Whippe or Spring Trappe" (Leonard Mascal, 1590).

Source: Leonard Mascal, *A Booke of Engines and traps to take Polcats, Buzardes, Rattes, Mice and all other kindes of Vermin and beasts whatsoever, most profitable for all Warriners, and such as delight in this kind of sport and pastime* (London: John Wolfe, 1590), p. 63.

If husbandry manuals were the new purveyors of agrarian improvement, then images of proper and efficient plows and horses were important devices in their discursive toolbox. For example, Gervase Markham, a one-time captain in the English army in Ireland, discussed at length the mechanical qualities of good plows in different types of ground in his manual of 1613 *The English Husbandman*. Markham warned that just as a good musician has to tune his instrument properly in order to play good music, so it is with a husbandman and his plow. "Even with a good plough," Markham warned,

> if the Husbandman have not the cunning to temper it and set it in the right way, it is impossible that ever his labour should come to good end.[71]

Horses, too, were used and wielded as great symbols of nationalism. Beginning with Elizabethan times, the English preferred not to grace Irish

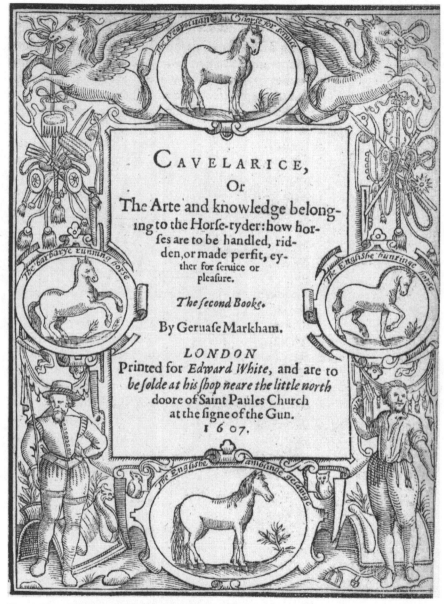

Figure 1.3. "Horses and Horsemanship" (Gervase Markham, 1607).

Source: Gervase Markham, *Cavelarice, or the English Horseman: Contayning All the Arte of Horse-manship, As Much As Is Necessary for Any Man to Understand* (London: Edward White, 1607), Book II, title page, p. i, opposite Book I, p. 88; 4° M 39 Art. Reproduced with permission of the Bodleian Library, Oxford University.

equines with the name "horse," instead contemptuously referring to them as "hobbies" (and, in Scotland, "prickers"). Edmund Spenser condemned the Irish for "their riding," moreover, and he advocated their deployment of English "horse-furniture"—stirrups, bit, bridle, and saddle.[72] Fynes Moryson complained that the Irish tended to use inefficient bridle snaffles on their horses rather than the bits favored by the English.[73] Among the best-known and most aggressive tracts to promote Englishness through cultural imagery involving horses and good horsemanship were Gervase Markham's book *Cavelarice, or the English Horseman* of 1607 and his military training manual *The Souldiers Exercise* of 1625. *Cavelarice*, for example, was explicitly dedicated by Markham to the cultivation of good horsemen and good horses "in this Empire of great Brittaine."[74] Complaining about the rude ways in which they were handled, Markham seldom referred to Irish horses in *Cavelarice*, but, when he did, he generally did so in a disparaging way. Like their rude and lazy riders, Irish horses Markham placed last in his assessment of horses bred in different countries: "The *Irish Hobbie. . . .* This horse, though he trot very wel, yet he naturally desireth to amble."[75]

Against such slovenliness, Markham instead recommended

> the vertue, goodnesse, boldnesse, swiftnesse, and indurance of our true bred English Horses, [which are] equall with any race of Horses whatsoever. . . . [For] infinite labour, and by indurance, which is easiest to bee discerned in our English hunting matches, I have not seen any horse able to compare with the English horse.[76]

Echoing these sentiments, the policymaking 1622 commission recommended the introduction of "husbandry . . . which might engender industry, peace and civility" as a solution to "the heathenish and brutish manner of living in Ireland."[77] In fact, the tripartite hegemonic rallying cry of the English occupiers was "husbandry," "hard work," and "surveying." Husbandry was intended to improve the efficiency of agricultural production; hard work to combat the many Irish vices associated with their natural laziness; and surveying, embraced by the harsh logic of colonialism, "for its capacity to ensure that the colonial settlers and the English government would 'extract maximum value out of the available land.'"[78]

Plowing by tail therefore contravened the emerging English practices associated with good husbandry. Indeed, Edmund Spenser himself had strongly urged the use of proper plows by Irish farmers,[79] and, according to another commentator, "The English settlers who saw these (short) ploughs at work thought them both 'uncivil' and unprofitable."[80] There is no doubt that the stealthy Wentworth was a most enthusiastic champion of the superiority of Englishness and of English husbandry practices and, therefore, of the English view of the proper use of horses and plows— and of all these being forced on an Ireland still in the process of being conquered.

Early Modern State Formation and the Regulation of Human–Animal Relationships

To move closer to the 1635 Act's language "the cruelty used to the beasts," it must be stressed that both in law and in reality, the master status of animals from centuries before the 1635 Act, up to and during the early modern era and far beyond, including the present, has been that of humans' private property. It bodes us well to remember this status when, looking backward, we try to decipher the meaning of any sixteenth- or seventeenth-century legislation that refers to animals—to be misled by some apparent concern with animals' welfare, for example, and thereby to forget their objective master status as property. This mistake would be an easy one to make were we to read the text of an act of 1545 that made it a felony for anyone to cut out an animal's tongue.[81] The framers of this statute were worried not about animal welfare but about the destruction and the spoiling of property. Indeed, besides outlawing the excision of live animals' tongues, the three other mischiefs outlawed by the act were setting fire to carts laden with coal, the (de)barking of fruit trees, and the burning of timber made ready for houses. Then and now, the very word "cattle" derives from animals' status as chattel or property. It was applied not only to cows but also to bulls, chickens, donkeys, geese, goats, mules, oxen, sheep, and, of course, the horses that command attention in the pages of this chapter.[82]

As property, animals had no statutory or common-law right to protection in the seventeenth century except if they were another's property, if they were used by state apparatuses like the army and the postal system, or if, as in the case of bullbaiting, an owner's animals were involved in some human-organized disturbance or melee or one that was defined by the police and local magistrates as a breach of the peace or of public order. The English legal system was interested mainly in horses, for example, when as items of property they were stolen from their owner or maimed or otherwise misappropriated. Horse stealing was seen as a serious form of theft from at least the reign of Henry VIII. One Henrecian statute of 1545 decreed that horse theft was punishable with execution, and, at the same time, it removed the offence from benefit of clergy (though not for crimes involving murder).[83] A statute of 1548 denied horse thieves the protection of sanctuary.[84] There were a number of factors associated with the increased punitiveness of these new statutes. Among them, J. M. Beattie has suggested, were the seriousness of the offense, horses' high value, and the ease with which they could be stolen.[85] As property, in other words, horses mattered greatly.

From the middle of the sixteenth century on, a great variety of social institutions and practices involving human–animal relations began to be regulated by law. Emerging piecemeal at times and more systematically at others, new laws addressed human–animal relations in agriculture and husbandry, the import and export of animals and animal products, and the regulation and licensing of farming, hunting, fishing, slaughtering, transportation, leather tanning, markets, weights and measures, and so on. It also included the development of abattoirs and their movement away from densely populated areas; the disposal of nonhuman animals' wastes from towns and ports; hygiene practices; regulations about animals used as carriers of goods and transporters of humans; the provision of shelter, food, and water for cattle; and even, in the case of sumptuary laws, how many animals, which species, which parts, and on what occasions civilized people might eat and wear them.

Like other animals, whether designated as domesticated or wild, horses inhabited contested sites toward and within which changing attitudes and practices were visible in proclamations issued by the monarchy and by the Privy Council. Typical of these was an order of 1609 regulating the use of horses by carriers and by the embryonic postal system.[86] This law tried to limit a horse rider's maximum speed to seven miles per hour in summer and six in winter and to restrict a horse's maximum load to thirty pounds. Its stated intent was to prevent "injury of the beast." Another instance of a seeming concern with horses' welfare is a proclamation issued in 1627 by Charles I. This stated that "horses employed on service are fitter to ride when used to bit than to snaffles" and that, henceforth, no riders would be allowed to use a snaffle on pain of contempt.[87]

On the surface, therefore, a few early seventeenth-century regulations do seem to have addressed horses' welfare. Were they intended to improve a public service or to reduce animals' suffering at the hands of humans? In the case of the 1609 order, for example, it is most likely that its aim was to develop an efficient means of communication by which the state could more rapidly detect and defeat conspiracies and rebellions.[88] About the 1627 proclamation, it must be said also that it had far more to do with the practical aim of extracting the most efficient use of horses' labor than with affording nonhuman animals moral consideration. In both cases, animals' welfare was a secondary phenomenon, an instrumental by-product of new rules that encouraged humans to maximize efficiency in their use of horses' labor. In neither case does the language of the regulation express or hint at a concern for cruelty.

Concepts of Cruelty

Among the stated justifications for criminalizing plowing by tail, the 1635 Act included "besides the cruelty used to the beasts . . ." What did cruelty mean in this specific context? Until the late medieval period, the concept of cruelty (*crudelitas*) was a rather vague and abstract one. In any given cultural and lexical context, its content and meaning tended to derive from its attachment either to the evil intentions of foreign or religious others or to the large-scale nature of its stage. The "Mongol hordes," for example, were therefore seen as cruel. So, too, depending on the circumstances and who was viewing them and with what intent, were barbarians, cannibals, Catholics, Jews, Protestants, Turks, and tyrants.[89] In the medieval period, the term "cruelty" might include a variety of forms of wickedness, excess, various wartime practices, tyranny, divine justice, and even the disregard of certain obligatory acts of kindness. At the same time, cruelty (*saevitia*, *atrocitas*, and *feritas*) was also employed in scriptural passages to refer to the animalistic qualities displayed by wild animals and beasts and demons.

Some early modern thinkers tried to rework and sharpen the application of the concept of cruelty, moving it from its elevated level of the grand stage of national and religious conflict downward to certain aspects of everyday life. Varying in both place and time and longevity, among cruelty's many companions were intensity, hard-heartedness, verity, severity, strictness, and rigor. Cruelty was also used as an antonym of indifference, mercy, and courtesy; as a superlative akin to "very" or "bloody" (as in "cruelly" hot); and as a synonym of crude and crudeness (i.e., raw, uncooked, undigested, uncivil, or rough).

These numerous notions of cruelty were almost exclusively applied to human actions. At some point, when the perception of human–animal relationships intersected with the notion of taking pleasure in another's pain or distress, cruelty began to be used as a concept that described the killing of animals. Erasmus, Thomas More, Montaigne, and the Calvinist Jean de Léry all described the killing of animals as cruel, especially when it involved a pleasurable spectacle, as it did in hunting. For example, in an essay of 1580 on cruelty, Montaigne suggested—with one eye fixed on the ancient Romans and the other on the Conquistadores—not only that we humans wrong animals when we hunt and kill them but also that those who grow accustomed to the slaughtering of animals are more likely to proceed to the killing of humans.[90] "There is," Montaigne urged, "a certain respect, a general duty of humanity, not only to beasts that have life and sense, but even to trees and plants."[91] In the writings of Jean Crespin and John Foxe particularly, cruelty became more and more associated with how others derived pleasure from the infliction of pain on their victims ("martyrs"), as it did also in the plays of Shakespeare and in some hunting manuals of the time, such as George Turberville's 1576 *Book of Venerie*.[92] In the gradual unfolding of the humane predicates of this trajectory, the germination of new attitudes to human–animal relationships first appeared in the case of animals used in sports and games. These included, most famously, blood sports like cockfights, the running of bulls, and the baiting of badgers, bulls, bears, dogs, monkeys, and, on occasion, horses.

To which of cruelty's many meanings was the 1635 Act directed? In trying to answer this question, it is tempting to look for a single meaning of cruelty that denoted a homogeneous moral or practical object in both Britain and Ireland. But that temptation would at once be deflected because it wrongly assumes that the employment and perception of the term did not vary with different audiences and with different socioeconomic and cultural strata. Reference must therefore now be made to concepts of cruelty that were invented and enacted in the seventeenth century, first in Britain and then in Ireland.

English Puritanism and God's Other Creatures

In Britain, there were two developments whose respective trajectories might have had some anticipatory relevance for the prohibition of animal cruelty in Ireland. Both became visible in the late Elizabethan period. As has just been indicated, the first development was the regulation of human–animal relations in early modern state formation. The second was the possible ameliorative influence of English Puritanism.

Lurking in the background as obvious precedents for the 1635 Act are the well-known attempts of English Puritans to regulate the manners and habits of English social life. The Puritans' attempts to reform manners and to forge a culture of discipline can be characterized in several ways. Two predominate. One is that Puritan reformism was quite varied in the objects of its concern. The other is that it was intense in the number and ardor of prosecutions, especially at the local level.

The Puritans' regulatory activity was associated with a broad range of social behavior, including speech, religion, sex, and labor.[93] In late sixteenth-century East Anglia, for example, among the extraordinary range of practices that Puritan-dominated towns sought to ban were adultery, fornication, sodomy, buggery, prostitution, idleness, drunkenness, profanity, gambling, wrestling and grinning matches, dancing and fiddling, theaters, puppet shows, and bowls. Interestingly enough, it was precisely in this region, in the heavily Puritan counties of Essex, Suffolk, and Norfolk, that the new principles of husbandry were the most developed in seventeenth-century England.

One of Puritanism's most powerful dimensions was radical sabbatarianism. Indeed, nestled between two chapters in Exodus, each praising the sacrificial slaughter of animals, was a third that decreed that the Sabbath was a day of rest not only for daughters, manservants, and maidservants but also for cattle.[94] Popular Sunday recreations were therefore condemned because they interfered with the piety required for proper observance of the Sabbath. Courts routinely prosecuted Sunday violations by dancers, dicers, bear baiters, bowlers, and football players.[95] Sabbatarianism was also one of the Puritans' most contested and despised platforms, managing to provoke James I's extraordinary *Declaration of Sports* of 1617, which actively encouraged Sunday revels, though only if they took place in the afternoon. Indeed, sabbatarian legislation was debated without statutory conclusion in every parliament between 1584 and 1621.[96] Eventually, under direct Puritan influence, the Sunday Observance Act (1625) emerged. This act was directed at "a disorderlie sort of people" who engages in "many quarrels [and] bloodshedds . . . neglecting divine service."[97] The act forbade participation in any extraparochial gatherings for sports on the Sabbath and any intraparochial gatherings for "any Bearebaiting, Bullbaiting, Enterludes, comon Playes, and other unlawful exercises and pastimes." If they threatened public order, banned recreations also included cockfights, the baiting of badgers and dogs, and, eventually, the use of horses to race.

The importance of these new regulations is obvious. Why the Puritans enacted them is not. Invariably, these gravitate toward one of three emphases. The first is that they were aspects of the broad civilizing process of manners and personalities, as identified and popularized in the writings of Norbert Elias.[98] Evidence for this viewpoint lies in the numerous contemporary declarations that animal baiting was bad manners, bad taste, and conducive to interhuman violence that included, especially, drunken revelry, rioting, and other offenses against public order.

The second explanation, overlapping often with the first, is that the criminalization of animal baiting was a prelude to or even an aspect of the attempt by the state to regulate and monopolize the means of violence, including sports, in the early modern era. This competitive thrust occurred in the context of newly emerging class struggles, and it intersected, for example, with a need to curtail the various dangers associated with the vagabondage of masterless men. Because the early modern state was in the process of embourgeoisification, perhaps the outlawing of some forms of animal cruelty did not embrace fox hunting and other pursuits and sports of the rich and powerful, though the evidence in this regard is not straightforward (e.g., though attendance at violent entertainment and sports involving animals was almost exclusively gendered—men did attend, women generally didn't—the audience for some sports, such as cockfighting, drew on the support of all social classes).

Whichever of these tendencies better explains the banning of animal baitings and what it portended for the rapidly deepening fractures in mid-seventeenth-century British society, their resolution lies well beyond the scope and aim of this chapter. However, organized as sport and as entertainment, the continued existence of animal baitings was seen as a threat to the champions of law and order. Animal baitings were noisy, messy, and disrespectful events that were vulnerable to the state's increasing tendency to regulate human–animal relations. They involved actions that threatened public order. They directly challenge the state's tendency to monopolize violence. They were seen as "cruel."

In trying to understand why they did what they did, it is tempting to read backward from the Puritans' actions to their possible motives and intentions. There is thus a third explanation of a possible link between, on the one hand, the Puritan-led criminalization of animal baiting in England and, on the other, the emergence in Ireland of the 1635 Act and its justificatory phrase "besides the cruelty used to the beasts." This explanation hinges on the answer to a single, irritatingly difficult question: What motive did the Puritans have for opposing animal cruelty?

The Puritans' most likely source of motivation was the inspiration afforded by Calvin's theology of Reformism. In this respect, a rereading of Calvin's 1562 *Laws and Statutes of Geneva* is a little disappointing. Concerned chiefly as it was with early modern forms of capitalist organization, Calvin's *Laws and Statutes* offers little by way of principled guidance for how humans should treat animals. Not much of relevance can therefore be read into its short paragraphs that seek to regulate the trade of butchers, for example, about honest weights and measures and about the disposal of animal blood.[99] These were common regulations set up by guilds and boroughs in early modern societies throughout Europe, and they had little or nothing to do with the cultivation of humane attitudes to animals.

A text with more likely motivating appeal is Calvin's 1541–1559 *Institutes of the Christian Religion*. The *Institutes* contain its author's lively polemics against his detractors and theological rivals. Here, Calvin's elegant and flowery prose is replete with animal imagery and animal metaphors and with barbed testimony to the diversity of creatures in God's kingdom, including humans ("ye devious snakes," "filthy dogs," "stupid asses," and so on).

To a seventeenth-century Puritan campaigning against animal baiting, however, exactly what message could or should be gleaned from Calvin's text is not at all clear. Confusingly, the *Institutes* might have pointed the faithful not in one but in several directions. Consider two. On the one hand, for Calvin animals are part of God's creation, and we humans are therefore obliged to treat them with respect. Thus, in discussing God's creation of the world, Calvin stated that God "sustains, nourishes, and cares for, everything he has made, even to the least sparrow."[100] Again, quoting the Lord's word with approval, Calvin promised that "I will make for you a covenant with the beasts of the field, with the birds of the air, and the reptiles of the ground."[101]

On the other hand, the *Institutes* unequivocally demanded obedience to the Old Testament injunctions about the hierarchy in the Great Chain of Being. These injunctions dictate that humans are by nature superior to beasts and that animals' labor, skin, and flesh are at our disposal when and as we should need them. But even in drawing these ultimately rigid boundaries between humans and animals, Calvin left open a door for more refined discussion. At one point in the *Institutes*, he seemed to make an ally of Plutarch's Gryllus, who suggested that in the absence of religion, "men are in no wise superior to brute beasts, but are in many respects far more miserable."[102] Moreover, in his *Commentaries*, Calvin stated flatly that "the bodies of dumb beasts . . . and donkeys and men come from the same clay"[103] and that "men are required to practice justice even in dealing with animals . . . *a just man cares well for his beasts*."[104]

However, the attempt to read backward from actions to motives is a treacherous path. At times, of course, it is nearly impossible to distinguish motive from self-interest and this from self-glorification. At others, inconsistency or simple error may lie between motive and action, further complicating discovery of the Puritans' source of inspiration. For our purposes, the result is uncertainty about why, precisely, the Puritans opposed animal cruelty.

In different ways, this inconclusiveness about Puritan intent is reinforced by some of the arguments of two important and well-known books.
Their common focus is human–animal relations. One is Keith Thomas's
magisterial *Man and the Natural World*, the other Erica Fudge's insightful
Perceiving Animals. To take *Man and the Natural World* first, Thomas documents, often in excruciating detail, a great variety of human cruelties to a
great variety of animals. He tries to show that a transformation in human(e)
sentiments toward animals unfolded gradually in England over a long period of time. One among many of Thomas's illustrations of cruelty is the
example of Queen Elizabeth's delight at the screeching of cats burning on
bonfires and her giddy love of hunting deer.[105] Others are provided by
various sorts of animal baiting and are indulged in mostly by males but also
by members of all ages and social classes.

To Thomas, the growth of pro-animal sentiments is not, strictly speaking, a purely modern achievement. On the contrary, he insists, arguments
against cruelty have existed in England from very early times. As evidence
of this longevity, Thomas quotes a passage from the moral treatise *Dives
et Pauper*:

> And therefore men should have ruth [i.e., pity] of beasts and birds and not
> harm them without cause . . . and therefore they that for cruelty and vanity
> . . . torment beasts or fowl more than . . . is speedful [i.e., expedient] to
> man's living . . . they sin . . . full grievously.[106]

This was written "no later than 1410," and Thomas somewhat aggressively adds that "this is a notable passage and a very embarrassing one
to anybody trying to trace some development in English thinking about
animal cruelty."[107] He proceeds very successfully to catalogue how in late
Elizabethan and early Stuart England, animal cruelty was vociferously opposed in pamphlets, newsletters, and sermons by a clamor of Protestant
and Puritan reformers, including Quakers, Dissenters, and Latitudinarians.
Over the next 200 years, he continues, and aided by the rise of the natural
sciences and their inherent antianthropocentric tendencies, these challenges were pushed onward, expanded in scope, and consolidated. Even
wrapped in the relative safety of quotation marks, Thomas is quite upbeat
about this triumph of inevitability:

> Animals had thus moved from being mere "brutes" or "beasts" to being
> "fellow beasts," "fellow mortals" or "fellow creatures" and finally to being
> "companions," "friends" and "brothers."[108]

Two relevant points should be made about Thomas's history of the triumph of animal protection. The first is that this history was by no means an uncontested one. Like battles in the English civil war itself, victories could easily be reversed. Thus, as evidence of forward progress, Thomas records that, given the lack of direction by Parliament,

> some municipalities had already begun to act. Maidstone banned cock-throwing in 1653 as "cruel and un-Christianlike" [while] Chester had prohibited bear-baiting on similar grounds. Other local authorities followed suit.[109]

Thomas also fails to emphasize how very mixed is the evidence about the effectiveness of the outlawing of such cruelties to bears, bulls, and cocks. It is worth recording here that, propelled by the zeal of the Puritan Mayor Henry Hardware, it is true that bearbaiting was prohibited in Chester in 1599, partly because it was accompanied by public displays of drunkenness and violence. Nevertheless, this prohibition was effectively reversed by Hardware's successors when bearbaiting was officially sponsored in Chester in 1610 and bullbaiting in 1620.[110] In fact, Chester did not formally abolish bullbaiting until 1803 (and Britain as a whole, by statute, not until 1835).

It is also not easy to agree with Thomas's logic when he confronts the question of the Puritans' beliefs about cruelty to animals and a little lamely concludes that, yes, the Puritans believed animal cruelty to be wrong and that, because of this belief, they opposed it.[111] This reasoning enlightens us about neither the derivation of the Puritans' opposition to cruelty nor why their opposition arose when and as it did. But both of these are among the necessary conditions of understanding the emergence of cruelty laws. Within the same trajectory, consider also the Cromwellian Protectorate's Ordinance for Prohibiting Cock-matches (March 31, 1654). What was the Puritans' specific intent in this ordinance?[112] Was it singular? Twofold? More? The ordinance's language clearly indicates that, in declaring cock-fighting matches unlawful assemblies, its framers did not have in the front of their minds a reduction in animals' suffering. Rather, such matches were explicitly to be prohibited, the ordinance stated, because it was believed that cockfighting often led to disturbances of the public peace and to the dishonor of God and were often accompanied by gaming, drinking, swearing, quarreling, and "other dissolute practices" and often produced the ruin of the participants and their families.

Surely, if the Puritans had opposed animal cruelty for theological or utilitarian or aesthetic reasons, that would have been one thing. But if Thomas is suggesting that the Puritans opposed animal cruelty because they believed that animals have *a right* to be free from human cruelty, that is something else altogether and, moreover, it is false. Before that right was properly articulated and even partially recognized in law, 250 years more were to go by. In fact, as Thomas himself indicates, those who attacked animal cruelty *in itself* were rare exceptions and were regarded by their contemporaries as eccentric.

In her book *Perceiving Animals*, Erica Fudge takes an opposite tack to Thomas's large-scale teleology. In so doing, she manages adroitly to place her readers in the very midst of the seventeenth-century audience at the London Bear-Garden. Fudge's method of representation is to rely on observations by the Bear-Garden's awed or frightened visitors and treatises on them by well-known Puritans Robert Bolton, Phillip Stubbs, and William Perkins. She documents that members of the Bear-Garden audience admired baiting for a large number of reasons because—when they reacted to a screaming monkey on horseback who was chased and attacked by dogs—it is "an enjoyable parody"; "a comedy"; "the disturbing spectacle . . . becomes a reminder of the superiority of humanity"; the monkey is both like members of the audience and not like them . . . humanity is constantly being reinforced";[113] and in particular types of baiting, such as bears by dogs, the cruelty to animals is a metaphor of the poor and oppressed rising up against social inequality.[114]

Similarly, Fudge also shows that the Puritans opposed London's animal baiting for a great variety of reasons. Among them were that "it is not very pleasant to watch," "it is dangerous," "it reminds humans of their weakness in the face of wild nature," "it is the fruit of the rebellion against God," "it is a reminder . . . of the essential depravity of postlapsarian humanity," and "it shows our natural propensity to cruelty."[115]

Given the great variety of attitudes consistent with or leading to opposition to cruelty, it is therefore hard to know exactly what influence Calvinism exerted on the dividing line for English Puritans between acceptable and unacceptable behavior in human–animal relations. Certainly, Sunday observance enjoined Puritan families to rest cattle on the Sabbath. But did they observe the Sabbath because they felt obliged to care for quadrupeds one day a week or because they wanted to fill their churches with off-duty farmers? Certainly, too, Puritans opposed most forms of animal baiting. But did their views and practices derive from their opposition to the infliction of pain and suffering on animals? Or did they emerge because the Puritans saw cruelty as conducive to idleness and to sins of the flesh? It is also likely true that roughly the same number of Puritan English women and men decried bearbaiting as approved of bullbaiting and bull running. The heinousness of these cruelties was apparently outweighed by the carnivorous Puritans' desire to tenderize the meat and thus to improve its texture and flavor (cravings quite consistent with the robust recipes on display in a cookbook by Oliver's wife, *The Court and Kitchen of Elizabeth Cromwell*).

How can the curious position of English Puritanism in the early history of animal protection be summarized? In doing this, we do not need to travel as far as Macaulay did when he cynically complained that the Puritan hated bearbaiting "not because it gave pain to the bear but because it gave pleasure to the spectators." Indeed, he generally contrived to enjoy this double pleasure."[116] Suspicions can legitimately be raised about the reformers' political motives, however, and it can also be asked whether their sincerity was altogether pure. Inconsistencies can also be pinpointed between their beliefs and actions. Regardless of how these particular questions are resolved, we can say, definitely, that the seventeenth-century Puritan notion of cruelty differed profoundly from the rights-based one that was to appear only much later—at the earliest not until the 1880s. Whereas the Puritan notion was inspired by theological reformism and articulated in anthropocentric terms, a full-fledged understanding of cruelty would be one based on a recognition of animals' interests for their own sake, not ours.

The Meaning(s) of Cruelty in the 1635 Act

Three clear explanations have been given for the 1635 Act's criminalization of plowing by tail. First, plow fines were a useful source of income for the English administration in Ireland. Second, criminalization was an act in a deadly cultural drama the outcome of which was routinely determined by the power of the English conquerors to impose their will on the Irish. Its dramatic focus was the English belief that most Gaelic Irish customs were vastly inferior to their own and manifest, especially, in their failure either to breed good horses or to plow in an efficient and productive manner. Third, the 1635 Act was but one of many mechanisms pursued by the state to regulate human–animal relationships. A fourth, more contentious explanation—and one that will soon be revisited—is the relationship between early modern state formation and the motivations that English Puritans might have had for outlawing animal baitings.

The meaning of cruelty in the 1635 Act can now be addressed more or less directly. About the attaching of "short ploughs . . . to the tails of ponies walking abreast," it has been observed that history shows how even the most obvious and reasonable reform may be resented when it involves a change in the habits of country people. . . . The English settlers who saw these ploughs at work thought them both "uncivil" and unprofitable; and the cruelty was obvious, Chichester stating that many hundreds of beasts were killed or spoiled yearly.[117]

Chichester's claim is not only condescending, of course, but probably also a bloated exaggeration; if "many hundreds of beasts were killed or spoiled yearly," then the practice would have expired of its own volition. Moreover, even if in 1613 Chichester actually believed, in respect of plowing by tail, that "the cruelty was obvious," then the problem still remains: what did such usages of the word "cruelty" mean? Whatever "cruelty" was, it was not obvious. Commensurately, what should be understood by the 1635 Act's phrase "besides the cruelty used to the beasts"? It may be assumed that the term "beasts" is restricted to animals that were used to plow. These would have included horses, mares, geldings, garrans, and colts and possibly also oxen and donkeys, It may also be assumed that the word "besides" had no more devious meaning than "in addition to" or "an obvious reason that" or, even, "it goes without saying that."

It is probably also correct to assume that in the act, cruelty referred either to an accounting principle such as "lacking in profit" or to an action that was wrong because it caused animals to suffer. The choice appears to be a stark one. To put it in another form, when James I complained about plowing by tail in Ireland that it was "a rude and hurtful" custom,[118] did he mean thereby that it was a disservice to good husbandry and hurtful to English revenues? Or that it was painful to horses? On balance, it was the former. And again, consider that in *Cavelarice*, the husbandry purveyor Gervase Markham expressed great concern about horses' "swellings, brushings [and] blisterings."[119] Markham would probably not have described the mental state of someone who had intentionally inflicted those injuries as cruel. However, were he to have condemned such equine injuries as cruel—whether intentionally inflicted or not—it is likely that by that term he intended waste and inefficiency and a violation of husbandry principles.

Some insight into the difficulty of interpreting cruelty's meaning in the 1635 Act in Ireland can be found in a few paragraphs in two important contemporary texts. The first is the *View of the Present State of Ireland* by Edmund Spenser, a fierce critic of Irish backwardness and a champion of English husbandry principles. Consider the juxtaposition of two scenes in the *View*, the central dramatic form of which is the dialogue between Eudoxus and Irenius. In the first, Irenius relates a number of Irish customs to Eudoxus. He does this in order to show that the Irish derived much of their culture from the ancient Scythians—including, for example, the habit of those in the north who capture wolves and then "boil the blood of the beast living and to make meat therof."[120]

Having listened to Irenius's telling of this custom, Eudoxus remarks only that he was "all that while as it were entranced and carried so far from myself as that I am now right sorry that ye ended so soon."[121] Notice that Eudoxus did not reply to Irenius that the practice of boiling wolves alive was wrong or that it was in any sense cruel. Rather, Eudoxus merely said that he was sorry that Irenius's story "had ended so soon."

Contrast this scene with another in the *View* where Spenser described in detail the weapons of Irish warriors

> whose . . . bows are not past three quarters of a yard long with a string of wreathed hemp, slackly bent, and whose arrows are not above half an ell long, tipped with steel heads made like common broad arrow-heads, but much more sharp and slender, that they must enter an armed man or horse most cruelly, notwithstanding that they are shot forth weakly.[122]

In his description of how Irish-made arrows enter an armed man or horse "most cruelly," Spenser was surely not articulating a concern for humans' or horses' welfare. Rather, he was describing a practice that in this particular case had been undertaken efficiently, effectively, and lethally and, therefore, cruelly.

Now consider the pamphlet *A New Description of Ireland*, published in London in 1610. Its author was the peripatetic Barnabe Rich, a pensioned English army officer with strong Puritan leanings who had once been imprisoned by the Dublin sheriff for writing a hostile tract on popery. Throughout his text, Rich considered Ireland basically a good and a godly place. But he also saw it as trapped between, on the one hand, the twin incivilities of popery and priests and, on the other, predictably enough, various backward Irish customs. One of these customs was plowing by tail:

> I can see a number of defects, and that in the most principall points of their Husbandry; as in the manner of the Tilling of their grounde . . . they have no other means whereby to draw the Plough, but every Horse by his own taile, so that when the poore beast by his painfull labour, hath worne the haire of his tail so short, as it can no longer be tied, the Plough must stand.[123]

Rich's description of plowing by tail is not simply the standard English fare of the backwardness of the Irish and their violation of good husbandry practices. It is that, indeed, and more. In the previous quotation, for example, Rich shows himself sympathetic to the plight of Irish farmers who, wanting to till their land, have no choice other than to opt for the economy of horses' tails. But Rich also displays concern for horses' welfare. In fact, following a discussion of "civility, humanity, or any manner of Decencie," the reader is momentarily breathless, turning the page to see if these three virtues might collectively embody the antonymy of some never-before-voiced notion of cruelty in itself. Excitement has its eventual reward. After some barbed, well-rehearsed comparisons between the Irish, Scythians, and cannibals titled "That the Irish are by nature inclined unto cruelty," Rich writes,

> The extreamest point whereunto the crueltie of man may stretch, is for one man to kill another, yea Divinity it selfe, willeth us to shew favor, and not to be cruelly inclined, no not to bruit beastes, which the Almighty hath created and placed amongst his other creatures, as well for his glory as for his service, and hath himselfe said do be merciful respect unto them. . . . *We see here God himself had some commiseration to the poore cattell, and it was not without respect, that he prescribed to Moses,* in the first Table of the Commandementes, that as well the cattell as the stranger within thy gates, should cease from their labour, and rest on the Sabaoth day. If it hath pleased God the Creator of all things to be thus regardful to the worke of his handes, I am awfully persuaded, that such as by nature do shew themselves to be no lesse bloudy minded towards men, then towards beasts, do shew themselves to be naturally inclined to cruelty, the ugliness whereof, is to be abhorred and detected amongst men.[124]

Although this particular excerpt is not directed to plowing by tail as such, it clearly expresses the Puritan sentiments described earlier in this chapter. The excerpt—indeed, Rich's entire pamphlet—is ruled by the Godly might of English Puritanism, thus its repetition of the Almighty's command to respect animals, to care for them, to have mercy on them, to rest them on the Sabbath, and "and not to be cruelly inclined, no not to bruit beastes, which the Almighty hath created." However, even though Rich's text is a clear expression of one sort of Puritan sentiment about animals, those sentiments were themselves ambiguous and inconsistent. Were they voiced from a position that championed the interests of animals? Well, yes, no, and perhaps. Or do they reflect a fear of a disorderly public, a drunken, animal-baiting congregation that might not observe the Sabbath? It is uncertain.

If the anonymous English draftsmen of the 1635 Act had in mind what Spenser's Irenius and Eudoxus meant by the term "cruelty," then they would not have intended something akin to "suffering" or "pain" let alone sentiments involving moral condemnation. Perhaps, as Governor Chichester has been credited with saying, the term was meant to deplore a whole chain of events that began with plowing by tail, led next to the spoiling of horses, and, ultimately and most wastefully, ended with horses' deaths.

Suppose, instead, that the draftsmen's intentions were less materialistic and more spiritual (though in the case of Calvinism, for example, these tendencies were intimately intertwined). In this projection, the inspiration would not have been prompted by Roman Catholicism, indifferent almost to a point of principle as this persuasion's dogma was to animals' suffering.[125] The substantial Ulster population of Scottish Presbyterians and among them, in particular, Scottish Calvinists were the most likely source of what at this time might have passed as an enlightened attitude to animals. However, tolerated in Ireland until the early 1630s, Scottish Presbyterians were increasingly targets of Wentworth's wrath. In part, this was because Scottish Presbyterianism was not the version of Protestantism he sought to encourage but rather the Puritan-leaning Church of Ireland. This church demanded that all recusants and Nonconformists swear an oath of loyalty to the English monarch.[126] In this case, too, that is where, as this chapter has been at pains to stress, most seventeenth-century Irish roads led.

Aftermath

At the end of one of the several rebellions against English rule in the 1640s, a condition of peace insisted on by the Irish Confederates was the repeal of the penal laws, including the 1635 Act. By General Ormond and a disingenuous Charles I, this condition was agreed to in return for the Confederates' provision of an antiparliamentary standing army in Ireland.[127] Article 22 of the Ormond Treaty of 1649 proposed to rescind all the earlier legislation that forbade plowing by tail. The secretary for foreign tongues to the Council of State, John Milton, passionately condemned the 1649 treaty and reserved special vehemence for article 22. Milton condemned plowing by tail and sought to uphold the existing law against it not because he saw the practice as cruel to animals—an idea that he did not mention—but because he thought it a custom that showed the Irish to be primitive, savage, idiots, and fools. His anti-Catholic, colonialist rhetoric helped forge the ideological groundwork for the imminent Cromwellian "reduction" of Ireland, even though it was less the Irish than the Scottish and, perhaps, the English Presbyterians whom Milton regarded as the most serious threat to English rule. Despite the promise held forth in the Ormond Treaty, forfeitures and fines for plowing by tail nevertheless continued.[128] The unpopular law was not actually repealed until August 31, 1828.[129]

Much about the 1635 Act is still unknown.[130] How were individual cases of plowing by tail brought to the attention of the authorities and with what results? How were appeals administered? How was recidivism addressed? Barring some unforeseen discovery, the complete absence of relevant judicial records implies that these interesting questions of enforcement and administration cannot be pursued with much success.

Nor is it known in what ways the downtrodden Irish resisted the provisions of the 1635 Act. Herein lies a major puzzle. Why would horses' tails be used for plowing if those who plowed knew that the practice would lead, sooner or later, to the animals' destruction? Perhaps those who plowed with horses' tails tended not to use their own horses—a possibility completely ignored in the discourse of English administrators, contemporary diarists, and the 1622 commission. If poor Gaelic farmers owned neither their own horses nor the meadows and fields required for pasture, then did the conditions of their servitude mean that sometimes plowing by tail was a form of resistance? If so, it anticipated the more widespread mutilations of the horses and cattle of Anglo-Irish landlords that were to be condemned by the latter as agrarian outrages.

How successful was the 1635 Act in its criminalization of plowing by tail? Much of the answer hinges on the yardstick of success. The 1635 Act was very far from being a neat and tidy triumph of humane reason over various sorts of barbarism. It had much more to do with English political will, cultural chauvinism, and the pursuit of private profit than the protection of animals—and perhaps very little at all to do with the latter. The act's usage of the term "cruelty" mostly referred to something akin to uncultivated, uncouth, wasteful, lethal, primitive, and Other. It was, in short, synonymous with how seventeenth-century English administrators and settlers tended to look at or look down on the native Irish, especially the Irish poor.

Did the 1635 Act succeed in raising money for the English in Ireland? Yes, undoubtedly. Did it succeed in eradicating plowing by tail? No. According to the peripatetic John Dunton, plowing by tail had disappeared or had "been given up" in Ireland by 1698, even in remote districts like western Connacht.[131] However, another observer reported that in 1777 it was "done in every season" and "all over Cavan."[132] Yet another report stated that the practice existed in Roscommon as recently as 1809 "and probably much later,"[133] while the distinguished Irish ethnographer E. E. Evans has written that it was certainly in use in County Galway in 1820 and that "as late as 1938, in Donegal, [she] spoke to a man who told me that the tail was secured by a difficult knot which in his youth only a few men knew."[134] In 1949, in an interview in County Cavan, a laborer, Pat Smith, recalled,

> I heard of them ploughing with bulls and bullocks in olden times. . . . They had another way of ploughing—they'd tackle the plough to the horse's tail. I don't know how it was done unless they had a rope tied around the tail. I heard of my grandfather doing it, and a yeoman or some class of a policeman came into the field and challenged him about it. My grandfather ordered him out of the field and said he'd prosecute him for trespass or something like that. The horse would have a long tail.[135]

Notes

1. The 1635 Act (10 & 11 Car. I, chap. 15) required that sheep's wool should be clipped or sheared rather than pulled. Before I dispense altogether here with the crime of pulling the wool from sheep, I should say that the 1635 Act was not the first legislation emanating from London to outlaw the practice. It was preceded by a proclamation (*Against Pulling Wool . . .*) for Scotland of March 18, 1617, that outlawed "pulling wool from sheep instead of clipping it." The prohibition was inserted into the 1635 Act partly on the recommendation of the Irish Commission of 1622, one of whose specific charges had been to inquire "whether the pulling of wool from the sheep's back with their hands and with sticks split and twisted, whereby many sheep do perish and much wool is lost . . . be not a barbarous and hurtful usage" (p. 57).

2. My thanks to Ber ó Muirí in Galway for her generous advice with this translation.

3. See also Bernadette Cunningham (1986), "Native Culture and Political Change in Ireland, 1580–1640."

4. Fergus Kelly (2000), *Early Irish Farming*, p. 477.

5. On the possible Neolithic origins of plowing by tail, see P. J. Fowler (1969), "Early Prehistoric Agriculture in Western Europe: Some Archaeological Evidence," p. 158.

6. W. Pinkerton (1858), "Ploughing by the Horse's Tail," p. 216. However, I have been unable to substantiate Pinkerton's claim about an image of the use of a short plow on the Piercefield bronze in England. It is apparently true that several Roman bronze pieces were unearthed by archaeologists in Piercefield. However, the Piercefield in Pinkerton's account is probably not the one in Yorkshire but rather the one in Monmouthshire in Wales. On the Piercefield, Monmouthshire, discoveries, see Anonymous (1840), "May 21," pp. 634–36.

7. See Roger Robertson (1792), "Observations and Facts concerning the Breed of Horses in Scotland in Ancient Times," p. 278. Similarly, see Hugh Miller (1850), *Scenes and Legends of the North of Scotland*.

8. Robert Kemp Philp (1859), *The History of Progress in Great Britain*, p. 89.

9. In his *Historical Account of the Plantation in Ulster*, George Hill (1877) has claimed that plowing by tail "prevailed from a remote period, not only in Ireland and Scotland, but throughout many other regions of Europe" (p. 459, n. 32). Although Hill offers no evidence in support of it, his claim is probably correct.

10. On the development of horse-draft practices in Ireland, see especially A. T. Lucas (1973), "Irish Ploughing Practices," pp. 67–71, and Fergus Kelly (2000), *Early Irish Farming*, p. 21. My thanks to Raymond Gillespie for alerting me to Anthony Lucas's very detailed article on plowing by tail.

11. The curious case of using a camel's tail to plow is documented as follows in *The Annals of Connacht* (1472): "Extraordinary animals arrived in Ireland from the King of England, viz. a kind of mare, yellow in colour, with bovine hooves, very long neck, very large head and a very long ugly, scanty-haired tail. She . . . would draw any load, however heavy, that was attached to her tail" (p. 561).

12. Fowler (1969), "Early Prehistoric Agriculture in Western Europe," has claimed "since the ploughman is dressed up in some form of bird garment and is also bearing a prominent, albeit reversed phallus, the fertility overtones are unmistakeable" (p. 158).

13. See, for example, J. J. McAuliffe (1943), "Ploughing by Horses' Tails." See also John O'Donovan (1858), "Notes" (p. 135), who tried to argue that plowing by tail was "impossible." The year following O'Donovan's note, the *Irish Times* (September 23, 1859) felt compelled to record that "if our grandfathers had any regard for truth, we must believe that in their young days it was not uncommon to yoke horses to plough by the tails in parts of Ireland" (p. 1).

14. Barnabe Rich (1610), *A New Description of Ireland*, p. 26. The original forms of spelling, punctuation, and syntax have been retained except where clarity requires their modernization.

15. A mid-eighteenth-century illustration from Orkney of several ponies loaded with peat on their backs, with the bridle of one tied to the tail of another, has been reproduced in Alexander Fenton (1978), *The Northern Isles: Orkney and Shetland*, p. 247.

16. William Lithgow (1632), *The Totall Discourse of the Rare Adventures and Painefull Peregrinations*, p. 377.

17. Thomas Dineley (1680), "Dineley's Journal," p. 545.

18. Edward MacLysaght (1979), *Irish Life in the Seventeenth Century*, p. 174. Jonathan Bell (1987), "The Improvement of Irish Farming Techniques since 1750: Theory and Practice" (pp. 37–38), has with some delicacy deduced that "as harnesses, tails were not very reliable and certainly very difficult to repair."

19. A passage in the *Annals of Ulster* conveys the humiliating torture inflicted on a group of Norse captives by Gilla-MoChonna, king of southern Brega: "The king yoked most of his captives to a plough, and forced two others to follow, harrowing (*ic foirsed*) from their scrotums (*asa tíagaib*)" (cited in Kelly [2000], *Early Irish Farming*, p. 478).

20. Arthur Young (1780), *Tour in Ireland*, p. 258; see also pp. 211, 235.

21. Young, *Tour in Ireland*, p. 249. Cuthbert Bede (1878), "Note," has suggested that "for harrowing . . . when the tail had become too much docked for the work, it was artificially lengthened by twisted sticks" (p. 503). Presumably, this method would also have been applied to plowing by tail.

22. For an influential plea for the development of the Irish law along the lines of the institutions that the Norman conquest imposed on Britain, see Sir John Davies (1612), *A Discovery of the True Causes Why Ireland Was Never Entirely Subdued*. A concise and very helpful guide to the lawmaking process in Ireland is provided in W. N. Osborough (1995), "Introduction" to *The Irish Statutes 1310–1800*. The complexity of the process of lawmaking confronting English Lord Deputies of Ireland is profusely instantiated in John McCavitt (1998), *Sir Arthur Chichester: Lord Deputy of Ireland 1605–1616*.

23. On this, see "The King to Arthur Chichester, November 30, 1612," in *Calendar of State Papers, Ireland* (hereinafter *Cal.S.P.Ire.*), *1611–1614*, p. 305.

24. "Acts in Next Parliament," pp. 188–93, in *Cal.S.P.Ire.*, *1611–1614*, p. 193. In 1615, ostensibly on the grounds that fines were having no effect, the Irish House of Commons petitioned that corporal punishment be awarded those convicted of plowing by tail. See also George O'Brien (1919), *The Economic History of Ireland in the Seventeenth Century*, p. 39.

25. On the commission's brief, see Victor Treadwell (2006), "Introduction" to Irish Commission of 1622, pp. xxix–xxxvi.

26. Irish Commission of 1622, p. 57.

27. Irish Commission of 1622, pp. 6, 15, 57, 523, and 731, respectively.

28. Irish Commission of 1622, p. 258.

29. On this proposed extension to "other beasts," see "Fines for Ploughing by the Horses' Tails, March 15, 1625," in *Cal.S.P.Ire.*, *1615–1625*, p. 572.

30. The complex political causes of the relative lack of response to the recommendations of the 1622 commission are identified in Victor Treadwell (1998), *Buckingham and Ireland, 1616–1628: A Study in Anglo-Irish Politics*, and Nicholas Canny (2001), *Making Ireland British: 1580–1650*, pp. 243–58.

31. See also Treadwell, "Introduction," p. xxxix. Wentworth arrived in Ireland with eighty horse carriages, and, according to C. V. Wedgwood (1961), *Thomas Wentworth, First Earl of Strafford, 1593–1641: A Revaluation*, London: Jonathan Cape, his first sight of Ireland depressed him. Dublin, for example, seemed to Wentworth to be sinking into the mud, and he saw no possibility of indulging "his favourite sport of hawking, as not a partridge had been seen near Dublin within the memory of man" (p. 137).

32. The Articles of Plantation required Irish farmers to plow after the manner of the English Pale, or, in other words, with the use of the long plow. See Irish Commission of 1622, p. 608.

33. See *Royal Proclamations of the Tudor and Stuart Sovereigns 1485–1491*, vol. 2, pp. 145–51.

34. Hugh Kearney (1959), *Strafford in Ireland 1633–41*, p. 63.

35. On Wentworth's possible intentions, see J. F. Merritt (1996), "Power and Communication: Thomas Wentworth and Government at a Distance during the Personal Rule, 1629–1635," p. 116. See also Kearney, *Strafford in Ireland.*

36. The group included the Connacht lawyers Patrick Darcy and Richard Martin (forebear of Richard "Humanity Dick" Martin, M.P.); the former agents Sir Edward Fitzharris, Sir Henry Lynch, and Sir Thomas Luttrell; and Sir Nicholas White, Nicholas Plunkett, Sir William Sarsfield, and Maurice Fitzgerald. For more on the composition of this group, see Aidan Clarke (1991), "The Government of Wentworth 1632–40," pp. 247–48.

37. Kearney, *Strafford in Ireland,* p. 62. Among the other Graces of lesser importance were those licensing aqua vitae, wine, ale, beer, and the tanning of leather (p. 63).

38. Irish Commission of 1622, pp. 248–49.

39. "The King to Sir Arthur Chichester, November 30, 1612," in *Cal.S.P.Ire., 1611–1614,* p. 305. The fines were levied at least in Ulster and Connaught ("Cornwalis to Lord Northampton, October 26, 1613," in *Cal.S.P.Ire., 1611–1614,* p. 432).

40. "Answer of the Lord Deputy Chichester and the Privy Council to the Petition of the Recusant Lords and Others in Ireland, August 31 1613," pp. 413–18, in *Cal.S.P.Ire., 1611–1614,* pp. 417–18.

41. Irish Commission of 1622, "Revenues," pp. 366–67.

42. *Desiderata Curiosa Hibernica* (1772), 1, p. 242. In 1625, Uvedall sold his license for plowing by tail for the large sum of 1,250 pounds; see "The King to Sir Arthur Chichester, November 30, 1612," in *Cal.S.P.Ire., 1611–1614,* p. 305.

43. While advocating the favored English long plows, some of the English administrators complicated the issue by wrongly referring to the use of short plows when what they actually meant was "ploughing after the Irish method," which was with the use of horses' tails. For example, see "Cornwaley to Lord Northampton," in *Cal.S.P.Ire., 1611–1614,* p. 432.

44. Irish Commission of 1622, p. 248.

45. "The King to St. John, May 18, 1620," in *Cal.S.P.Ire., 1615–1625,* p. 282.

46. "Letter from Lord Falkland to the Privy Council, December 10, 1627," in *Cal.S.P.Ire., 1625–1632,* p. 292. See also "Letter from the King to the Lord Deputy for Sir Francis Annesley, November 21, 1627," ordering him "to issue warrants for the collection of the penalty imposed upon such as should plough by the tails or rumps of their beasts" (*Cal.S.P.Ire., 1625–1632,* p. 283).

47. Cited in Clarke (1966), *The Old English in Ireland, 1603–1660,* p. 240.

48. See appendix 1.

49. Irish Commission of 1622, pp. 248–49.

50. "Sir Charles Cornwaleys to Lord Northampton, October 22, 1613," in *Cal.S.P.Ire., 1611–1614,* p. 430.

51. "Sir Charles Cornwaleys to Lord Northampton, October 22, 1613," in *Cal.S.P.Ire., 1611–1614,* p. 430.

52. To some unrecorded Irish grievances, one commission responded that "the natives pretend a necessity of continuing this manner of ploughing as more fit for stony and mountainous grounds, yet the Commissioners think it not fit to be continued." This appears in *Commission to Examine the Abuses in Parliament and Country* (November 12, 1613), *Cal.S.P.Ire.*, pp. 436–55, 448–49.

53. *Commission to Examine the Abuses in Parliament and Country* (November 12, 1613), *Cal.S.P.Ire.*, pp. 447–48.

54. *Commission to Examine the Abuses in Parliament and Country* (November 12, 1613), *Cal.S.P.Ire.*, p. 448.

55. Leonard Mascal (1620), *The Government of Cattel*, p. 2.

56. T. W. Moody (1939), *The Londonderry Plantation 1609–41*, p. 342. Although describing plowing by tail "as bad husbandry because an efficient system of harnessing was within the resources of even small farmers," Jonathan Bell (1987), "The Improvement of Irish Farming Techniques since 1750: Theory and Practice," has also commented that "collars made from *súgañ* (twisted straw), and traces made from straw or withies were recognized by contemporaries as easily made, cheap and effective" (pp. 37–38).

57. In 1613, one English official ("Sir Charles Cornwaleys to Lord Northampton, October 22, 1613," pp. 431–32, in *Cal.S.P.Ire., 1611–1614*) stated that "the Irish affirm that are of their experience, they find that in ground hilly, stony, &c, full of bulrushes, where a long plough will not go, it is the most profitable way for them to use the share, and that it is more easy for the garrans to go up the mountains, where it is all liberty, than where it is loaded by English 'horse-colars.'" (p. 430).

58. Richard Bagwell (1909), *Ireland under the Stuarts and during the Interregnum*, p. 65.

59. On plowing by tail in Ulster, see Raymond Gillespie (1985), *Colonial Ulster: The Settlement of East Ulster 1600–1641*, pp. 64–65, 75, 218. For an estimate of the prevalence of plowing by tail in the Ulster plantation ("more prevalent . . . than elsewhere"), see Moody, *The Londonderry Plantation 1609–41*, p. 342, and Philip Robinson (2000), *The Plantation of Ulster: British Settlement in an Irish Landscape 1600–1670*, pp. 30–31, 179, 188.

60. On this, see E. E. Evans (1976), "Some Problems of Irish Ethnography: The Example of Ploughing by the Tail," pp. 34–35. According to Evans, it is clear from the early literature that horses were occasionally used in pre-Norman Ireland and that "if the implements they used were light the tail would have been the most efficient and even perhaps the most humane means of traction" (p. 35). However, it remains unclear what Evans meant either by "early" or by "humane." A similar worry should be attached to the claim by Pinkerton, "Ploughing by the Horse's Tail," that "in justice to those who continue the practice of *harrowing by the tail,* I beg to observe that, as far as cruelty is concerned, I really can see no objection to it; for if you gave the animals any pain, I do not think they would submit to it as quietly as they do; indeed there are people who assert it to be the most *humane* way of doing the work!" (p. 217, n.).

61. Edward MacLysaght (1979), *Irish Life in the Seventeenth Century*, p. 174. Moreover, Arthur Young (1780), *Tour in Ireland*, recorded that the Irish "insist that, take a horse tired in traces, and put him to work by the tail, he will draw better: quite fresh again" (p. 211).

62. On the influence of Cambrensis on Spenser, see Canny, *Making Ireland British 1580–1650*, p. 47. On a variety of preformed notions of Irish incivility, see Patricia Coughlan (1990), "'Cheap and Common Animals': The English Anatomy of Ireland in the Seventeenth Century." See also Nicholas Canny (1976), *The Elizabethan Conquest of Ireland: A Pattern Established, 1565–76*.

63. "Glibbes," Spenser complained, "which is a thick curled bush of haire, hanging down over their eyes, and monstrously disguising them, which are both very bad and hurtfull" (*View of the Present State of Ireland* [1633], pp. 60–61). Spenser's association of mantles with outlawry continued to be accepted by subsequent generations of English observers of rural Irish life; see, for example, James Brewer (1826), *The Beauties of Ireland: Being Original Delineations, Topographical, Historical and Biographical, of Each County*, p. 183. A nuanced and authoritative account of Spenser's *View of the Present State of Ireland* is Canny, *Making Ireland British 1580–1650*, pp. 1–58. Spenser's influence on Wentworth is discussed in Raymond Gillespie (2006), *Seventeenth-Century Ireland*, pp. 105–7, and Canny, *Making Ireland British 1580–1650*, pp. 281, 287.

64. Spenser, *View of the Present State of Ireland*, p. 149.

65. Fynes Moryson (1617), *Itinerary*, p. 51.

66. Moryson, *Itinerary*, p. 51.

67. William Lithgow (1632), *The Totall Discourse of the Rare Adventures and Painefull Peregrinations*, p. 377. The second of Lithgow's remarkable sights was that "of women going about their work with their babes behind their backs, and with breasts of such capacity and length that they were laid over their shoulders to feed the infants" (p. 377). McAuliffe, "Ploughing by Horses' Tails," has used the unlikelihood of Lithgow's second sight (an obvious male fantasy) to suggest that, in combination with the notion of plowing by tail—"these stories match each other"—"it seems to me quite likely that this enactment [i.e., the 1635 Act] was suggested by Lithgow's quaint story" (p. 9).

68. Andrew McRae (1996), *God Speed the Plough*, pp. 1–17.

69. Mr. Robert Cecil, "Proceedings in the Commons, December 9, 1601," *Historical Collections*, History of Parliament Trust.

70. Gervase Markham (1625), *The Inrichment of the Weald of Kent*, p. 20. Andrew McRae (1996), in *God Speed the Plough*, plots in great detail how the English legal concept of "approve" was gradually appropriated by the husbandry movement and reworked into a notion that signified pecuniary and profitable "improve(ment)." "'Agrarian improvement' was consolidated as a concept," writes McRae, "which conflated qualitative changes in agricultural productivity with increases in financial returns. In this form, it became the catchcry of a new age of agrarian change" (p. 137).

71. Gervase Markham (1613), *The English Husbandman*, chap. 4, p. c2.

72. Spenser, *View of the Present State of Ireland*, p. 66. For his disparaging comments on the slightness of Irish military horse furniture, see Rich, *A New Description of Ireland*, p. 96.

73. Moryson, *Itinerary*, p. 48. The use of snaffles was soon to be officially banned in England on order of Charles I—see *Royal Proclamations* (November 20, 1627), I, no. 1521, p. 179.

74. Gervase Markham (1607), *Cavelarice, or the English Horseman*, p. 2 in the dedication. The importance of Markham's bellicose English nationalism was originally made known to me by Elspeth Graham (2004) in her essay "Reading, Writing and Riding Horses in Early Modern England." Graham comments that "the importance of benevolence toward horses . . . is a semispoken tenet of all that Markham writes" (p. 32).

75. Markham, *Cavelarice*, bk. 1, pp. 16–17.

76. Markham, *Cavelarice*, bk. 1, pp. 8–10.

77. Irish Commission of 1622, p. 57.

78. McCrae, *God Speed the Plough*, p. 196. With its precise logic so suitable to colonialist plunders and the elimination of vague customary titles, surveying played no small part a few years later, in the retaliatory aftermath of the 1641 uprising, in prising some two and half million acres of Irish land from their customary owners.

79. Spenser, *View of the Present State of Ireland*, p. 149.

80. Bagwell, *Ireland under the Stuarts and during the Interregnum*, p. 125. Also on the prohusbandry agenda enacted in 1635 was the *Act to Prevent the Custom of Burning of Corne in the Straw* (10 & 11 Car. I, chap. 17). This attributed the dearth of cattle to "the ill husbandrie and improvident care of the owners" and the "natural lazie disposition of the Irish . . . [who tried] to deceive his Majestie of such debts as they may be owing at any time, and their landlords of their rents" (p. 171). In terms of husbandry principles, the statute objected to the practice because, instead of threshing corn, burning it "consum[ed] the straw, which might relieve their cattell in winter, and afford materials towards the covering or thatching their houses, and spoiling the corne, making it black, loathsome and filthy" (p. 171).

81. *Act Against Burning of Frames* (1545), 37 Hen.VIII c.vi,3.

82. Sometimes legal distinctions were made between "great cattle" and smaller quadrupeds and between cattle and sheep. Most other animals were either "wild" or "vermin" (and sometimes both, as in the case of creatures like badgers and foxes).

83. *Benefit of Clergy Removed From any Person Stealing a Horse, etc.* (1545), 37 Hen.VIII, c.8, s.2. See also *An Act for the Repeal of Certain Statutes Concerning Treasons, Felonies, etc.* (1547), 1 Edw.VI c.12, s.9. Benefit of clergy was the custom of granting lesser penalties to first-time offenders who could claim clerical status. Successfully claiming this benefit required no more proof than an ability to read the "neck verse" (Psalms 51:1). Keith Wrightson (1982), *English Society 1580–1680*, using Essex Assizes data for 1579–1603, has shown that 80 percent of

first-time offenders convicted of stealing sheep or cows claimed clerical status and that, rather than hanged, they were branded.

84. *An Act that No Man Stealing Horse or Horses Shall Enjoy the Benefit of His Clergy* (1548), 2 & 3 Edw.VI c33.

85. J. M. Beattie (1986), *Crime and the Courts in England, 1660–1800*, pp. 168, 423. Beattie also argues that the theft of sheep and cattle was never regarded as seriously as the theft of horses because they were of less value than horses, harder to fence, and therefore less likely to involve gangs (p.170).

86. "By the King: Orders decreed upon for the furtherance of our service, as well in writing, as riding in Post: 15th May, 1609," pp. 221–24, in *Stuart Royal Proclamations*, vol. I, p. 223. For an earlier yet similar example, see "King's Proclamation: Orders for thorow Posts, and Curriers, riding in Post in our affaires: March 25, 1604," pp. 77–79, in *Stuart Royal Proclamations*, vol. I, p. 79.

87. *Royal Proclamations* (November 20, 1627), I, no. 521, p. 179.

88. See Larkin and Hughes (1973), *Stuart Royal Proclamations*, p. 77, n. 1.

89. See also Daniel Baraz (2003), *Medieval Cruelty.*

90. Michel de Montaigne (1580), "Cruelty," pp. 187–88. See also Montaigne's (1576) epistemologically skeptical *Apology for Raimond Sebond.*

91. Montaigne, "Cruelty," p. 191.

92. The identification of sixteenth-century challenges to the human–animal boundary is undertaken especially well in Matt Cartmill (1993), *A View to a Death in the Morning: Hunting and Nature through History.* See also, for example, Cartmill's discursive analysis of early hunting manuals and of Shakespeare, whom, he claims, employed the hunt as a symbol of murder, usurpation, and rape (pp.78–80).

93. The number and fortitude of the pockets of Puritan concentration varied considerably throughout England and among social classes, as did their successes and failures. On the Puritans' regulatory activity, see Steve Hindle (2000), *The State and Social Change in Early Modern England, 1550–1640*, pp. 177–201.

94. Exodus 20:8–10, 23:12.

95. See Robert W. Malcolmson (1973), *Popular Recreations in English Society 1700–1850*, pp. 5–6.

96. See Steve Hindle (2000), *The State and Social Change in Early Modern England, 1550–1640*, p. 191.

97. *An Act for Punishing of Divers Abuses Committed on the Lord's Day Called Sunday* (1625), 1 Car. I, I. The act more or less directly opposed the Jacobean *Declaration of Sports* (1617) and the *Book of Sports* (1618).

98. For a small sampling of Elias's writings, see Norbert Elias (1994), *The Civilising Process*, and Norbert Elias and Eric Dunning (1986), *The Quest for Excitement: Sport and Leisure in the Civilizing Process.* For how this literature relates to human–animal relations, see Adrian Franklin (1999), *Animals and Modern Cultures: A Sociology of Human-Animal Relations to Modernity*, pp. 17–26. See also Ted Benton (2007), "Ecology, Community and Justice: The Meaning of Green," and Keith Tester (1991), *The Humanity of Animal Rights*, pp. 68–73.

99. John Calvin (1562), *Laws and Statutes of Geneva*, pp. 85–86.

100. John Calvin (1541–1559), *Institutes of the Christian Religion*, I:XVI, 1, pp. 197–98. See also John Rawlinson (1612), *Mercy to a Beast: Sermon Preached at Saint Maries Spittle in London*. Rawlinson urged that a "righteous man is mercifull to the life of his beast" (pp. 2–3). Among this man's duties are "not to exact more of his beast than the strength of it is well able to beare" (p. 15), to ensure that the beast is "not over-travelled . . . [or]over-burdened" (p. 25), "not to be over-milked" (p. 26). Mercy to beasts requires compassion . . . for the[ir] needs and distress" (pp. 27–28). In the closing pages of *Mercy to a Beast*, Rawlinson places his entreaties in an overall proprietary context: the righteous man should "regard the life of his beast . . . because it is *his* . . . and of his wife because she is *his* . . . and of his children, because they are *his*" (pp. 50–51) (emphasis in the original).

101. Calvin, *Institutes of the Christian Religion*, IV:I, 20, p. 1034.

102. Calvin, *Institutes of the Christian Religion*, I:IV, 3, p. 47. An editorial footnote in Calvin, *Institutes of the Christian Religion* (n. 13), prises open another view on Calvin's point, namely, that he was probably referring to Plutarch's *Bruta animalia ratione uti*, in which examples are given of animals' superiority compared with assorted human perversions.

103. Calvin (n.d.), *Commentaries*, p. 294.

104. Calvin, *Commentaries*, p. 329 (emphasis in the original).

105. Keith Thomas (1983), *Man and the Natural World: Changing Attitudes in England 1500–1800*, pp. 146–47.

106. Thomas, *Man and the Natural World*, p. 153.

107. Thomas, *Man and the Natural World*, p. 153.

108. Thomas, *Man and the Natural World*, p. 172.

109. Thomas, *Man and the Natural World*, p. 158. Thomas instantiates Bristol and Portsmouth as other towns following this pattern (p. 360, n. 41).

110. These back-and-forth regulatory missteps are chronicled in David Mills (1998), *Recycling the Cycle: The City of Chester and Its Whitsun Plays*, pp. 69–72. For a history of the rise and decline of bullbaiting in Britain after the mid-seventeenth century, see Emma Griffin (2005), *England's Revelry: A History of Popular Sports and Pastimes 1660–1830*. See also Moira Ferguson (1998), *Animal Advocacy and Englishwomen, 1780–1900: Patriots, Nation, and Empire*.

111. Thomas, *Man and the Natural World*, pp. 143–65.

112. Two events illustrate the clear difficulty in identifying the Puritans' motives when they opposed animal baiting. The first is described in an extract from an anonymous newspaper report of 1643 on parliamentary proceedings and on other political matters of the day, as follows (Anonymous, 1643, "A perfect Diurnal of some Passages of Parliament, and from other Parts of the Kingdom"): "Upon the Queen's coming from Holland, she brought with her, besides a company of savage-like Ruffians, a company of savage Bears, to what purpose, you may judge by the sequell, for these Bears were left about Newarke, and brought into Country Towns constantly on the Lords Day to be baited (such is the Religion these Re-

formers would settle amongst us). And if any went about to hinder or but speak against this damnable profanation, they were presently noted as Roundheads, and Puritans, and sure to be plundered for it. But some of Colonell Cromwell's Forces coming by accident into Uppingham, a Town in Rutland on the last Lord's Day, found the Bears playing there in the usuall manner, and in the height of their sport, caused them to be seized upon, tied to a tree, and shot to death."

The second event occurred in 1653 when Sir Thomas Pride, then the Sheriff of Middlesex, killed all the bears and cocks at the Bankside bear garden in London. By some sarcastic wag, this event was reported in a newsletter just afterward as follows (Anonymous, 1653, "Advertisement from London"): "Besides the Massacre of the poore bears by that knight Errant Sir Tho. Pride, there went to the Pott also about 60 Cocks of the Game, all this being don for preventing of any great meeting of the people."

T. B. Macaulay's *History of England* (1848) reports one, presumably royalist or, at least, anti-Puritan representation of the last speech and dying words of Thomas Pride defending the act thus: "The first thing that is upon my spirits is the killing of the bears, for which the people hate me, and call me all the names in the rainbow. But did not David kill a bear? Did not the Lord Deputy Ireton kill a bear? Did not another lord of ours kill five bears?" (vol. 1, p. 159).

113. Erica Fudge (2002), *Perceiving Animals: Humans and Beasts in Early Modern English Culture,* pp. 11–13.

114. Fudge, *Perceiving Animals,* p. 17.

115. Fudge, *Perceiving Animals,* pp. 11–15. In a more recent book, Fudge (2006), *Brutal Reasoning: Animals, Rationality, and Humanity in Early Modern England,* very skillfully documents that, even though they were uninterested in animals or in animals' well-being as such, self-controlled and reason-controlled Puritans ultimately opposed cruelty to animals for the *self-interested* reason that compassion toward animals reflected well on themselves.

116. Macaulay, *History of England,* vol. 1, p. 159. Macaulay's opinion should be compared with Calvin's (*Commentaries,* p. 329) own view about Deuteronomy's commandment that "Thou shalt not muzzle the ox when it treadth the corn": "To prevent anyone from applying it to oxen, rather than to men, he [i.e., Paul] adds that God gave it, not because he was concerned about the oxen, but for the sake of the laborers."

117. Bagwell, *Ireland under the Stuarts and during the Interregnum,* vol. 1, pp. 124–25.

118. "The King to St. John, May 18, 1620," *Cal.S.P.Ire., 1615–1625,* p. 282.

119. Markham, *Cavelarice,* pp. 63–64. Thus, Elspeth Graham (1994), "Reading, Writing and Riding Horses," has written about Markham's husbandry: "Cruelty finds many forms but manifests itself not as a moral fault but in practical ways. Cruel or erroneous practices lead to the production of horses that are not useful or manageable (as in the instance of Irish horses)" (p. 132).

120. Spenser, *View of the Present State of Ireland*, p. 57.

121. Spenser, *View of the Present State of Ireland*, p. 57.

122. Spenser, *View of the Present State of Ireland*, p. 57.

123. Rich, *A New Description of Ireland*, p. B2 in the epistle (emphasis in the original). Rich and his pamphlets were actually once referred to in state correspondence, not altogether in a favorable way, as follows: "A new description of Ireland, with the disposition of the Irish" by Barnabie Rich, gent. A.D. 1610, p. 26. He served (he says) 47 years in Ireland" (See "Cornwalis to Lord Northampton, October 26, 1613," in *Cal.S.P.Ire., 1611–1614*, p. 432, n. 2).

124. Rich, *A New Description of Ireland*, pp. 20–21 (emphasis in the original).

125. For example, at the time of the 1635 Act, during the papacy of Urban VIII (1623–1644), rumor had it about the pope that "[his] worries made the pontiff so restless that he ordered all the birds in his garden killed because they disrupted his sleep with their nocturnal calls." I am grateful to Mike Webb at the Bodleian Library for alerting me to this nicety of Roman Catholic history. See also William R. Shea and Mariano Artigas (2003), *Galileo in Rome: The Rise and Fall of a Troublesome Genius*, and http://www.unav.es/cryf/galileoaffair.html.

126. On the intricacies of religious politics in Ireland in the 1630s and beyond, see Raymond Gillespie (1995), "Dissenters and Conformists, 1661–1700."

127. John Milton (1649), "Observations on the Articles of Peace, 1649." On Milton's "Observations," see Micheál Ó Siechrú (1999), *Confederate Ireland 1642–1649*, chap. 6. That Milton would not have supported Cromwell's slaughter of the Irish is convincingly argued in Joad Raymond (2004), "Complications of Interest: Milton, Scotland, Ireland, and National Identity in 1649." On the influence of Edmund Spenser on Milton, see Maureen Quilligan (1983), *Milton's Spenser: The Politics of Reading*.

128. According to a warrant of 1662, the king granted George Hamilton the right during his lifetime to collect all penalties and forfeitures accruing from plowing by horses' tails and from the burning of corn in the straw ("Warrant issued from Dublin Castle, 19th September, 1662," *Carte* MSS 165, fol. 27v, Bodleian Library).

129. *Act to Repeal Several Acts and Parts of Acts In Force in Ireland* (1828), 9 George 1V, c.53,437.

130. After 1606 and before the 1635 Act, the crime of plowing by tail was likely tried at the county assizes and quarter sessions. The text of the 1635 Act indicates that the court of jurisdiction was the assizes held before justices of the peace. This is also the opinion of Moody, *The Londonderry Plantation 1609–41*, p. 342, though it is hard to know if this extended beyond [London]derry. Another source implies that, by the 1650s, trials for plowing by tail might have been limited to quarter sessions ("Bishop of Killaloe to the Duke of Ormond, September 1st, 1662," Bodleian Library, MSS. Carte 31, fol. 612).

131. On the disappearance of plowing by tail given in John Dunton's *Conversation in Ireland*, see Edward MacLysaght (1979), *Irish Life in the Seventeenth Century*, p. 27, n. 22.

132. Arthur Young (1780), *Tour in Ireland*, p. 211.

133. George Hill (1877), *An Historical Account of the Plantation in Ulster at the Commencement of the Seventeenth Century, 1608–1620*, p. 493, n. 127. John Stuart Mill poured scorn on the Irish practice of plowing by horse's tail as late as 1825; see his "A Hitherto Unprinted Speech on the Influence of Lawyers," p. 4.

134. E. E. Evans (1976), "Some Problems of Irish Ethnography: The Example of Ploughing by the Tail," pp. 35, 37.

135. "Interview with Pat Smith, 15th December, 1949," recorded in Lower Killinkere, County Cavan, *Irish Folklore Collections*, Ms. 1176, p. 310.

The Prosecution of Animal Cruelty in   **2**
Puritan Massachusetts, 1636–1683

THE PREVIOUS CHAPTER LAMENTED that much is still not known about the Irish Act Against Plowing by the Tayle of 1635.[1] In particular, it is unclear precisely what was intended by the 1635 Act's usage of the term "cruelty" as one of its stated justifications. But the evidence points unmistakably to the conclusion that the 1635 Act had little or, more likely, nothing to do with a desire to ameliorate the lives of animals used in agriculture. Moreover, given the complete absence of relevant judicial records for seventeenth-century Ireland, it is doubtful if a variety of interesting questions of legislative intent and of enforcement can ever be pursued with much success in this regard.

In his account of the British domination of Ireland, Nicholas Canny has pioneered the idea that Ireland was a British experiment and that the personal experiences there of Humphrey Gilbert, Sir Walter Raleigh, Martin Frobisher, and others were later used by them for interpretation, for identity formation, and for the conquest of the New World.[2] Those who sailed from Ireland and England for Virginia of course shared with those who went to New England hopes for a better life. They also had in common a long sea voyage from the motherland, confrontation with indigenous peoples, territorial conquest, plunder of raw materials, and struggles with the landscape. But Virginia was not New England. Although both places were seen by newly arrived colonists as frontier societies, many of the settlers in Virginia, often royalist sympathizers down on their luck in England, expected eventually to return to England, having made their fortunes in the New World.

For most of the settlers in New England, however, the move from England was viewed as a permanent one. Their commitment to a new life in the colonies was thus far more intense. This is not to say that seventeenth-century migrants to New England always had similar motives for leaving England. Some were seeking to escape repressive royal absolutism, others papism. Some sought to be rid of both. Some left England simply because their friends or family had done so. Others fervently wished to construct the Genevan city on the hill.

This chapter is concerned mainly with the Puritan experiment in the Massachusetts Bay Colony. In particular, it examines the emergence and enforcement of "Of the Bruite Creature." Within the *Body of Liberties of 1641* in Puritan Massachusetts, Liberties 92 and 93 ("Of the Bruite Creature") criminalized cruelty and neglect of domesticated animals. It would surely be an extraordinary historical coincidence if the 1635 Act and the 1641 "Of the Bruite Creature" were not part of the same historical process of state formation and changing human–animal relationships in England, Ireland, and Massachusetts. Separated by nearly 3,000 miles of Atlantic Ocean, these two laws were enacted in peripheral societies within six years of each other. The texts of both laws formally stated their respective framers' intentions to criminalize animal cruelty.

In what follows, I first sketch the emergence of the 1641 "Of the Bruite Creature" in the Massachusetts Bay Colony. Against this background, I then examine certain aspects of the enforcement of this legislation. I do this with the assistance of narratives from the records of the Quarterly Courts of Essex County, Massachusetts, between 1636 and 1683.

Governing Brutes in the Massachusetts Bay Colony

Little in England's deforested landscape or in its safe countryside served to prepare migrant Nonconformists for their arrival in the wooded wilderness of what was to become the Massachusetts Bay Colony. William Bradford, the governor of Plymouth Colony, described the Pilgrims' frightened reaction to their first sight of the Cape Cod landscape in November 1620 as follows:[3]

> Being thus passed ye vast ocean . . . they had now no friends to welcome them, nor inns to entertain or refresh their weatherbeaten bodys, nor houses or much less townes to repaire too, to seeke for succoure. . . .
> Besids, what could they see but a hideous and desolate wilderness, full of

wild beasts and willd men? And what multitude ther might be of them they knew not.

Poisonous snakes, lions, bears, and wolves were the wild beasts most feared by the colonists, a fact confirmed even by the promoters of the New England colonies in their advertisements, tracts, and sermons. The howling of wolves especially terrified them.[4] Although wolves had been extinct in England for several generations, their ubiquity was more than compensated for by the profits to be made from their plentiful skins and from those of the other furry creatures that inhabited the wilderness: foxes, raccoons, beavers, otters, and bears. As it happened, the extermination of predators agreed nicely with the Puritans' desire to strike a blow for civilization by taming the wilderness.[5]

The economic centrality of livestock and agriculture in Massachusetts Bay was obvious from the very beginning of colonization there—thus John Winthrop's almost prosaic summary of events for one day in 1630 that "the wolves killed some swine at Saugus; a cow died at Plimouth, and a goat at Boston with eating Indian corn."[6] Many of the colonists were originally farmers who had emigrated from rural and coastal areas in Puritan-dominated East Anglia—Essex, Suffolk, and Norfolk—and in which husbandry principles were the most progressive in England. Among these East Anglian exiles were the Massachusetts Puritan leaders John Winthrop, John Winthrop Jr., Thomas Hooker, John Davenport, Thomas Shepard, Nathaniel Ward, William Pynchon, and John Eliot. The arrival of these ardent settlers, combined with the presence in Massachusetts Bay of appropriate raw materials, living or fossil, and willing investment from English capitalists, from merchant adventurers, and from arriving settlers, led directly to a thriving mixed economy of agriculture, fishing, shipbuilding, and timber. Within a decade, the colonists had managed to create a vigorous network for the production and distribution of cattle, at first for the local economy and then, from the early 1640s, for the West Indies. Indeed, one economic historian has written about the domestic trade in cattle, in particular, but also that in pigs and sheep, that it "kept New England's economy afloat during the 1630s."[7]

Within this agricultural-based economy, the construction of regulations about human–animal relationships was one of the most urgent priorities for capitalist entrepreneurs and small farmers alike. One of the first areas of regulation concerned the killing of wild animals, especially wolves. Besides terrifying the English colonists with their nocturnal howling, wolves also made the bad judgment to prey on the colonists' cattle, pigs, and goats. Considerable bounties were therefore often paid to those who hunted wolves.[8] Bounty was usually paid to those who killed wolves, the level of which varied according to how and how many wolves were killed and how many cattle were thereby saved. Sometimes, no bounty was paid at all for killing wolves ("to neither English nor Indians").[9] On rare occasions, a bounty was also paid for the killing of foxes[10] and wild swine.[11] On other occasions, courts ruled on whether colonists should be allowed to fish with nets near weirs,[12] for example, and whether colonists might employ Indians to shoot fowl[13] or deer[14] with guns.

Another area of public regulation was the danger posed to health and hygiene and human sensibilities by the slaughtering of cattle in close proximity to the citizenry. From the mid-1630s on, ad hoc public hygiene regulations emerged on a town-by-town basis. Many of these had as their focus animals and their waste products. Indeed, in the very first entry of the Boston Town records, in 1634, the selectmen banned the leaving of any fish or garbage near the bridge or town landing place.[15] Detailed regulations were issued about the working environments of tanners, shoemakers, and curriers.[16] For example, it was declared that in respect of oxen, bulls, steers, and cows, "no butcher shall gash, cut, impair or hurte their hides."[17] Specific areas were set aside for the messy trades of lime burners and blubber boilers,[18] and actions were taken to quell the odors of a mismanaged slaughterhouse.[19] In one complaint, "tan Fatts" were declared to be "of great annoyance."[20] A Boston butcher, Robert Nash, was ordered

> to be give[n] speedy notice . . . that with all speed he remove the Stinking garbage out of his yard, nere the street, and provide some other remote place for slaughter of Beasts, that such loath-some smells might be avoided, which are of great annoyance unto the neighbours, and to strangers.[21]

Regarding animals, the most contentious conflicts involved the transport and movement of cattle. Some rules addressed the loading and unloading of cattle and their by-products onto sailing vessels. Others emerged for the construction of adequate and safe roads and bridges so that carts and horses could travel safely and be used to get their goods to market.[22] Innkeepers were instructed to provide shelter for carriers' horses between points of production and embarkation, "having one inclosure for summer, & hay and p[ro]vender for winter."[23]

During the first three decades of colonization, agriculture comprised considerably more cattle production than it did the cultivation of wheat and grain. Given the relative scarcity of human labor in Massachusetts Bay, cattle were allowed to wander unattended. Moreover, on the assumption that their animals would thereby eat more food and grasses, mate more often, and produce more offspring, colonists not only condoned but also insisted on the free roaming of their cattle. This violation of accepted husbandry principles led to an interesting reversal—while colonists' cattle were allowed to wander, it was corn and grains that had to be fenced in. How, where, and with what consequences cattle grazed therefore soon emerged at the heart of a number of serious conflicts.

In situations where animals are regarded as humans' private property, it should be stressed, the regulation of human–animal relationships is never between humans and animals as such but rather between one human and another human. In the particular circumstances of Puritan Massachusetts Bay, therefore, serious conflicts quickly emerged between one colonist and another on the one hand and between colonists and the indigenous peoples on the other. For purposes of grazing, cattle did not much discriminate between land owned by colonists and land inhabited by Indians. Colonists' cattle were obviously a major source of irritation for the Indians. The colonists typically solved this rivalry simply by appropriating Indian land so that their cattle could then graze there freely and, if necessary, with the forces of law and order to assist them. John Winthrop transformed this practice into legal principle with devastating ruthlessness. "As for the Natives in New England," he divined,

> they inclose noe Land, neither have [they] any settled habytation, nor any tame Cattle to improve the Land by, and soe have noe other but a Naturall Right to those Countries, soe as if we leave them sufficient [land] for their use, we may lawfully take the rest.[24]

This created enormous problems not only for the Indians, when settlers' animals wandered into their traps or trampled their corn,[25] but also for the colonists themselves. It was not only cattle causing harm but also trespassing swine, hogs, sheep, and goats.[26] In 1638, it was ordered that swine would be forfeited if they were found trespassing in cornfields, meadows, or pastures[27] or in or adjacent to town commons.[28]

The early records of the General Court and of the Court of Assistants are therefore rife with disputes to do with the havoc caused by grazing cattle, trespass, and fences (whether in need of repair or completely lacking).[29] Moreover, those who interfered with the procedures for impounding trespassing cattle were ordered to be whipped ("all breaches very offensive and injurious").[30]

The Criminalization of Animal Cruelty

The combination of court decisions and ad hoc municipal laws was clearly too haphazard and unsystematic for the Puritans' taste for orderliness and predictability. One of the first references to the Massachusetts Bay colonists' preference for a formal system of laws is contained in an order of May 3, 1635, by Governor John Winthrop. Specifically, Winthrop ordered that "some men should be appointed to frame a body of grounds of laws, in resemblance of a *Magna Charta*."[31] The next year (1636), two competing draft laws began to circulate in the Massachusetts Bay Colony. One draft, titled *Moses his Judicialls*, was devised largely by Parson John Cotton. The *Judicialls* comprised a fire-and-brimstone biblical literalism. The other draft was a set of common-law–based rules drawn up by the Puritan Nathaniel Ward, a Cambridge-educated lawyer and excommunicated fugitive from the wrath of the Archbishop of Canterbury, William Laud. Although Cotton's *Judicialls* was adopted by the New Haven Colony, it was rejected in late 1639 by a special committee of the Massachusetts Bay Colony. The compendium that finally emerged in November 1641 was formally enacted by the General Court of the Massachusetts Bay Colony as the *Body of Liberties*.

Although its precise combination of influences has been open to endless interpretation and debate, the *Body of Liberties* was an experimental mixture of English common law, equity, Mosaic commandments, and localized pressures.[32] While the *Liberties* generally defined crimes according to English law or, at least, what the antilawyerly Puritans knew of English law and could remember of it, capital punishment followed Mosaic rules. None of the legislation would have been at all unacceptable to English judges and lawmakers. Not surprisingly, therefore, when the General Court ordered that copies of law books be procured, these were English books supportive of and based on English common law.[33]

Animals are explicitly mentioned five times in the ninety-eight liberties.[34] Cruelty to animals was formally criminalized in Liberties 92 and 93. Without precedent in English law and among the most innovative provisions of the *Body of Liberties*, Liberties 92 and 93 were collectively titled "Of the Bruite Creature"[35]:

> Of[f] the Bruite Creature
> 92 No man shall exercise any Tirranny or Crueltie towards any bruite Creature which are usuallie kept for man's use.
> 93 If any man shall have occasion to leade or drive Cattel from place to place that is far of, so that they be weary, or hungry, or fall sick, or lambe, It shall be lawful to rest or refresh them, for a competent time, in any open place that is not Corne, meadow, or inclosed for some peculiar use.

Liberties 92 and 93 seem self-evidently both to forbid "cruelty" to nonhuman animals and also to promote their protection. The language of "Of the Bruite Creature" indicates that Liberties 92 and 93 were intended to apply both to positive acts of "Tirranny" or "Crueltie" against domesticated animals and to omissions of some of their basic needs for rest, food, and water. However, it is unclear whether the language of this indisputably Puritan legislation was intended to be broad and inclusive or, rather, deliberately vague. What counted as acts of "Tirrany" and "Crueltie," and how did Puritans in Massachusetts understand the distinction implicit in Liberty 93 between "creatures which are usuallie kept for man's use" and, presumably, "wild" animals?

There are at least two aids for unlocking the meaning of cruelty in "Of the Bruite Creature." The first concerns the additional insight that can be gleaned from how the term was employed elsewhere in the *Body of Liberties*. The second derives from the written records of animal cruelty prosecutions in the Massachusetts courts.

Besides its appearance in "Of the Bruite Creature," the notion of cruelty also appears in several other places in the *Body of Liberties*: implicitly in Liberties 43 and 45 and explicitly in Liberties 46 and 85. Liberty 43 might fairly be taken to mean that excessive punishment was unjust or cruel.[36] Liberty 45 barred the use of torture in judicial interrogations unless it was in a capital case and the accused had already been convicted or if it was used to identify accomplices. However, in neither circumstance was torture permitted if it was "barbarous and inhumane." In this context, "barbarous" and "inhumane"—when applied to interhuman practices— seem to be synonyms delineating the unjustifiable infliction of physical pain. They are also synonyms, we might say, for cruelty. It is true that in 1641, opposition to torture could be embedded in several oppositional discourses, including the probabilistic notion that torture produced mathematically unreliable confessions. But the opposition to torture in Liberty 45 seems just as much grounded in the Puritans' perception that torture was morally unjustifiable, except in very rare circumstances. To this interpretation it might be added that the very next liberty—Liberty 46—forbade the use of any bodily punishments that were "inhumane Barbarous or cruel."

The term "cruelty" is used on one other occasion in the *Body of Liberties* in Liberty 85. Titled "Liberties of Servants," this states,

> If any servants shall flee from the Tiranny and cruelty of their masters to the howse of any freeman of the same Towne, they shall be protected and susteyned there till due order be taken for their relief.[37]

It is surely no coincidence that the language of "Liberties of Servants" is identical to that used in "Of the Bruite Creature." Indeed, other than in Liberty 85 and in "Of the Bruite Creature," the phrase "Tiranny and Cruelty" occurs nowhere else in the *Body of Liberties*. It is therefore tempting to think that servants and domesticated animals were placed in somewhat similar categories. Servants and domesticated animals were subordinates to whom their owners nevertheless owed certain obligations.

It is worth stressing that the liberties and rights enumerated in the *Body of Liberties* are structured according to the Puritan insistence on hierarchy in social relationships. Gods sits atop. Beneath Him are the Massachusetts Bay Colony and its judicial organization and proceedings, and beneath them, in descending order of importance according to their "place and proportion," are free men, then women, children, servants, foreigners, strangers, and, finally, "any bruite Creature which are usuallie kept for man's use." Moreover, while the rights attached to free men (Liberties 58–78),[38] women (79 and 80),[39] children (81–84),[40] servants (85–88),[41] and foreigners and strangers (89–91)[42] are explicitly listed as liberties, the obligation placed on humans not to tyrannize domesticated animals, not to be cruel to them, and to provide for their basic bodily needs are not listed as "Liberties" as such. The human obligations toward domesticated animals are listed after the enumeration of the liberties; they are given the title "Of the Bruite Creature" and two numbers (92 and 93).[43]

In other words, in the *Body of Liberties*, animals are part of the "*Body*," though they do not have liberties in the same way that humans do. The *Body of Liberties* placed certain obligations on the owners of domesticated animals, and criminalization was stated to apply to the actions of owners who physically mistreated their animals or who failed to provide them with sustenance. Puritanism and Calvinism demanded that animals would be kept firmly in their respective allotted places—last in the pecking order—but, at the same time, treated with respect and kindness according to that power and prudence given by God.

The records of relevant judicial prosecutions here are another resource for examining what animal cruelty might have meant to the citizens and judiciary of Puritan Massachusetts Bay Colony. These include the following:

1. The five-volume *Records of the Governor and Company of the Massachusetts Bay in New England* (*RGCMB*). However, there are no cases in the General Court in which any defendant was charged with animal cruelty and no evidence offered of animal cruelty where the charge was dismissed. There is one possible case

of neglect, with very scanty facts: in 1647, a complaint was made in the General Court against Edmund Bridges "for his neglect of shoeing Mr. Symond's horse."[44]

2. Two sets of records of the Court of Assistants: *Records of the Court of Assistants, 1641–1644* (*RCA*) and *Records of the Court of Assistants of the Massachusetts Bay 1630–1692*[45] (*RCAMB*). Neither in the *RCA* nor in the *RCAMB* are there any obvious examples of prosecutions for animal cruelty. This is not to say definitively that there are no animal cruelty cases in the *RCA* and *RCAMB*, but if there are any, then they are very difficult to identify without further details. Most often this is because the offense with which a defendant was charged was not stated. Thus, in 1641, "John Vocar was censured to pay ten shillings, or bee whipped." In the same year, "Pesons, or George the Indian, was banished and not to come among the English after a weeke."

3. The eight-volume *Records and Files of the Quarterly Courts of Essex County Massachusetts 1636–1683*. The *Quarterly Courts of Essex County* (*QCEC*) derived their legal powers from the corporate charter of the Massachusetts Bay Company. The colonial equivalent of the Quarterly Sessions in England, the *QCEC* contain very few references to English law, perhaps because law books were scarce, because the Puritans were not well versed in English law, or because, given their recent political and legal troubles in the motherland, they put little faith in practicing lawyers. The *QCEC* exercised jurisdiction over criminal, civil, and administrative matters in Essex County, Massachusetts. Were they actually to exist, recorded cases of animal cruelty might be found not only in the presentments of grand juries but also in court transcripts of legal disputes between private citizens. We now turn to these in more detail.

Animal Cruelty Prosecutions in the Quarterly Courts of Essex County, Massachusetts, 1636–1683

The nonhuman animals named in the pages of the *QCEC* include asses, bears, beasts, beavers, bees, boars, bullocks, bulls, calves, a cat, cattle, colts, cows, deer, dogs, ewes, geldings, goats, heifers, hogs, horses, kids, kine, lambs, livestock, mares, moose, otters, oxen, pigs, racoons, rams, sheep, shotes, sows, steers, swine, and wolves. One is left with the strong impression that in their first two decades, Massachusetts courts adjudicated more cases involving animals than any other category. Perhaps this is only to be expected in a society the economy of which was overdetermined by agricultural relationships.

Reading the QCEC

At first glance, the omens for finding information on animal abuse in the *QCEC* are not especially favorable. Only one case of animal abuse was identified by Samuel Morison in his once-authoritative book *Builders of the Bay Colony* ("an interesting case of condemnation for cruelty to an ox").[46] Quite opposite conclusions have been reached by two well-respected and more recent studies. On the one hand, Emily Leavitt and Diane Halverson claim that Liberty 92 was used successfully for prosecution.[47] But, other than referring to Morison's finding, they offer no support for this bold claim. Were there other prosecutions for animal cruelty? Did prosecution operate as a deterrent to would-be animal abusers? On the other hand, in her book *Creatures of Empire*, Virginia DeJohn Anderson finds that "there is no evidence that any Bay colonist was ever prosecuted for violations that almost certainly occurred."[48] However, Anderson does not tell her readers how she reached this conclusion.

On matters specifically to do with crime and deviance, the *QCEC* records have been searched in some depth on at least two occasions. First, in his book *Wayward Puritans* Kai Erikson constructed an otherwise-useful typology of seventeenth-century deviance. But his typology included no clear space for possible cases of animal cruelty cases.[49] Second, in his study of 793 criminal cases in Massachusetts between 1629 and 1650, Howard Schweber uncovered two prosecutions for animal cruelty. Both cases were held at Salem Quarterly Court on November 7, 1649, one against Ann Haggett, the other against William Flint.[50] However, Schweber came on these cases accidentally and in passing, as it were, in the course of his search for crimes committed in households. Had he intended to look specifically for them, Schweber would have perhaps found more animal cruelty prosecutions.

Several caveats must be offered about reading the *QCEC*. One is that, in trying to find animal cruelty prosecutions by looking for them in each volume's index, the existing index categories are not especially helpful. Constructed as they were nearly a century ago, their compilers could not realistically have foreseen what information researchers several generations later would have wanted to find in the *QCEC*. The indices should therefore be viewed with skepticism. Instead, the entire text of each volume needs to be read line by line and page by page so as either to read between the lines, so to speak, or to look for categories other than the obvious "Animals, cruelty to" or "Crimes, cruelty to animals" (one case in eight volumes in 1660) and so on.

Another difficulty is that most of the cases recorded in the QCEC provide precious few details of court proceedings or of events before and after court hearings. A great many of the entries in the QCEC are one line or less in length, such as "William Pritchett of Lynn discharged."[51] Very often, even when entries are longer than one line, their contents are quite cryptic: for example, "Richard Norman testified that Goody Peach told him that she spoke only what she said to Goody Blancher."[52] Sometimes if a charge and verdict are stated, then precious little evidence is given: for example, "Guido Baly admonished for beating his wife."[53] In some cases, even when the charge and evidence are provided, it is impossible to know the nature of the offense: for example, "Thomas Wheeler testified that he had goats of Wm. James, one of which was yellow."[54] Similarly, "Thomas Rowell fined for taking tobacco out of doors and near a house. His wife was admonished for cruelty."[55] Rowell's wife was admonished for "cruelty," but whether this was to a servant, a child, or an animal is not stated.

Animals tend to be visible in QCEC texts in one of three ways: in wills and estates, when they have been stolen or otherwise misappropriated or damaged by a defendant, or when a plaintiff alleged that his property had been damaged by the defendant's animals—by goats,[56] for example, or by bees,[57] swine,[58] sows,[59] or horses.[60] Especially before the enactment of "Of the Bruite Creature" in 1641, even when cruelty or neglect might have been present, QCEC cases involving animals were overwhelmingly seen as property offenses. Thus, "Peter Paltrey's servant Jane Wheat whipped for killing his neighbor's poultry, for lying and loitering and running away from her master."[61] And "John Stacy v. Richard More. For killing his swine."[62] And "Mr. Gervas Garford hired a cow of John Pease for a year; Pease then being absent, Garford was ordered to keep the cow till Pease returned."[63] But what should be made of the following entry? "Thomas Rowell fined for taking tobacco out of doors and near a house. His wife was admonished for cruelty."[64] And Francis Ussellton was fined for cursing a swine of Henry Haggett, saying "A pox a god upon her & the divill take her."[65]

Another difficulty with reading the QCEC derives from the powerful and complicating influence of sabbatarianism. The broad range of offenses associated with popular pastimes and work that had been banned in the seventeenth century by English Puritans was also banned in Puritan Massachusetts. These included not only gaming offenses, drinking, swearing, and so on but also certain practices that, though they might have been permitted on the other six days of the week, were crimes if committed on Sundays. Examples of such sabbatarian offenses were most forms of labor, such as haymaking, gathering peas or wood, driving cattle, loading or unloading ships, and hunting, and failure to attend congregation and absence from public ordinances. Penalties for offenses committed on Sundays were typically higher than if committed on other days.[66]

Sabbatarian offenses involving human–animal relationships were quite numerous throughout the seventeenth century.[67] Most sabbatarian offenses, when recorded in the *QCEC*, seem quite straightforward, even if disarmingly brief. Thus, "Mathew Coe . . . for hunting raccoons on the Lord's Day during public service, fined."[68] The hunting of raccoons, which were regarded as wild animals and therefore belonging to no one, became an offense only if done on Sundays. But the meaning of sabbatarian cases involving animals is not always so obvious. Consider the case of William Robinson, who was charged with "carrying a fowling piece on the Lord's Day."[69] Can we safely assume that Robinson's action became an offense only because he was hunting on a Sunday? Perhaps it was a trespass on Robinson's part that led to the sabbatarian charge or a neighbor's animosity. Without further documentation, these questions cannot be answered. Consider also Harklackenden Symonds, who was fined for driving cattle on the Sabbath.[70] Was Symonds prosecuted only because he engaged in driving cattle on a Sunday, a sabbatarian offense for which he was found guilty? Or was he prosecuted because he had violated Liberty 93, which forbade the causing of cattle to be weary or hungry while they were being driven from one place to another, and this just happened to be done on a Sunday? We cannot know. Consider, finally the judicial decision that "whosoever shall offend in riding or running their horses fast to or from the meetings [on the Lord's Day] shall forfeit 20s., unless it be upon some extraordinary occasion or necessity."[71] Was riding horses "fast" seen as cruel or neglectful, and does this mean that it was permissible to ride horses to congregation slowly on the Sabbath?

Animal Cruelty Prosecutions Possible and Probable

The previously mentioned caveats notwithstanding, there are six instances in the *QCEC* where a notion of animal cruelty might have been part of or even a central theme in prosecutorial evidence:

1. In 1644, John and Stephen Talbie were admonished for "unbecoming speeches about a dog in the water, though not

proved the baptizing of him."[72] Was this a religious offense? Did it involve cruelty?

2. In 1649, William Flint "was presented for beating a bull and cow and his son at one time in a cruel manner." Flint was discharged.[73]

3. In 1651, Edward Coleburne and others were presented to the court for "several railing and scandalous speeches" against Joseph Fowler, among which was the allegation that Fowler had wounded a hog with a knife.[74] Although no verdict is recorded in this case, wounding a hog with a knife would clearly have fallen within the scope of Liberty 92.

4. In 1669, "Edward Brag complained of Benjamin Marshall for threatening his house and cattle, etc."[75]

5. In 1672, Robert Bartlet's mare was found dead with a wound behind the shoulder, where it had impaled itself on a piece of sharp stake where the fence had broken and had not been properly repaired.[76] The main theme of this case might have been a boundary dispute, it might have involved cruelty, and, though no verdict or disposition is given, probably the defendant would have at least been liable for the value of the horse.

6. In 1682, Nathan Webster was charged with killing a tame deer.[77] What the offense in this case was is uncertain. Did the killing of the deer involve cruelty? Was it a breach of the peace or an offense against public order? Was it a property offense (though wild animals could not be owned, a deer presumably could be, if tamed after capture, and the killing of her might lead to a suit for damages).

Besides these six cases, there were also fourteen cases that very likely or surely did involve cruelty to animals. In chronological order, they are the following:

1. In 1649, John Leech Jr. was fined for beating Samuell Allin, son of William Allin, and setting his dog on cows, "to the pulling of their tayles."[78]

2. In 1649, Ann, wife of Henry Haggett, was fined for beating her child and calf in a cruel manner with an ax.[79]

3. An interesting case occurred in 1662, which is unusual in the length and the detail of the court record:

> William Bartoll, aged about thirty-two years, and Marke Pittman, aged about forty years, deposed that some time the last May they

saw Joseph Daliver on a Lord's day morning where a young foal, said to be Mr. Walton's, was found dead in the afternoon by Bartoll. The latter thought it had been knocked in the head, as the skull was beaten flat and the brains lay on the ground. Pittman further deposed that about three weeks after that, on a second day of the week at sunrise, he saw said Daliver going along with a gun under his arm. . . . Pittman, having occasion to go the same way to look for his cows, followed said Daliver, although keeping out of sight. Presently he heard a gun go off about eight rods before him, and with it the neighing of horses and saw them run, but he did not think then that the man had killed them. Pittman then went over to the stage about his business and about two or three hours after, one of deponent's children came to him and told him that Goodman Connant's mare was killed, and he went over after to see, sending his boy to tell said Connant of it. When deponent came to the place where he heard the gun go off, he saw the mare newly killed, and plainly saw where she was shot on the thigh in the near flank.

Erasmus James, aged twenty-seven years, and Josiah Walton, aged about twenty years, deposed that going with Richard Rowland to view his mare that was dead, they found that she had been shot in the breast, for there were twenty holes in her body. At the same time they saw one shot taken out of lote Connant's mare that was found dead. [80]

Galiver was convicted of having killed two mares. He was fined ten pounds, required to compensate the horses' owners a total of twenty-five pounds, and to pay the court costs; finally, he was bound over to good behavior and to remain in prison until the fine was paid.

4. In 1666, Abraham Fitt was condemned for abusing an ox. The record states the following:

Writ: Moses Pengry v. Abragam Fitt; for abusing an ox, so that it died. . . . Samuell Eyrs of Ipswich deposed that he saw Abraham Fitt come with a load of wood upon a sled by his house, a reasonable load for two cattle. Going over the gutter near his barn, the off bullock slipped upon the ice and he could not get him up until he had unyoked him and he was forced to call his dog to raise him, and the bullock shook the bullock by the ear. After the bullock was dead, Fitts desired deponent to help him draw him to Decon Pengre's, but the latter refused it, and he went to three men to take the hide, but could get none to do it. . . .

Thomas Burnum deposed that he saw Fitt with his sled near Mr. Huberd's barn and he noticed that the bullock was very white with frost, the weather being very cold and the bullock being in a greast sweat. Deponent told him that he should put the bullock in a warm place as soon as he could. . . .

John Lee deposed that the ox ran so fast that he could hardly catch him. . . .

Robert Colines deposed that he was asked to strip the bullock and he thought death was caused by beating. . . .

William Danfford deposed that Fitt beat his cattle.[81]

5. In what appears to be a civil action of trespass—though listed in the *QCEC* index as a crime—animal cruelty arose in a case of 1659 against William Dellow. In this, Robert Shatswell successfully sued William Dellow for forty-four shillings for trespass and for "cruelty in beating his ox, whereby he is much diminished, the ox being dead."[82] In this case, the cruelty was variously described by several witnesses as follows:

> Dellow beat Shatswell's ox "so he died" (Witness Richard Shatswell).
>
> Shatswell's bullock "[was] so beaten that the hair was off. William Dellow did it with a small walnut stick" (Witness Joseph Browne).
>
> Shatswell said to Dellow "'Now William you may see the froots of crooilty.' Dellow agreed to pay for half of the beast, and said he hoped it would be a warning to him not to beat any so again" (Witness Richard Brabrocke).
>
> Upon examination after the beast was dead [they] saw that there was a bruise on the side near the heart, etc. (Witnesses Edmon Bridges and John Apelford).[83]

6. In 1660, a complaint was filed against John Leigh for wounding an ox and killing a pig belonging to John Fuller.[84] Fuller and Leigh were neighbors in Ipswich and became involved in a dispute about Fuller's cows grazing in Leigh's pasture. Fuller himself and other witnesses testified that Leigh retaliated against Fuller by injuring Fuller's animals: a dead hog was found "with his foot in the yoke and his head broken to a jelly." Two witnesses, Thomas and Sarah Low, complained that they found one of their cows "with her ear pulled off," probably by Lee's dog. Thomas Low also testified

that he saw Lee "throw a stick at his sheep," that Lee "broke the leg of one of his lambs," and that he "had lost fourteen head of cattle, sheep and swine by such means." Although numerous other witnesses also made similar accusations against Leigh, the jury found him not guilty of the main charge. However, because "great suspicion" remained, Leigh was bound over to appear at the next court for further examination.

7. In 1660, John Pinder was fined five pounds for "cutting a mare." The facts reported for this case were as follows:[85]

> Samuel Graves, aged about thirty-eight years, testified that John Pinder, jr., told him and one of his children that he wished deponent's house and all he had would burn, and that his father wished so too. Deponent found a match lying near the groundsel of his barn with the burned end touching the hay, and he had often told said Pinder of his naughty tricks and he would reply "You lye, Graves." Deponent had also heard him go along the street muttering and threatening his children, hogs and fowls, saying that he would knock them in the head. Said Graves had several fowls knocked in the head, lying in Pinder's yard, his pigs wounded and a shoat of three quarters old stabbed with a pitchfork. Deponent had often told Pinder's father of his tricks, but he would not believe it.[86]

Pinder was found guilty of cutting the mare. For unknown reasons, part of his fine was waived.

8. In 1662, George Farough confessed that he had taken six hogs and shoats and converted them to his own use. For this the court ordered him to pay restitution of ten pounds to the owners of the animals. Additionally, for his other offenses of "stealing, deceitfully removing a landmark and cruelty in drowning a mare," Farough was ordered to be severely whipped and disenfranchised.[87]

9. In 1669, John Chub, "for killing Renold Foster's horse, was sentenced to pay 5li to said Foster and 5li to the county or else to be whipped. Also to pay Thomas Low 10s."[88]

10. In 1669, "Moses Worcester, presented for cruelty to cattle, was ordered to have a legal admonition."[89]

11. In 1672, "Francis Young was presented upon complaint of Caleb Kimball for using cruelty in treatment of said Kimball's oxen."[90]

12. On March 30, 1675, Joseph Selden was charged with "cutting a horse" in the Massachusetts Bay (New Hampshire).[91] No further details are provided.
13. In 1676, John Smith, a tailor, was found guilty and fined five groats "for an act of cruelty to a swine, using more violence than was necessary to the driving of the swine to the pound."[92]
14. In 1682, Walter Fairefield of Wenham was ordered to appear in court "for cruelty abusing and striking his servant about six years ago whereby he was unable to perform his work, also for abusing one of his swine and, to conceal it, threw it into a swamp."[93]

Drawn from an unknown universe of violations, these QCEC cases show that animal cruelty prohibitions were sometimes accompanied by criminal prosecution in seventeenth-century Puritan Massachusetts. Of the roughly 3,000 QCEC cases between 1636 and 1683, fourteen of them more or less directly concerned animal cruelty. Between the enactment in 1641 of Liberties 92 and 93 ("Of the Bruite Creature"), there was on average, therefore, roughly one conviction for animal cruelty in Essex County every three years up to 1683. In these cases, those on trial were accused of using knives, guns, stakes, and other means to torment, wound, maim, and kill dogs, cows, calves, horses, oxen, pigs, swine, hogs, shoats, and lambs. The motives of the accused appear to have ranged from revenge and retaliation to boundary disputes and simple viciousness. Those aberrant souls convicted of animal cruelty were sanctioned with warnings, fines, restitution, temporary incarceration, whippings, and disenfranchisement.

What do these cases suggest about the prosecution of animal cruelty under the terms of Liberty 92? To what extent was animal cruelty prosecuted, with what consequences, and for whom? Were the lives of animals ameliorated? Why were there no prosecutions recorded for neglect of animals according to the provisions of Liberty 93?

To all these questions, the resounding answer must be that it's hard to say. Official narratives of arrests, prosecutions, and convictions probably tell us less about the prevalence of animal cruelty and its amelioration than they do about the activities of agents of social control. Indeed, it is quite possible that, like acts of bestiality, incidents of animal cruelty, if detected, were less likely to make their way into the criminal justice system than they were to be handled informally and in private. In seventeenth-century Puritan Massachusetts, some laws, such as those regulating political and religious dissent,[94] sexual deviation, and alcohol use, were consistently enforced with passion and with punitiveness. Other laws were enforced little or not at all. Perhaps it was that way with Liberties 92 and 93.

Taking Stock

Chapter 1 examined the emergence and meaning of the problematic preamble "the cruelty used to the beasts" in the 1635 Irish Act Against Plowing by the Tayle. This chapter has examined another law the stated justification of which was opposition to animal cruelty, namely, Liberties 92 and 93 ("Of the Bruite Creature") enacted in 1641 in Puritan Massachusetts. Both laws emerged as moments in the expanding tendency of the early modern English state to regulate human–animal relationships. Both were mechanisms wielded in a twofold process of colonization: on the one hand, of animals and native Irish and, on the other, of animals and native Americans.

The language in "Of the Bruite Creature" was the same as the language that migrating Puritans had brought with them from England and that had been developing pockets of concentration there since the late sixteenth century. Wherever they lived, all Puritans would surely have agreed with Cotton Mather's recommendation on how to "Serve God with *Priestly Glory*, free from Sin":[95]

> Tutors be *Strict*; but yet be *Gentle* too:
> Don't by fierce *Cruelties* fair *Hopes* undo.
> The Lads with *Honour* first, and *Reason*, rule;
> *Blowes* are but for the *Refractory Fool*.

But it remains unclear whether Puritans condemned and criminalized violent human–animal relationships such as blood sports because they saw them as cruel or, instead, because they were thought to encourage idleness, sins of the flesh, and displays of violence that threatened public order. Although the doctrinal influence of Calvinism on the 1635 Act, if any, remains a mystery, its effects are much easier to see in Puritan Massachusetts. In law, at least, and if only during the first one or two generations of settlement and before the rot of unintended consequences set in, the distance in Massachusetts between Puritan intention and criminalization appears to have been a relatively short one. Yet there were no laws prohibiting animal cruelty in Plymouth Colony's 1636 Laws or in statutory revisions there in 1658 and 1672. A provision in the Providence (Rhode Island) Colony's 1647 Code of Laws forbade "cut[ting] out the tongue of a beast being alive," though this offense was categorized not as cruelty but as theft and, specifically, as larceny.[96] There were no anticruelty provisions in the New Haven Code of 1656.[97] Only Connecticut Colony followed suit, nine years after the emergence of "Of the Bruite Creature" in Massachusetts, by enacting an almost identical anticruelty provision in its 1650 *General Laws and Liberties*.[98]

At least two questions should be pursued further. The first is why the first animal cruelty legislation emerged in Puritan Massachusetts rather than, say, elsewhere in the New England colonies. Perhaps the answer to this question lies in the nature of the different and competing Puritanisms in New England and in their respective effects on legislative activity. Although in *their* own time the practitioners of each of the various Puritanisms recognized each other as Puritans, as did their religious and political opponents, there were nevertheless severe doctrinal disagreements about the Word of God and the outward signs of election among Presbyterians, antinomians, independent separatists, Baptists, and Quakers. Perhaps the answer lies somewhere in this heady ideological conflict. Perhaps it lies just as much in the realm of historical accident and in the malevolent workings of the goddess Fortuna.

Another question has to do with the existence in Puritan Massachusetts of certain attitudes toward human–animal relationships that would seem to us, if held together, to be quite incompatible. On the one hand, consider that certain forms of animal cruelty and neglect were outlawed by "Of the Bruite Creature." Moreover, as this chapter has demonstrated, this legislation was not just symbolic but was accompanied by criminal prosecutions (though their intensity must remain a matter of dispute). On the other hand, consider that "Of the Bruite Creature" emerged in an early modern culture where cruelty to animals was so extensively embedded in everyday life that it was not even recognized as such by its inhabitants. On one, arguably less significant level, these cruelties can be found not only in the unkind death meted out by the criminal justice system to trespassing dogs and to a variety of other animals after the occasional trial of humans convicted of bestiality or witchcraft but also in local customs like that in Eastham, Massachusetts, which held that no man was allowed to marry until he had killed either six blackbirds or three crows.

Much more significant than these were the cruelties whose reflections appear in the culinary recipes of seventeenth-century Massachusetts. As anthropologists have long known, how people prepare and cook their food conveys hugely significant cultural messages about who they are and how they see animals. The everyday cooking methods used in Puritan Massachusetts would doubtless have been based on some mixture of recipes the colonists brought with them from England, the culinary practices of the indigenous peoples, and their own local adaptations. There were several popular seventeenth-century English cookbooks, among them John Wecker's *Secrets of Art and Nature*, which recommended in grotesque detail various techniques for the softening and roasting, while alive, of the flesh of eels, geese, ducks, and pigs.[99] Others included Gervase Markham's *English Huswife*, John Murrell's *New Booke of Cookerie*, and Robert May's *Accomplisht Cook* (which contained "expert ways for the dressing of all sorts of Flesh, Fowl, and Fish"). The recipes most likely to be in vogue among Massachusetts Puritans would have been those disseminated by Elizabeth Cromwell (who had the considerable advantage of being able to try out new delicacies on her husband Oliver). Her book of 1654, *The Court and Kitchen of Elizabeth Cromwell*, has recipes for soups, stews, fresh roasts, preserved meats (bacon, ham, and salt pork), and local fare, such as mollusks, fish, wild game, fowl/birds, domesticated hogs, deer, turkey, chicken, and lamb. Although Cromwell avoided any description of the proper methods by which animals should be killed for the table, these can be found in other cookery books of the time.[100]

Finally, it must be said that "Of the Bruite Creature" did not represent a key moment in the gradual unfolding of the predicates of some humane worldview. Nor was it a stepping-stone to a future where cruelty to animals was condemned either for the sake of the animals and their pain or because, especially, cruelty was seen as a wrongful breach of the moral circle of beings to whom rights should be extended. Like the 1635 Act Against Plowing by Tayle, "Of the Bruite Creature" was enacted and understood entirely in terms of the supremacy of human interests over those of animals.

Notes

1. Most of the court records referred to in this chapter originally used the Julian, old system of double dating between January 1 and March 24 inclusive. These have been modernized here by conforming them to the New Style, Gregorian calendar.

2. See Nicholas Canny (1976), *The Elizabethan Conquest of Ireland: A Pattern Established, 1565–76*, esp. pp. 154–63; Nicholas Canny and Anthony Pagden, eds. (1987), *Colonial Identity in the Atlantic World, 1500–1800*; and Nicholas Canny, "The Permissive Frontier: The Problem of Social Control in English Settlements in Ireland and Virginia, 1550–1650." See also Denis O'Hearn (2005), "Ireland in the Atlantic Economy."

3. William Bradford (1650), *History of Plymouth Plantation*, p. 78. The English colonialist discourse on Indian "willd men" in New England echoed strongly Edmund Spenser's prejudiced perceptions of Irish wildness and incivility. See also, for example, Sir Vincent Gockins's letter to the new Lord Deputy of Ireland, Thomas Wentworth, offering advice about the characteristics of the Irish: "They are as bloody as a wolf when they can overcome. They live in houses more beastly than barbarians or Indians." "Sir Vincent Gockins to Lord Wentworth, middle of 1633," in *Calendar of State Papers, Ireland, 1647–1660, addendum for 1633*, p. 184.

4. According to Jon Coleman (2004), *Vicious: Wolves and Men in America*, "Wolves had enough sensibility to retreat from people, but they had no way of knowing that some humans' notion of territoriality extended to the exotic beasts they imported. When they sank their teeth into cows, goats, pigs, and sheep, wolves committed sins unimaginable to them" (p. 34).

5. On notions of civilization and wilderness in seventeenth-century New England, see John Canup (1990), "Out of the Wilderness: The Emergence of an American Identity in Colonial New England."

6. John Winthrop (1650), *A Journal, 1630–1644*, entry for September 20, 1630.

7. Stephen Innes (1995), *Creating the Commonwealth: The Economic Culture of Puritan New England*, p. 280. See also Stephen Innes (1983), *Labor in a New Land: Economy and Society in Seventeenth-Century Springfield*, pp. 30–34.

8. Abraham Whitheire was allowed ten shillings for a wolf he killed (*Quarterly Court of Essex County*, hereinafter *QCEC*), July 6, 1647, Salem, vol. 1, p. 118. In the case of *Thomas Thulay v. Wm. Ilsly, selectman of Nubury*, the plaintiff was awarded fourteen pounds for seven wolves he had killed (*QCEC*, March 26, 1667, Ipswich, vol. 3, p. 388).

9. The General Court decreed that those who killed wolves with the use of hounds should receive four times the reward (forty shillings/ten shillings) of those who killed them "with trap, peece, or other engine" (*Records of the Governor and Company of the Massachusetts Bay in New England* (hereinafter *RGCMB*), October 7, 1640, vol. 1, p. 304. Sometimes, towns paid bounty if wolf hunters successfully protected cattle from wolves: "one penny [per wolf] for "any beast & horse [saved]" (*RGCMB*, November 9, 1630, vol. 1, p. 81); another case stipulated two pounds per wolf killed (*RGCMB*, November 7, 1632, vol. 1, p. 102).

10. *RGCMB*, September 3, 1632, vol. 1, p. 156.

11. *RGCMB*, May 18, 1631, vol. 1, p. 87.

12. *RGCMB*, September 3, 1634, vol. 1, p. 127.

13. *RGCMB*, September 3, 1634, vol. 1, p. 127.

14. *RGCMB*, March 13, 1639, vol. 1, p. 252.

15. *Record Commissioners of the City of Boston: Second Report, 1634–1661* (1877), p. 1. On June 12, 1637, George Woodward "was found a delinquent for an

unlawful entry upon some of the Towne's ground and for digging holes and annoying the high Way with stinking fish" (p. 18).

16. *RGCMB*, June 14, 1642, vol. 2, pp. 18–20.

17. *RGCMB*, November 11, 1647, vol. 2, p. 220.

18. *RGCMB*, November 11, 1647, vol. 2, p. 118.

19. Cited in John B. Blake (1959), *Public Health in the Town of Boston, 1630–1822*, p. 13.

20. Blake, *Public Health in the Town of Boston*, p. 148.

21. *Record Commissioners of the City of Boston* (1877), p. 70. Evidence that this notice was not altogether successful can be found in the Boston Town Records of May 26, 1647: "It is ordered that the annoyance that is made by Robt. Nash in his slaughter howse, by his killings of beasts in the street now lay'd out, that hee shall remove that annoyance on penaltye of 19*s*. 6*d*. for evry defect iustly complained of" (p. 91). In 1652, Boston banned the "throw[ing] forth or lay[ing] any intralls of beast or fowles or garbidg or Carion or dead dogs or Catts or any other dead beast or stinkeing thing, in any hie way or dich or Common" (pp. 110–11).

22. For example, see the instruction in *RGCMB*, October 7, 1641, vol. 1, p. 338. According to the *Records of the Court of Assistants* (October 28, 1641, p. xxviii), the towns of Dorchester and Boston were fined 5 shillings and 10 shillings, respectively, for having defective roads.

23. *RGCMB*, May 14, 1645, vol. 2, p. 100.

24. John Winthrop (1629), "Reasons to be Considered, and Objections with Answers," pp. 140–41.

25. To their detriment, Indians occasionally appear in court records when colonists' pigs wandered into their traps. In one case, the Indian Nahanton was ordered to give two beaver skins to Mr. Blackesone for this offense (*RGCMB*, April 7, 1635, vol. 1, p. 143). Similarly, Winthrop, *A Journal*, reported that "at a court Jo. Sagamore and Chickatobot being told at last court of some injuries that their men did to our cattle, and giving consent to make satisfaction, now one of their men was complained of for shooting a pig for which Chickatobot was ordered to pay a small skin of beaver, which he presently paid" (p. 26). Courts occasionally ruled in the favor of Indians. For example, in 1632, Sir Richard Saltonstall was ordered to give Saggamore John a hogshead of corn for the damage that his cattle did to the latter's corn (*RGCMB*, November 7, 1632, vol. 1, p. 102).

26. In 1639 in Boston, the stated penalty for animals caught trespassing or doing damage on another's property was five shillings for swine and twelve pence for goats, with half to be given to the town and half to the victimized landowner. On this, see *Record Commissioners of the City of Boston: Second Report, 1634–1661* (1877), pp. 40 and 131.

27. *RGCMB*, September 6, 1638, vol. 1, p. 238.

28. *RGCMB*, September 6, 1638, vol. 1, p. 239.

29. On the problems created by roaming cattle, see the excellent commentary by Virginia DeJohn Anderson (2004), *Creatures of Empire: How Domestic Animals*

Transformed Early America, pp. 226–28. On issues to do with fences in particular, see William Cronon (1983), *Changes in the Land: Indians, Colonists, and the Ecology of New England*, chap. 7.

30. *RGCMB*, June 14, 1642, vol. 2, p. 17.

31. Winthrop, *A Journal*, p. 82.

32. Theodore Bozeman (1988), *To Live Ancient Lives: the Primitivist Dimension in Puritanism*, pp. 168–84. Kai Erikson (1986), *Wayward Puritans: A Study in the Sociology of Deviance*, had an unfussy grasp of what the Puritans were trying to accomplish in the *Body of Liberties* when he suggested that they intended that the new colony would be both a legal extension of old England and a spiritual revision of everything that was wrong at home.

33. In 1647, the General Court ordered copies of the following books for "the use of the Court from time to time: two of Sir Edward Cooke upon Littleton; two of books of Entryes; two of Sir Edward Cooke upon Magna Charta; two of New Tearmes of the law; two Dalton's Justice of the Peace; two of Sir Edward Cooke's Reports." See *RGCMB*, November 11, 1647, vol. 2, p. 212. The several meanings that the Puritans themselves attached to the notion of liberty are described in David Fischer (1989), *Albion's Seed: Four British Folkways in America*, pp. 199–205. Of the four meanings identified by Fischer, "liberty" is perhaps best and most simply translated as "law."

34. Besides their appearance in "Of the Bruite Creature," animals are also referred to in Liberties 8, 16, and 32. Liberty 8 stated that a man should be compensated at a reasonable rate if, while they were pressed into public use or service, his cattle or goods perished or suffered damage (*Body of Liberties*, p. 34); Liberty 16 allowed householders free fishing and fowling in all ponds, bays, coves, and rivers (p. 36); and Liberty 32 provided for recovery of cattle impounded or seized (p. 40).

35. "Of the Bruite Creature" (1641), p. 53. Among those who have suggested that "Of the Bruite Creature" was the first anticruelty statute are Richard Ryder (1989), *Animal Revolution: Changing Attitudes to Speciesism*; Emily Stewart Leavitt and Diane Halverson (1990), "The Evolution of Anti-Cruelty Laws in the United States"; Simon Brooman and Debbie Legge (1997), *Law Relating to Animals*; Joseph Sauder (2000), "Enacting and Enforcing Felony Animal Cruelty Laws to Prevent Violence against Humans"; and Mike Radford (2001), *Animal Welfare Law in Britain*. Steven Wise (2000), *Rattling the Cage: Toward Legal Rights for Animals*, states that the 1641 *Body of Liberties* "enacted not just pathbreaking protections for women, children, and servants but the West's first animal protection laws" (p. 43). But he then dismissively suggests—correctly—that the Puritans were still trapped in the Great Chain of Being and never wavered from their belief that animals were created solely for humans' purposes. See also the cautions recommended in Diane Beers (2006), *For the Prevention of Cruelty: The History and Legacy of Animal Rights Activism in the United States*, p. 20.

36. Liberty 43 ordered that "no man shall be beaten with above 40 stripes, nor shall any true gentleman, nor any man equall to a gentleman be punished with

whipping, unles his crime be very shamefull, and his course of life vitious and profligate" (*Body of Liberties*, 1641, p. 43). Note also, of course, the hierarchical distinctions of social class referred to in this liberty.

37. *Body of Liberties*, 1641, p. 51.

38. *Body of Liberties*, 1641, pp. 46–60.

39. *Body of Liberties*, 1641, p. 51.

40. *Body of Liberties*, 1641, p. 51.

41. *Body of Liberties*, 1641, pp. 51–52.

42. *Body of Liberties*, 1641, p. 53.

43. In 1648, Liberties 92 and 93 became chapters 32 and 38, respectively, of the *Charters and General Laws of the Colony and Province of Massachusetts Bay*. Chapter 32 ("An Act Against Cruelty to Brute Creatures") stated, "It is ordered by this court, that no man shall exercise any tyranny or cruelty towards any brute creatures, which are usually kept for the use of man" (p. 95), and chapter 38 ("An Act As to Driving Cattle, and Right to Feed Them in Open Places") stated, "It is ordered by this court and the authority thereof, that if any man shall have occasion to lead, or drive cattle from place to place that is far off, so that they be weary, or hungry, or fall sick or lame, it shall be lawful to rest and refresh them for a competent time in any open place that is not corn, meadow or inclosed for some particular use" (p. 100).

It is moot whether the word "lambe" in Liberty 93 was a simple misprint of "lame" or else indicated ewes who were "in lambe" or "lambing" (*Body of Liberties*, 1641, p. 52). Liberty 93 addressing drovers contained the word "lambe" in 1641, while in the revised laws of 1660, this is rendered as "lame." On this small textual change, see also William Whitmore's "Introduction" to the 1890 imprint of the *Body of Liberties* (p. xxiii, n. 16).

44. *RGCMB*, May 26, 1647, vol. 2, p. 196. Bridges was ordered to answer the complaint at the next County Court, though there seems to be no further record of the case against him.

45. The Court of Assistants first met on August 23, 1630. At first, its meetings coincided with those of the General Court (the first record of which is for October 19, 1630, and which met only four other times). The powers and duties of the Court of Assistants from 1629 to 1641 included not only the trial of civil and criminal cases but also the functions of a legislature. From October 1641 to March 5, 1643, crimes of all degrees of seriousness were handled by the Court of Assistants, from capital cases to misdemeanors. From May 16, 1649, on, the Court of Assistants refused to hear cases that could be handled in County Courts, except for appeals. On the respective powers of the General Court and the Court of Assistants, see John Noble (1904), "Preface" (*RCAMB*, vol. 1, pp. iii–xiii).

46. Samuel Eliot Morison (1932), *Builders of the Bay Colony*, p. 232, n. 1. The case Morison referred to is *QCEC*, March 27, 1666, Ipswich, vol. 3, p. 305. Jerrold Tannenbaum (1995), "Animals and the Law: Property, Cruelty, Rights," also claims that "there is a record of at least one prosecution under these statutes"

(the Liberties #92 and 93)" (p. 565). Tannenbaum based his claim on Morison's statement above.

47. Emily Stewart Leavitt and Diane Halverson (1990), "The Evolution of Anti-Cruelty Laws in the United States," p. 1.

48. Virginia DeJohn Anderson (2004), *Creatures of Empire: How Domestic Animals Transformed Early America*, p. 93. Anderson appears to base her claim on Edgar J. McManus (1993), *Laws and Liberty in Early New England: Criminal Justice in Early New England*, app. C, pp. 200–210, whose survey of court cases also found no animal cruelty prosecutions in seventeenth-century New England.

49. Erikson, *Wayward Puritans*, pp. 171–181. Erikson's typology included crimes against the church, contempt of authority, fornication, disturbing the peace, crimes against property, and crimes against persons. Had he discovered an animal cruelty prosecution, in which of these categories would it have been inserted? Probably none. See also David Konig (1979), *Law and Society in Puritan Massachusetts: Essex County, 1629–1692*, esp. pp. 141–42. Konig's study, as its title suggests, is concerned with law in general in Puritan Massachusetts.

50. Howard Schweber (1998), "Ordering Principles: The Adjudication of Criminal Cases in Puritan Massachusetts, 1629–1650." Schweber's scheme included violence and deceit, order in court, breaches of the calendar, order in the public square, breaches of regulation, speech offenses, sexual misconduct, and offenses against household order. The two animal cruelty cases Schweber discovered he uses to suggest only that "the casual way in which the beating of a child is listed among—and after—the enumeration of beatings given to animals in the Flint and Haggett cases may be taken to support the thesis that filial relations in the 17th century were not what we would hope them to be today" (p. 388, n. 37).

51. QCEC, November 1, 1645, Salem, vol. 1, p. 91.

52. QCEC, July 8, 1645, Salem, vol. 1, p. 79.

53. QCEC, December 27, 1642, Salem, vol. 1, p. 49.

54. QCEC, February 18, 1645, Salem, vol. 1, p. 91.

55. QCEC, September 26, 1654, Ipswich, vol. 1, p. 365.

56. Thus, "Mr. Willia[m] Brown's goats came near Mr. Baxter's farm, and Mr. Verrin's maid set a little dog on them. Mr. Batter's great dog fell upon the goats and killed one. Mr. Batter was ordered to pay for the goat." QCEC, June 30, 1640, Salem, vol. 1, p. 18.

57. "William Edwards fined 20s 'for untrue and falce dealing about Bees,'" QCEC, January 25, 1641, Salem, vol. 1, p. 29.

58. "John Stacy v. Richard More. For killing his swine," QCEC, January 25, 1641, Salem, vol. 1, p. 30.

59. Peter Pettford . . . deposed that he killed a sow for Mr. Keans which had a black spot under one of its eyes before it was killed. . . . He scraped the spot off after the sow was killed." QCEC, June 30, 1641, Salem, vol. 1, p. 27.

60. "The Lady Debora Moody v. Frances Ingers," QCEC, January 25, 1641, Salem, vol. 1, p. 33. Lest it be said that the rich and powerful always had their way,

one might consult a case of October 27, 1642, that reported that Lady Deborah Moody of Lynn was presented for not believing in infant baptism (*QCEC*, vol. 1, p. 48). She did not appear in court, moreover, because "she was in a way of conviction before the elders" (*QCEC*, vol. 1, p. 48). Only 6.8 percent of those convicted of crimes in Middlesex County Court were nonwhite, and the majority were not drawn from the poverty stricken and the bottom of Puritan society (Eli Faber [1978], "Puritan Criminals: The Economic, Social, and Intellectual Background to Crime in Seventeenth-Century Massachusetts"). Faber's findings are generally supported by Schweber, "Ordering Principles."

61. *QCEC*, April 27, 1637, Salem, vol. 1, p. 5.

62. *QCEC*, January 25, 1641, Salem, vol. 1, p. 30.

63. *QCEC*, April 25, 1639, Salem, vol. 1, p. 11.

64. *QCEC*, September 26, 1654, Ipswich, vol. 1, p. 365.

65. *QCEC*, July 1, 1657, Salem, vol. 2, p. 50.

66. For example, more severe penalties were mandated for those "who robbed dwelling houses on the Lord's day, when the inhabitants are gone to the worship of God" (*RGCMB*, June 14, 1642, vol. 2, p. 22). Again, "Though burglars were commonly punished by having the letter 'B' branded on their foreheads, for good measure in Suffolk County they also had one ear cut off if their crime was committed on the Sabbath" (Samuel Eliot Morison [1933], "Introduction," in *Records of the Suffolk County Court 1671–1680*, pp. lxxx–lxxxi).

67. In 1630, for example, John Baker was ordered to be whipped for shooting at fowl on the Sabbath (*RGCMB*, November 30, 1630, vol. 1, p. 82).

68. *QCEC*, November 30, 1652, Salem, vol. 1, p. 273.

69. *QCEC*, February 21, 1643, Salem, vol. 1, p. 51.

70. *QCEC*, May 9, 1666, Ipswich, vol. 3, p. 320.

71. *QCEC*, May 1, 1672, Ipswich, vol. 5, p. 39. Major Robert Pike was convicted of traveling by horse and for "lying and wicked speaking" on the Sabbath after sunset. He was ordered to be "severely whipped, once at Ipswich and also at Newbury" *QCEC*, May 4, 1680, Ipswich, vol. 7, pp. 376–77. Somewhat similarly, John Gamage was admonished for "breach of the Sabbath fetching a horse from Jeffrey's neck before the sun was set" (*QCEC*, April 13, 1675, Salisbury, vol. 6, p. 26).

72. *QCEC*, July 10, 1644, Salem, vol. 1, p. 65.

73. *QCEC*, September 7, 1649, Ipswich, vol. 1, p. 174. A short-term epidemic of piety must have broken out in Ipswich because two other defendants were found guilty of cruelty to animals on the very same day.

74. *QCEC*, June 3, 1651, Ipswich, vol. 1, p. 226.

75. *QCEC*, January 26, 1669, Salem, vol. 4, p. 99.

76. *QCEC*, June 25, 1672, Salem, vol. 5, p. 41.

77. *QCEC*, May 9, 1682, Ipswich, vol. 8, p. 299.

78. *QCEC*, September 7, 1649, Ipswich, vol. 1, p. 174.

79. *QCEC*, September 7, 1649, Salem, vol. 1, p. 174.

80. *QCEC*, September 30, 1662, Ipswich, vol. 2, pp. 441–42. At the next hearing of the court, Galiver's good behavior was noted, and he was discharged, presumably having paid his fine and compensation. *QCEC*, November 13, 1662, Salem, vol. 3, p. 16.

81. *QCEC*, March 27, 1666, Ipswich, vol. 3, p. 305.

82. *QCEC*, March 29, 1659, Ipswich, vol. 2, pp. 147–48.

83. *QCEC*, March 29, 1659, Ipswich, vol. 2, pp. 147–48.

84. *QCEC*, May 10, 1660, Ipswich, vol. 2, p. 199. A brief entry in the Ipswich court records on September 25, 1660, states that on further examination, "John Leigh was released of his bond" (p. 248).

85. *QCEC*, September 25, 1660, Ipswich, vol. 2, pp. 248–49. In the original docket, lodged on March 27, 1660, Pinder was charged with "cutting two mares" (p. 197).

86. *QCEC*, September 25, 1660, Ipswich, vol. 2, pp. 248–49.

87. *QCEC*, March 25, 1656, Ipswich, vol. 2, p. 373. On his petition and humiliation, Farough voided the sentence of whipping on paying the sum of three pounds.

88. *QCEC*, March 30, 1669, Ipswich, vol. 4, p. 124.

89. *QCEC*, April 13, 1669, Salisbury, vol. 4, p. 132.

90. *QCEC*, June 25, 1672, Salem, vol. 5, p. 40.

91. Selden's case is recorded in *Pynchon Waste Book for Hampshire* and cited by Joseph H. Smith (1961), "Introduction: Criminal Jurisdiction," p. 116. Selden failing to appear in court, Judge John Pynchon ordered that he be sent for, examined, and dealt with accordingly. However, there is no record that Pynchon ever took further action in this case.

92. *QCEC*, November 14, 1676, Salisbury, vol. 6, p. 209.

93. *QCEC*, November 28, 1682, Salem, vol. 8, p. 410.

94. Animals and notions of animal cruelty also worked their way into Puritans' perceptions of witchcraft. Thus, in events that might have foreshadowed the Salem witchcraft panic, various citizens alleged that they had been abused by animals. Jobe Tyller of Andover, for example, complained of "a bird coming in to suck his wife . . . in the first night a Humbl bee [appeared], the next night a beare ap[peare]d w[hich] grouned the teeth and shooke the claw . . . the next was the ap[par]ition of a great snake" (*QCEC*, June 28, 1659, Salem, vol. 2, pp. 158–59). In 1683, Mary Webster was charged with having been familiar with the devil in the form of a black cat, and prosecuted for witchcraft (*RCAMB*, 1683, vol.1, p. 283). Though the record does not state it, it is possible that—like in cases of bestiality—upon conviction of the human and just before their execution, offending animals also were killed.

Bradley Chapin (1983), *Criminal Justice in Colonial America, 1606–1660*, table 4.2, cites one Massachusetts Bay case of witchcraft involving animals: in 1656, goodwife Jane Walford, Mass (N.H.), "caused illness, animal familiars, bound over and not prosecuted." Chapin also lists three cases of witchcraft that might have involved

animal cruelty: in 1655, Elizabeth Godman, a New Haven gentlewoman, causing illness to humans and animals, three court appearances, admonished, briefly in
prison, and bound over to good behavior; in 1657, William Meaker, New Haven,
accused of bewitching pigs, bound to good behavior; and in 1658, Elizabeth Gar-
lick, Connecticut, servant, "harm to animals; death of humans," acquitted.

95. Cotton Mather (1780), "Elegy at Ezekiel Cheever's Funeral," pp. 29–30.

96. Basing itself on Henrecian and Elizabethan statutes, the provision "Trespass by Man or Beast" of the Providence (Rhode Island) Colony Code of Laws
(1647, pp. 38–39) stated,

> It is also agreed that he that shall maliciously and
> Unlawfully burn or spoil a cart-heap of wood prepared
> For coals, or otherwise cut out the tongue of a beast
> Being alive, cut off the ears of a man, bark fruit trees
> . . . . Being lawfully convict, as in larceny, he shall pay to the party grieved his costs
> and treble damages and forfeit to the king ten pounds. (39 Hen. 8,6)

> The same penalty doth he deserve, that put his beasts or others into another man's
> field . . . [and] for other trespasses either ignorantly done by the person himself or by
> his cattle. (43 Eliz. 7)

97. However, though it contained no offense of animal cruelty, the 1656
New Haven Code specified that "brutish folly" and "bestly cruelty" were among
the cases in which "[s]*tripes*, or whipping [is] a correction fit, and proper in some
cases" (p. 53).

98. The Connecticut General Laws of 1650 stated, "*Cruelty:* no man shall
exercise any Cruelty towards any Bruit Creature, which are usually kept for the
use of man, upon pain of such punishment as in the judgement of the Court the
nature of the offence shall deserve. Damages" (p. 523). See also Haskins and Ewing (1969), "The Spread of Massachusetts Law in the Seventeenth Century," who
write, contentiously, "That Connecticut did not strike out on its own, except for
a half dozen of its seventy-eight provisions, is an indication both of the completeness and the comprehensive of the earlier Massachusetts statute and its suitability
to the conditions of Puritan society elsewhere" (p. 189).

99. Wecker's (1582) *Secrets of Art and Nature* was translated from Latin into
English in 1660. See also the comments on gustatory gratification in Patricia Fumerton (1990), "Introduction: A New New Historicism," pp. 1–3.

100. Robert May (1685), *Accomplisht Cook*, for example, instructed his readers
how to "break that deer, leach that brawn, rear that goose, lift that swan, sauce
that capon, spoil that hen, fruit that chicken, unbrace that mallard, unlace that
coney, dismember that hen, disfigure that peracock, unjoint that bitturn, untach
that curlew . . . thigh all manner of small birds" (p. 9).

Toward a Sociology of Animal Sexual Assault

3

T HE THEME OF THIS CHAPTER emerged less from my wish to contribute to an embryonic sociology of animal abuse than from the practical needs of pedagogy. In trying to develop an undergraduate course on the sociology of animal abuse, I was immediately confronted with conveying to my students an adequate response to the deceptively simple question, What is animal abuse? Class time devoted to the specter of the dramatic and well-publicized horrors of agribusiness, slaughterhouses, vivisection, hunting, trapping, circuses, and so on would tend to stimulate among students, I believed, more of a visceral reaction than the desired goal of sustained inquiry about the nature of animal abuse.

It happened that, in casting a wide net for some heuristic device that would enable me to examine animal abuse in a pedagogic context, I stumbled on two unusual and quite intriguing representations of sexual relations between humans and animals. Separated by 300 years and inhabiting vastly different cultural universes, they forced me to rethink my understanding of bestiality. One was a censorious description of bestiality in a seventeenth-century diary. The other was a celebratory depiction of it in a film produced in the 1980s.

In an entry for 1642 in his diary *Of Plymouth Plantation, 1620–1647*, Governor William Bradford commented on the trial of one Thomas Granger for bestiality. According to Bradford, Granger, aged sixteen or seventeen, was indicted for "buggery with a mare, a cow, two goats, five sheep, two calves and a turkey."[1] Although he declined to enter many of the details of the case, Bradford related that Granger, who had been accidentally discovered while engaging in "a lewd practice towards the mare," had freely admitted "the fact with that beast at that time" and that he had also identified several sheep with whom he had been familiar. Under examination, Granger and another youth ("who had made some sodomitical attempts") had been asked how they first learned and came to "the knowledge and practice of such wickedness?" One of the pair confessed that he had long practiced it in England, where he had learned of it from others who kept cattle there. On these admissions, Bradford reflected "by which it appears how one wicked person may infect many, and what care all ought to have what servants they bring into their families."[2] Granger was found guilty and duly condemned to death. "A very sad spectacle it was," Bradford lamented, for "first the mare and then the cow and the rest of the lesser cattle were killed before his face, according to the law, Leviticus xx.15; and then he himself was executed."[3]

These entries in Governor Bradford's diary are compelling for several reasons, not least of which is that they betray the extensive ideological influence of Judeo-Christianity on attitudes toward human–animal sexual relations. Note, for example, that the legislation to which Bradford turned was not the prevailing English statute enacted in 1533 in the reign of Henry VIII. It was, rather, the Mosaic commandment contained in Leviticus (20:15): "if a man lieth with a beast, he shall surely be put to death: and ye shall slay the beast."[4] Assuming that Governor Bradford's musings about bestiality signify something other than the random scribbling of a bored colonial official, several questions about his commentary remain. For example, why were the transgressions ("accidentally discovered") of the unfortunate Granger reported to the authorities, while the "sodomitical attempts" of others were not? Were the circumstances of Granger's case representative of bestiality as a social practice or merely of those who happened to have been prosecuted for it?

At almost the same time as I stumbled across Bradford's seventeenth-century description of Thomas Granger's trial and execution for bestiality, a criminology student, knowing that I wanted to develop a course on the sociology of animal abuse, kindly suggested I take a look at a would-be-erotic video provocatively titled *Barnyard Love*. "I wonder what you'll think of this?" she asked, offering to lend it to me and informing me that she and her boyfriend had just viewed it.

I can report in all honesty that *Barnyard Love* was a difficult film for me to watch. It is a crudely produced German film of the mid-1990s that graphically depicts sexual acts engaged in by humans with animals. These acts include human males who engage in sexual intercourse with cows and hens and more often—given that heterosexual males are presumably the film's chief audience—human females who have sexual intercourse with dogs, who insert eels into their vaginas, and who perform fellatio on dogs and horses.

Even from my amateurish perspective and despite the obvious risks of anthropomorphism, I noticed how immensely varied were the filmed reactions of the different animals to attempted sexual union with and initiated by humans. At one extreme, the dogs in *Barnyard Love* who were engaged in sexual activities with women seemed energetically to enjoy such human attention. To me, at least, it did not seem possible that such canine enthusiasm could be feigned by off-camera training designed to suppress resistance or to hide more genuine emotions of grief and pain. At the opposite extreme, some animals, such as eels and hens, were manifestly unwilling recipients of human sexual advances. None of my students would have much trouble, I thought, in identifying as animal abuse the case of one unfortunate hen who was literally fucked to death, which for her was doubtless a terrifying consequence of enforced sexual intercourse with a human male. Yet, in the case of large quadrupeds, such as the horses and cows depicted in the film, their reaction seemed closer to boredom or perhaps indifference than it did to pain or to bliss—eating, urinating, and defecating as they were during intercourse or while their genitalia were being manipulated. Indeed, it was unclear whether these larger animals were even aware of the prolonged sexual relations that humans had foisted on them. In their case, however, what I saw as animals' indifference might actually have been calculated detachment on their part and, despite the possibility that we might never know it with much certainty, a coping strategy for numbing the pain inflicted on them by yet another of the myriad ways in which their lives are routinely invaded, inspected, and disposed of by humans.

Like the seventeenth-century case of Thomas Granger, the events depicted in films like *Barnyard Love* also raise interesting questions about the understanding of bestiality as a social practice. How should we approach bestiality: is it an outrageous and perhaps perverse act or, as the law's historical tolerance of it during modernity suggests, a relatively benign form of social deviance? Why have sexual relations involving humans and animals been so vociferously and ubiquitously condemned and so little studied?[5]

The Abominations of Leviticus

The cultural universe of bestiality is necessarily an anthropocentric one, though in many societies, past and present, it inhabits an ambiguous ideological terrain. On the one hand, it is exalted in myth and folklore. These favorable depictions of bestiality are often lodged in the sexual antics, in the conquests and the offspring of numerous gods, in the lineage of earthly monarchs and rulers, and in the texts of fairy stories and other morality tales. On the other hand, all known societies have likely applied some form of censure to human–animal sexual relations.

Very often, the censure of bestiality has been extremely severe.[6] The Hittite Laws (ca. 3,500 B.P.), for example, decreed that if a man had sexual intercourse with a pig, a dog, a sheep, or a goat, it was an abomination, and he should be put to death.[7] It also decreed, however, that there would be no punishment for sex with a cow, a horse, or a mule or, when soldiers were away at war for long periods of time, with horses and mules as alternatives to sex with their wives. In the case of a cow, if the man were to be led to the king, the king could spare his life. The first reference to the "offending ox"—the punishable, goring ox—also occurs in the Hittite Laws: "If an ox attacks a man [for sexual intercourse] and the ox dies and the man does not die (then) one sheep shall be brought as a substitute for the man, and they shall kill it. If a pig attacks a man, (there shall be) no punishment."[8]

From its inception, Judeo-Christianity applied austere standards and a strict discipline to those of its followers who violated its injunctions against the major sins of idolatry, the shedding of blood, and fornication, including bestiality.[9] In this tradition, the earliest and most influential justifications for censures of bestiality are provided in the Mosaic laws (ca. 3,000 B.P.), including Exodus, Deuteronomy, and Leviticus. Exodus (18:23), for example, stated, "You shall not have sexual relations with any animal to defile yourself thereby; nor shall any woman give herself to an animal to mate with it; it is a perversion." Deuteronomy (27:21) declared, "Cursed be he that lieth with any manner of beast," while Exodus (22:19) commanded, "Whosoever lieth with a beast shall surely be put to death"—"whosoever" here referring, at least in Leviticus (20:15–16), to both men and women. The fact that the list of forbidden sexual practices required two chapters of Leviticus (18:6–23 and 20:9–21) probably indicates, as Jacob Milgrom's authoritative *Leviticus 17–22* suggests, that the rabbis believed the violation of these laws to be widespread.[10]

Precisely what motives lie behind the various Mosaic bans on certain forms of sexual relationships is unclear. Probably they are not open to precise reclamation. Thus, while many of them are accompanied by words of disgust and condemnation, these utterances are not quite the same as motives. Milgrom speculates about the quintessential rationale that lies behind the list of forbidden sexual practices.[11] In his opinion, the most persuasive is that the common denominator of most of them is that they were intended to minimize family rivalries and quarrels and thereby maximize household peace. This explanation works well for the majority of the forbidden sexual practices, which are the incest prohibitions. But it does not explain some practices that are obviously private matters: sex with a menstruant, Molech, sodomy, and bestiality. In the eyes of Leviticus, these four categories are seen either as destroying the proper use of seed in the patriarchal family (as in the human sacrifice of children to Molech, often by burning) or the producing of no seed or as producing seed that is destructive of families. Milgrom notes that "it can well be that these rationales need no further rationale."[12]

For bestiality, Leviticus mandated death not only for guilty humans but also for offending animals. There are various reasons why it might have been believed that offending animals had to die. Possibly, if they were allowed to live, then they might serve as an unwelcome reminder of shameful acts. Or their continued existence might tempt another human into sin. Perhaps the burning of both guilty parties was a ritual purification, and their death would deprive them both of a decent burial.[13] Haltigar's pseudo-Roman, first-century penitential was even more specific about the fate of polluted animals: "If a man has sinned with a goat or with a sheep or with any animal, no one shall eat its flesh or milk, but it shall be killed and given to the dogs."[14]

Over the ages, three beliefs have persisted about the wrongfulness of bestiality: it ruptures the natural, God-given order of the universe; it violates the procreative intent required of all sexual relations between Christians; and it produces monstrous offspring that are the work of the Devil.[15]

Rupture of the Natural Order of the Universe

In her well-known analysis of social pollution in *Purity and Danger*, Mary Douglas stressed that in the Mosaic commandments, holiness is exemplified by completeness, by keeping distinct the categories of divine creation, and by defining them precisely. Prefaced by the general command, "Ye shall be holy: for I the Lord your God am holy," holiness requires that individuals conform to the class to which they belong.[16] This theme continues (Leviticus 19:19), "Ye shall keep my statutes. Thou shalt not let / Thy cattle gender with a diverse kind; thou / Shalt not sow thy field with mingled seed; neither / Shall a garment mingled of linen and woollen come upon thee." The rules that cattle should not "gender with a diverse kind" and that a field should not be sown "with mingled seed" lie at the heart of the

Mosaic injunctions about bestiality. If different classes of things must not be confused, then the mingling of humans and animals—bestiality—is confusion and should be condemned and prohibited.

On this very basis, the early Christian church regarded copulation with a Jew as a form of bestiality and sanctioned it with death. So, too, from the time of Leviticus to that of seventeenth-century English moralists and beyond, bestiality has been regarded as sinful or criminal because it represents a rupture of the natural order of the universe, the categories of which it is immoral to mix. Similarly, in Plymouth Plantation, Governor Bradford recorded the opinions of three ministers given in 1642 about the acts of "unnatural vice" to be punished with death, among which were to be women who commit bestiality.[17] Seeking affirmation in Leviticus, the ministers condemned bestiality, whether penetration had occurred or not, because it is "against the order of nature," "unnatural," and a "confusion." Again, Richard Capel, a seventeenth-century Stuart moralist, argued that bestiality is the worst of sexual crimes because "it turns man into a very beast, makes a man a member of a brute creature."[18]

Violation of Procreative Intent

In matters of sexual relations, "be thou holy" means more than "be thou separate," for Christian, especially Catholic, morality has long required that sexual intercourse should flow not from pleasure or play but exclusively from a procreative intent. Bestiality has thus also been condemned because it is held to be a violation of the Christian rule that procreation is the sole purpose of sexual intercourse. Crimes against nature have therefore been proclaimed to be those in which the emission of seed is not accompanied by a procreative intent, as in masturbation, anal and oral sex, incest, adultery, rape, and bestiality.

Monstrous Offspring

Bestiality has also been condemned because of the offspring a sexual union between humans and beasts is in some quarters thought to produce or because of the evil that such offspring are held to signify or portend.[19] This particular condemnation has itself been part of a complex cultural framework that includes animism, paganism, and a fascination with monsters. Classical antiquity, for example, provides numerous seemingly nonjudgmental references to human–animal sexual intercourse, including stories where animals were thought to be in love with humans. Such cases are very prominent in, for example, *De natura animalium* (ca. 1800 B.P.), the

Roman historian and sophist Aelian's miscellany of facts about animals and humans, genuine or supposed, that he gleaned from Greek writers, including Aristotle. Drawing on material from and about Rome, Greece, India, Libya, and Egypt, Aelian documented how widespread was the belief in the actual offspring of human–animal unions ("creatures of composite nature"): "many creatures are begotten with two faces and two breasts: some born of a cow have the foreparts of a man; others on the contrary spring up begotten of a man but with the head of a cow."[20]

Although Aelian provided his readers with no clues as to how such offspring were regarded, they cannot always have been viewed with disfavor given his ubiquitous and often reverential references to creatures such as satyrs, centaurs, and minotaurs. That the rigid hierarchical boundaries between animals and humans can easily become blurred is recorded in a spiteful history of Ireland by the twelfth-century chronicler Giraldus Cambrensis. Cambrensis related the practice of a certain Ulster people

> which is accustomed to appoint its king with a rite altogether outlandish and abominable. When the whole people of that land has been gathered together in one place, a white mare is brought forward into the middle of the assembly. He who is to be inaugurated, not as a chief, but as a beast, not as a king, but as an outlaw, has bestial intercourse with her before all, professing himself to be a beast also. The mare is then killed immediately, cut up in pieces, and boiled in water.[21]

Without further comment, Giraldus related how in the Glendalough mountains, a cow gave birth to a man-calf, the fruit of a union between the cow and a man, the local Irish folk "being especially addicted to such abominations."[22] Elsewhere, Giraldus reported that Irish men and women had sexual intercourse with cows, goats, and lions and that the populace believed that such unions were occasionally fertile. Indeed, Giraldus pondered whether it is murder to kill the product of a man–cow union, for "who can disallow the claims of a creature which stands erect, laughs, and goes on two feet to belong to the human species?"[23] Similar beliefs appear in seventeenth-century New England, one case being related in the New Haven court records.[24] Moreover, the poetry of John Donne and the speeches and sermons of John Winthrop, Cotton Mather and his brother John, Samuel Danforth, and William Bradford are infected with the fear that colonial agricultural society was a frontier existence not only beset with the internal dangers of alcohol, idleness, and lust but also surrounded by forests, wild animals, and savages.[25] Such beliefs operated in tandem with religious doctrine to assail bestiality and to portray its progeny as monsters resulting from the decay of civilization and the encroachment of the wilderness. Monstrous progeny were a visible reminder of how evil it was to transgress the God-given boundaries separating men from beasts.[26]

Occasionally, the judicial accusation of bestiality has blurred into or has been employed in concert with other charges, such as witchcraft. Thus, some early medieval European accusations of witchcraft involved the claim that the defendant had partaken in a ritual salute of the Devil's backside, the *osculum infame*, or obscene kiss.[27] In another case of unknown date, a certain Françoise Sécretain was burned alive because she had had carnal knowledge of domestic animals—a dog, a cat, and a cock—and because, she admitted, she was a witch and her animals were actually earthly forms of the devil.[28]

The social control of the object of such fears has been subject to great cultural variation in both style and volume. In some societies, surprisingly few prosecutions have accompanied the censure of bestiality. For example, despite the horror with which bestiality was viewed by Puritan zealots and legal writers in England and in colonial America, it was rarely indicted and was unlikely to result in a conviction.[29] In other societies, the number of convictions and executions is quite staggering. In Sweden, for example, from 1635 to 1778, there were as many as 700 executions for bestiality, and an even greater number of males was sentenced to flogging, church penalties, and public forced labor in chains.[30] On conviction, both human and animal were usually put to death, often by burning at the stake but occasionally by beheading or by hanging or from blows to the head. The bodies of the condemned, both human and animal, were finally burned or butchered and buried together.

If the penalties for bestiality and the entire range of unnatural acts had been strictly enforced, as Michael Goodich has noted, then Europe and colonial America would have become vast penal institutions inhabited by populations restricted in diet and dress, excluded from church ser-vices, and condemned to a joyless life of fasts, prayers, and flagellation.[31] The solution to this draconian morass was the hasty introduction in the twelfth century of mitigating devices like reservation, dispensation, and indulgences. Each of these devices effectively reduced the level of punish-ment while reaffirming penitents' dependence on the mercy of confessors, bishops, and popes. Although the thirteenth century saw a sharp growth in laws against bestiality, these were seldom prosecuted. Moreover, in the fourteenth and fifteenth centuries, despite the widespread belief that loose sexual habits were the peculiar traits of heretics, the canonical courts treated most sexual offenses, except homosexuality, rather lightly—

"considerably less harshly than offenses against ecclesiastical institutions and church property."[32]

According to biblical scholars, the rules of forbidden sexual practices in Leviticus 18 and 20 have had a larger impact on Western law than any comparable body of biblical commandments.[33] The earliest secular legislation on bestiality was probably enacted in Norway, where it was forbidden by the laws of *Gulathing* and *Fro stathing*, which punished it with castration and outlawry.[34]

In most European jurisdictions, once authority over cases of bestiality had passed, roughly speaking, from church to state, bestiality became a capital offense. In Sweden, it became a capital crime around 1400. In twelfth-century England, the moral reformer Peter Damian led a crusade directed at "sins against nature," which led to extraordinary legislation that classified all unnatural sex acts as "reserved sins." This designation entailed that acts such as homosexuality and bestiality were subject not to forgiveness by a priest in confession but to referral to the bishop of the diocese for penance and absolution.[35] The English theologian Thomas of Chobham provided a detailed treatment of bestiality in his *Summa Confessorum* (ca. 1214), which was specifically written for use by English clergy. Thomas ranked bestiality as the most heinous of all sins against nature, and he counseled that when a case of this kind was detected, the animal should be killed and its carcass burned or buried. Human offenders should be required to wear sandals without soles and could never wear linen, enter a church, eat meat or fish, drink intoxicants, or wear knights' garments.[36]

Bestiality became a capital offense in England in 1533,[37] a status it bequeathed to its colonies in America. Among the early English commentators on bestiality were the legal authorities Sir William Blackstone and Sir Edward Coke. To Blackstone, "the very mention of [the crime] is a disgrace to human nature."[38] To Coke—who followed St. Augustine's prescription that a sin by natural use, such as adultery or rape, is less shameful than one by unnatural use of "a member not granted for this"—bestiality was an instance of buggery, which, in the seventeenth century, was held to be more serious than rape. Coke wrote that bestiality "is a detestable and abominable sin amongst Christians not to be named, committed by carnal knowledge against the ordinance of the Creator, and order of nature, by mankind with mankind, or with brute beast, or by womankind with brute beast."[39]

The word "bestiality" entered the English language in the first half of the seventeenth century. There are at least two accounts of its origin. The first is that it derived from the Latin *bestialitas*, which was prominently employed by Thomas Aquinas in his thirteenth-century *Summa Theologica* severally to refer to primitive behavior, to human–animal sexual intercourse, and to the way in which animals copulate.[40] The second is that it derived from the Latin *animal*, which was originally translated into Old English as *beste* or *beast* from the French *bête*, which, in turn, probably came from the Sanskrit "that which is to be feared."[41] Until approximately the mid-nineteenth century, the term referred broadly to the beastlike, earthy and savage qualities allegedly inhering in animals. Today, bestiality tends exclusively to denote sexual relations between humans and animals.

Besides a hodgepodge of more or less polite colloquialisms, bestiality has also been termed "zoophilia," "zooerasty," "sodomy," and "buggery." Sometimes it is classified as a crime against nature (*peccatio contra naturam*); in this, it is a bedfellow of other crimes involving "pollution," such as sodomy, buggery, masturbation, and pedophilia. At other times, the terms "sodomy" and "buggery" are used interchangeably to describe bestiality, though they have also often been employed to denote homosexuality. Each of these terms carries with it pejorative baggage that varies in its moral bases, in its intensity, and in the duration of its condemnation. Moreover, in some societies, such as in New England from the Puritan 1600s until the mid-nineteenth century, bestiality has been generally regarded with such trepidation that even the very mention of the word is censured. Accordingly, it has also been referred to as "that unmentionable vice" or "a sin too fearful to be named" or "among Christians a crime not to be named."

The Drift to Tolerance

During and after the mid-nineteenth century, many nonreproductive sexual practices, including bestiality, were effectively decriminalized.[42] Following the early lead of Jeremy Bentham[43] and others, the social control of bestiality has formally passed from religion and criminal law to a medico-psychiatric discourse at whose center, it is claimed, lie diseased individuals who are often simpletons or imbeciles with a variety of characterological defects and who allegedly sometimes also have psychopathic personalities.

At once subverting this psychiatrization and also echoing certain aspects of the spirit of decriminalization, there has gradually emerged a pseudoliberal tolerance of bestiality. A key aspect of this tendency is that bestiality should be tolerated—within certain limits, even celebrated—both because it is harmless and because it is an interesting and vital part of almost every known culture.

Dearest Pet: *Midas Dekkers*

When I first encountered *Dearest Pet* in 1994, my initial reaction was that it closely resembled a well-thumbed tome that I had found in 1972 in a flea market in Durham, England. That book, titled *A History of the Rod: Flagellation and the Flagellants in All Countries*, proclaims on the frontispiece as its author an unlikely "Rev. Wm. M. Cooper, B.A." I suspect that the book was published in late Victorian London, though it is undated. I'm not sure how *A History of the Rod* managed to survive the prudish official ideologies of the time, though it does seem to conform well with the nineteenth-century passion for scientific classification. Its numerous woodcut illustrations and pen-and-ink and charcoal drawings of humans fornicating with animals seem designed more to titillate than to inform. Its libertine message was doubtless intended as an erotic commodity for consumption by a limited popular audience.

Like *A History of the Rod*, Midas Dekkers's book *Dearest Pet* is profusely illustrated, a veritable compendium of facts that can be read as a text of soft and, in places, not-so-soft pornography. But appearances can deceive. *Dearest Pet* is more than a simple work of titillation by the Dutch biologist and radio personality. Because there is so little else in the way of reading matter that addresses bestiality as an intellectual and social problem, it also serves to inform.

Without exaggeration, it was *Dearest Pet* that for me pierced the vacuum of intellectual neglect of bestiality that had been created by an amalgam of superstition, avoidance, and ignorance. Its 208 pages and wide-ranging bibliography provide a rich resource for any student of sexual deviance and social control. Certainly, several aspects of Dekkers's text have since been better researched and more tightly argued—and here I mean mainly the historical work of E. William Monter on France and Switzerland, Jonas Liliequist and Jens Rydström on Sweden, Joyce Salisbury on medieval Europe, and John Murrin on colonial America. But nothing approaches the broad sweep of *Dearest Pet*'s comprehensive perspective. *Dearest Pet* is a constructive text that employs interdisciplinary evidence to support its unitary project: the celebration of human–animal sexual relations as a form of sexual diversity. Throughout *Dearest Pet*, Dekkers relentlessly supports this project with a dizzying array of cartoons, paintings, and photographs taken from popular folklore, literature, religion, cinematography, biology, sexology, penology, and law.

But there is a compelling ambiguity at the heart of *Dearest Pet*. This must be recognized and, if possible, resolved by anyone concerned with sexuality and human–animal studies. It is this: is *Dearest Pet*'s ultimate quest—the normalization of bestiality as a form of sexual diversity—a logical addition to the justifiable extension of social acceptance and legal rights to gays, lesbians, and other sexual orientations, such as bisexualism and transsexualism? Or is it, instead, a piece of misplaced anthropocentrism whose plea for tolerance will simply lead to an increase in the myriad ways in which humans, lawfully and with widespread social acceptance, exploit and harm our fellow creatures?

"Heavy Petting": Peter Singer

The question of whether bestiality should be tolerated is long overdue for discussion. Indeed, a convenient vehicle for this discussion was provided by Professor Peter Singer's review of Dekkers's *Dearest Pet*. In his review titled "Heavy Petting," published in 2001 in the avant-garde, online magazine *Nerve*, Singer seems to promote an attitude of liberal tolerance toward bestiality.[44]

Singer's text, like the front cover of Dekkers's *Dearest Pet*, is announced with the image of a canine companion in an erstwhile erotic pose. His review of *Dearest Pet* can be summarized as follows. Singer begins by noting the disappearance, one by one, of the taboos against nonprocreative forms of sexuality. Although he does not identify the societies in which it is alleged that these taboos have largely disappeared, I suspect he must be referring to technologically advanced societies in the West. In these societies, homosexuality, lesbianism, and oral sex are practiced quite openly and to an extent unimaginable a century ago. However, Singer suggests that this is not true in the case of bestiality, which, "if Midas Dekkers . . . has got it right . . . is not because of its rarity."[45] Without completing this thought, Singer then notes that Dekkers has assembled "a substantial body of evidence" that suggests that bestiality is of long-standing duration (from "the Bronze Age") and that in many societies it is not an altogether uncommon practice.

Singer next asks how much of Dekkers's lengthy celebration of human–animal sexual relations is simple fantasy, "the King Kong-ish archetypes" of bygone eras. In trying to answer this question, he mentions Dekkers's references to various sexological studies—for example, the famous Kinsey surveys of the late 1940s and early 1950s—that imply that bestiality is quite widely practiced. Thus, while women having sex with bulls or rams is more myth than reality, Singer reports that "for three-quarters of the women who told Kinsey that they had had sexual contact with an animal, the animal involved was a dog, and actual sexual intercourse was rare. More commonly the woman limited themselves to touching and masturbating the animal, or having their genitals licked by it."[46]

How, then, Singer asks, should one explain the survival of the potency of the taboo against bestiality and the continued existence of human–animal sexual contacts? This apparent contradiction, he suggests, reflects our ambivalent relationship with animals. On the one hand, we humans believe that we are distinct from animals because we alone are made in God's image and have immortal souls. In Kantian terms, we are ends in ourselves. We have inherent dignity. On the other hand, we are also animals. There are thus many ways in which we inevitably behave as other animals do (mammals, anyway). They have penises and vaginas as we do, and they use them as we do. "The fact that the vagina of a calf can be sexually satisfying to a man shows how similar these organs are."[47] The persistence of the taboo against bestiality and the vehemence with which it is held, Singer continues, reflect "our desire to differentiate ourselves, erotically and in every other way, from animals."[48]

Singer then enters the most contentious section of his short review when he argues that some acts of bestiality described by Dekkers "are clearly wrong, and should remain crimes."[49] These include those cases where men use animals as sexual objects and do so with cruelty: "Some men use hens as a sexual object, inserting their penis into the cloaca, an all-purpose channel for wastes and for the passage of the egg. This is usually fatal to the hen, and in some cases she will be deliberately decapitated just before ejaculation in order to intensify the convulsions of its sphincter. This is cruelty, clear and simple."[50]

For Singer, bestiality is wrongful conduct only if it involves cruelty. This means, he adds, with the sort of valuable insight that he has provided in other venues, that the hen who is killed as a result of (human) male sexual advances suffers no worse harm than those egg-producing hens who are forced to live in wretched conditions all the time before they are strung upside down on a conveyor belt and slaughtered.

Singer abruptly ends his review of Dekkers's *Dearest Pet* with an extremely provocative final paragraph. In this, he comments on an event related to him by a woman who had visited Camp Leakey, a rehabilitation center run by Birute Galdikas ("the Jane Goodall of orangutans") for captured orangutans in Borneo:

> At Camp Leakey, the orangutans are gradually acclimatized to the jungle, and as they get closer to complete independence, they are able to come

and go as they please. While walking through the camp with Galdikas, my informant was suddenly seized by a large male orangutan, his intentions made obvious by his erect penis. Fighting off so powerful an animal was not an option, but Galdikas called to her companion not to be concerned, because the orangutan would not harm her, and adding, as further reassurance, that "they have a very small penis." As it happened, the orangutan lost interest before penetration took place, but the aspect of the story that struck me most forcefully was that in the eyes of someone who has lived much of her life with orangutans, to be seen by one of them as an object of sexual interest is not a cause for shock or horror. The potential violence of the orangutan's come-on may have been disturbing, but the fact that it was an orangutan making the advances was not. That may be because Galdikas understands very well that we are animals, indeed more specifically, we are great apes. This does not make sex across the species barrier normal, or natural, whatever those much-misused words may mean, but it does imply that it ceases to be an offence to our status and dignity as human beings.[51]

The immediate aftermath of Singer's review included heated objections from animal rights groups and think-tank discussion in newspapers and magazines such as the *New York Times* and *The New Republic*. Gary Francione, with Peter Singer one of the cosigners of the *Declaration on the Rights of Great Apes*, said that Singer could "no longer be trusted with the rights of apes."[52] The lone prominent defender of Singer's position was the president of People for the Ethical Treatment of Animals, Ingrid Newkirk, who supposed the rightfulness of some forms of human–animal sexual interaction.[53]

At first, having read and reread "Heavy Petting," I found it hard to believe that it had been written by Singer—he who is widely venerated as the author of *Animal Liberation, the* foundational text of the modern animal protection community. Was it a book review? Well, yes, but not exactly. Was it some ghastly postmodernist prank? What on earth did the scholar-activist imagine could have been achieved by it? Did it actually herald the birth of some liberal manifesto advocating the pleasures of bestiality? Probably not—or not intentionally so.

Trying to put a nonjudgmental spin on the general drift of the review, I wondered whether Singer had been quietly thinking about bestiality for some time. Perhaps his short review merely represented the logical conclusion to more intensive intellectual labors on his part.

On its face, however, "Heavy Petting" contains three obvious difficulties. First, it seems to believe that bestiality is not a rare phenomenon but an arguably legitimate orientation that has been consciously chosen and practiced by a few individuals in all societies since the dawn of time. This is, it should be noted, one of the possible planks in an agenda for tolerating bestiality. Thus, in *Dearest Pet*, Kinsey's evidence is trotted out by Dekkers and paraded, along with an obscure study of Austrian court proceedings from 1923 to 1965 (which estimates that 1 to 2 percent of rural males occasionally have sexual contact with animals), with the functionalist implication that bestiality can't be all that bad if in lots of places and times some people have always done it.[54] However, even if the prevalence of bestiality in a given society could be measured with some level of statistical confidence—which it cannot, as I argue toward the end of this chapter—neither Dekkers nor Singer would be able to draw one whit of comfort from this methodological advance because, unfortunately, from the mere existence of a social fact, however widespread, nothing can properly be inferred either about its functionality or about whether it is rightful conduct.

A second difficulty with "Heavy Petting" is that if bestiality is to be tolerated or not, then at some point we need to know what, precisely, bestiality is. Granted, defining bestiality is no easy matter. Singer himself mentions the obvious importance of the question of what bestiality is, and he rightly notes that "much depends, of course, on how the notion of a sexual relationship is defined."[55] Yet to this otherwise useful question, he responds uncritically either by repeating several of Dekkers's numerous examples or by making contentious innuendos about household dogs who grip the legs of visitors and rub their penises against them or about the habit of girls and young women who are attracted to riding horses. Singer claims that the latter practice "undoubtedly has a sexual undertone."[56] However, one must ask whether the claim itself stems from wishful thinking and threatened manhood.[57] Perhaps Singer and others have misidentified the habit of girls and young women who are attracted to riding horses as having a sexual component because it is a gendered social practice. At best, the claim trivializes the very complex social relationship between girls and horses. At worst, it insults the strong feelings of love and care that girls and women often feel for horses.

Consider also Singer's tale of the human woman at Camp Leakey who was seized by a large male orangutan with an erect penis. Against the implication of this story—that animals might desire humans—it should be pointed out that Camp Leakey is not the natural habitat of orangutans. It is, instead, a place where orangutans are in receipt of human compassion and largesse. There are no known cases where animals in their natural habitat display sexual desire for humans.

Moreover, though the sight of an orangutan's erect penis might appeal to human vanity, neither sexual desire nor the display of its physical symptoms necessarily connote informed consent by an orangutan. Singer suggests that because we humans are both animals and great apes, we should not be offended by an orangutan that makes a sexual advance to us. This seems to be an extravagantly marginal case of transferring potential victimhood. Suppose that the orangutan made sexual advances to a human that *did* offend her status and dignity as a human being. Would this affront require criminal prosecution of the offending animal? With benefit of court-appointed defense counsel? Singer relates that, fortunately, "the orangutan lost interest before penetration took place."[58] But one wonders how on earth his informant or even Singer himself could have determined that "the orangutan lost interest before penetration took place"—if penetration did not in fact take place?

Finally, and without wishing to misrepresent him, it is hard to know what to make of the general drift of Singer's review that bestiality might not be wrongful behavior if it does not involve cruelty. Because this is not offered with supporting argument, it is unclear which of several counterarguments to it might be relevant. However, it does seem to assume that there is no legitimate objection to bestiality unless cruelty is grafted onto it. In a nutshell, does this also mean that we should tolerate the actions of men who rape women or who molest infants and adolescents if they are not accompanied by mutilation and torture? Surely, over and above cruelty, we have a duty to avoid harming animals if there is any possibility—however unintentional—of our inflicting harm on them in the course of satisfying our sexual desires.

Whether we should tolerate bestiality, as Dekkers does and Singer seems to do (if it does not involve cruelty), hinges both on identifying what it is and also on answering one overriding question: is it consensual behavior, or does it involve coercion? In what follows, I suggest that "bestiality" should be understood as "animal sexual assault" and renamed as such. (Since we humans should not be in the business of policing interspecies sexual relations between nonhuman animals, my argument is limited to the sexual abuse of animals by humans.[59]) This view of bestiality differs radically from both from the abominable anthropocentrism of Judeo-Christianity and the pseudoliberal stance of tolerance.

Naming Animal Sexual Assault

Given the intense levels of coercive censures that have been applied to bestiality, it is remarkable that the social sciences have almost completely ignored a widespread social practice that is traditionally viewed with moral, judicial, and aesthetic outrage. An obvious reason for this neglect is that, to most of us, bestiality is a disturbing form of sexual practice that invites hurried bewilderment rather than sustained intellectual inquiry.[60] This helps explain why the topic of bestiality tends to surface in academic discourse only in lectures on the evolution of criminal law given by professors who, with embarrassed chuckles, refer to the declining volume of bestiality prosecutions since the early nineteenth century as an instance of the secularized tolerance and the supposed rationality of Western law.[61]

Is the drift to tolerance of bestiality a sign of increasing civility and social progress? A superficial answer to this question is yes, if by it is meant that censured humans are no longer brutalized by execution or by solitary confinement at hard labor. But that would be to look at bestiality solely from an anthropocentric viewpoint. Seldom, either in times past or now, do popular images of social control include recognition of the terror and pain that judicial interrogation and execution inflict on animals convicted of sexual relations with humans. Neither in the Mosaic commandments nor in the records of past or present court proceedings, neither in the rantings of Puritan zealots nor in psychiatric testimony, is bestiality censured because of the harm that it inflicts on animals. But, especially in the case of smaller creatures like rabbits and hens, animals often suffer great pain and even death from human–animal sexual relations. While researchers have seldom examined the physiological consequences of bestiality for humans, they have paid almost no attention whatsoever to the internal bleeding, the ruptured anal passages, the bruised vaginas, and the battered cloacae of animals, let alone to animals' psychological and emotional trauma and whether humans are capable of transmitting sexual diseases to them.[62] Such neglect of animal suffering mirrors the broader problem that, even when allowance is made for the discursive relevance of animal abuse to the understanding of human societies, it still tends not to be perceived, either theoretically or practically, as an object of study in its own right.

In principle, the attempt to understand bestiality as a form of animal abuse might profitably draw on the perspectives and insight of the three major tendencies that lie at the philosophical and theoretical heart of the animal protection community, namely, utilitarianism, rights theory, and feminism. Following rights theory, for example, it might be insisted that if bestiality is engaged in with a mammal, then it is a harm inflicted on a moral patient entitled to the fundamental right of respectful treatment. Quite apart from the problem of privileging mammals over all other species, discursive support for this specific task is very difficult to find either in the writings of the animal protection community or in its day-to-day activities.

Moreover, though feminism has made important contributions to the understanding of animal abuse, it has largely ignored the harmful effects of bestiality on animals. The major exception to this curious silence is the voice of Carol Adams.[63] She insists that we should understand bestiality as forced sex with animals because sexual relationships of unequal power cannot be consensual. In making this argument and in asserting that all forms of masculinist oppression are linked, Adams thereby begins to claim the perspective of animals as a central concern of feminism.

In seeking to replace anthropocentrism with an acknowledgment of the sentience of animals, Adams is surely correct to insist that we start with the fact that in almost every situation, humans and animals exist in a relation of potential or actual coercion. Whether as companions or as livestock, where they are thoroughly dependent on humans for food, shelter, and affection, or as feral creatures, where humans have the capacity to ensnare them and subject them to their will, animals' interaction with humans is always infused with the possibility of coercion. So it is with sex. Just as sexual assault against women differs from consensual sex because the former is sex obtained by one or some combination of physical, economic, psychological, or emotional coercion—any of which implies the impossibility of genuine consent—so, too, Adams's assertion that bestiality is always sexual coercion ("forced sex") is surely a correct description of most if not all human–animal sexual relations.

But I am not convinced that bestiality must entail sexual coercion simply because human–animal sexual relations always occur in a context of unequal power—however "unequal power" is theorized. If unequal power is the definitive criterion, then sexual coercion would be an essential characteristic not only of intercourse between human adults and infants or children but of most adult heterosexual and even gay and lesbian intercourse as well. Sexual coercion is not sex that occurs always and only in a context of unequal power, though on occasion, of course, situations of inequality imply coercion because, for a variety of reasons, the party with less power cannot freely dissent from participation. Ultimately, sexual coercion occurs whenever one party does not genuinely consent to sexual relations or does not have the ability to communicate consent to the other. Sometimes, one participant in a sexual encounter may appear to be consenting because she does not overtly resist, but that does not of course mean that genuine consent is present. For genuine consent to sexual relations to be present, all participants must be conscious, alert, fully informed, and positive in their desires.[64]

If genuine consent is a necessary condition of sex between one human and another, then there is no good reason to suppose that it may be dispensed with in the case of sex between humans and other sentient animals. Bestiality involves sexual coercion because animals are incapable of genuinely saying "yes" or "no" to humans in forms that we can readily understand. A different way of putting this is to suggest that, if it is true that we can never know what it is like to be a nonhuman animal, then presumably we will never know if animals are able to assent—*in their terms*—to human suggestions for sexual intimacy. Indeed, if we cannot know whether animals consent to our sexual overtures, then when we tolerate sexual relations between humans and animals, we are as blameworthy as when we fail to condemn adults who have sexual relations with infants or with children or with other "moral patients"—to use Tom Regan's term in *The Case for Animal Rights*—who, for whatever reason, are unable to refuse participation. If it is proper to regard unwanted sexual advances to women, to infants, and to children as sexual assault, then sexual advances to animals must surely be viewed likewise.

Moreover, like infants, young children, and other moral patients, animals are beings without an effective voice. Some animals, such as cows, hens, and other animals used in agriculture—including those I viewed in the film *Barnyard Love*—are not equipped to resist human sexual advances in any meaningful way because of their docile and often human-bred natures. Other animals, in trying to resist human sexual advances, can certainly scratch, bite, growl, howl, hiss, and otherwise communicate protest about unwanted advances. But in most one-on-one situations, an animal is incapable of enforcing its will to resist sexual assault, especially when a human is determined to effect his or her purpose. Moreover, animals are disadvantaged in yet another way, for when they are subjected to sexual coercion and to sexual assault, it is impossible for them to communicate the facts of their abuse to those who might give them aid.

In short, because bestiality is in certain key respects so similar to the sexual assault of women, children, and infants, it should be named *animal sexual assault*. Moreover, because for many of the same reasons that, as it applies to humans, the concept of sexual assault is more widely applicable than that of rape, so, too, animal sexual assault comprises a wider range of actions than those found in dictionary definitions of bestiality or in notions embedded in popular culture and in legal discourse, both of which tend to focus narrowly on penetration of the vagina, anus, or cloaca of an animal by a human penis. If the concept of animal sexual assault is not exhausted by penile or digital insertion, then how wide should its scope be? Surely not to those fantasies of human–animal sex identified in psychiatry and among "furries"; these may be statistically unusual, but they are neither perverse nor immoral. Should animal sexual assault include touching, kissing, and fondling? If it is extended to fondling, for example, then to the fondling of what, with what, and by whom?

Given animals' inability to communicate consent to human sexual overtures, it should be a general principle that *animal sexual assault comprises all sexual advances by humans to animals.* Admittedly, such a principle clearly has inherent problems. For example, how do we establish a general rule for identifying actions that are physically identical to those defined as animal sexual assault but that have a different intent? Consider, thus, the following tale related to me by a colleague:

> When I was a little girl I didn't take my dog to bed—she was too big for that—but instead lay regularly in her basket. I even sucked her nipples since I had seen her pups do that. She allowed it and didn't prevent it even though she wasn't suckling at the time. My mother, a doctor herself, was thank goodness not too narrow-minded and left us alone in our tactile relationship. This innocent and affectionate suckling was probably not sexual in nature, it certainly was not assaultive and it doubtless caused the dog no harm.[65]

Many actions like this can of course be either sexual or affective in nature, depending on their social contexts or on the physiological responses of the actors (for both human and nonhuman animals, innocent, nonsexual physical touching and stroking slow the pulse and respiration and lower the blood pressure, but quite the opposite responses are produced by sexual arousal). But where, precisely, should a line of demarcation be drawn between them? Clearly, the milking of a cow, for example, has nothing to do with sexual assault (though some vegetarians and vegans see milk production as assaultive). But how about electronically induced ejaculation for insemination? Is this animal sexual assault? Simple assault? Neither?

The argument that animal sexual assault comprises all sexual advances by humans to animals is of course not meant to lessen the severity of the censure of the sexual assault of one human by another. On the contrary, sexism and speciesism operate not in opposition to each other but in tandem. Animal sexual assault is the product of a masculinity that sees women, animals, and nature as objects that can be controlled, manipulated, and exploited. Thus, much of the sexist language that prepares the way for bodily sexual assault is voiced in speciesist terms.[66] When a man derogates women as cows, bitches, (dumb) bunnies, birds, chicks, foxes, or fresh meat and their genitalia in similar terms, he uses language to distance himself emotionally from his prey and to elevate himself above them. In so doing, he relegates women to a male-constructed category of "less than human" or, more important, "less than me." Reduced to this inferior status, both women and nonhuman animals are thereby denied subjectivity by male predators who can then proceed to exploit and abuse them without feelings of guilt. Unchallenged, sexist and speciesist terms operate in concert to legitimate sexual assaults on women and animals.

Toward a Sociology of Animal Sexual Assault

Thus far, in outlining and opposing conventional notions of bestiality, I have suggested their replacement with a concept of animal sexual assault. Although animal sexual assault often results from the same malicious masculinity and comprises the same harmful actions as those that constitute the sexual assault of one human by another, it is evidently not a unitary social practice but one with differing forms and variable prevalence. Indeed, the documented range of animals used in bestiality is quite diverse. It includes cows, horses, donkeys, sows, dogs, cats, ducks, sheep, goats, rabbits, hens, and eels.

In what follows, first, I try to identify some of the key categories of a typology of the forms of animal sexual assault. The typology includes commodification, adolescent sexual experimentation and gender socialization, aggravated cruelty, and zoophilia. These categories stem from variation in the degree of harm suffered by animals and the stated intentions of those who assault them.

A Typology of Animal Sexual Assault

COMMODIFICATION. This is the predominant element in animal sexual assaults that are packaged as commodities for sale in a market. It often involves a twofold assault. One assault is by a man on a woman who is assaulted and humiliated by being forced to have sex with an animal. The other assault is on the animal who is coerced, without the possibility of giving genuine consent, into having sex with a human (even the phrase "having sex with" in this sentence implies a sort of equality of choice between human and animal that does not exist in practice). Examples of commodified animal sexual assault include live shows of women copulating with animals in bars and sex clubs or depictions of animal sexual assaults in pornographic films such as *Barnyard Love* and *Deep Throat*. In the latter, for example, Linda Marchiano ("Linda Lovelace") was filmed having intercourse with a large dog resembling a German shepherd. Marchiano had agreed to be filmed in this two-hour episode only because her boyfriend and batterer threatened to kill her. She herself "felt nothing but acute revulsion" during the filmed sequence and for a long time after it.[67]

The Internet is the largest and most profitable venue for commodified animal sexual assault. Indeed, on March 5, 2008, a search of Google for "bestiality" displayed 6,180,000 results. In fact, there are thousands of websites and galleries depicting "bestiality" that can be accessed either for a one-time fee or by subscription for a month or longer by credit card boasting "guaranteed secure access." Some websites advertise a variety of "crush" videos for sale. Crush freaks are men who masturbate to the sight of high-heeled women who crush to death animals such as mice, frogs, lizards, and crickets. Another website announces that viewers may download crush videos, such as the one starring "Mistress Chloe":

> Mistress Chloe does it again, crushing crickets for fun. In this video, she crushes most of the crickets between her fingers. You will see super close-ups of the pitiful crickets dying between her fingers. You will see her torture them by pulling their legs off one by one, burning them with a cigarette lighter, crushing them on her beautiful legs, and squishing them beneath her feet and toes. 30 minutes, cost is $35.[68]

Also advertised on the Internet are animals placed by their owners in situations of sex work. For example, in 2002, the organization End Animal Abuse informed its listserv members that it had uncovered what it believed to be a prostitution ring operating in southern New Hampshire near the Massachusetts border.[69] The animal sex-work services offered were allegedly based at the self-proclaimed "Zootopia Ranch," which housed a variety of animals including domestic canines, equines, and other animals used on farms. Customers were offered a menu of items priced by length of time, species (for example, "male dog, one hour, $150; mare, one hour, $200"), type of sexual services, and instruction—and participation if desired—in sexual techniques by trained handlers.

In the category of commodification, consider, finally, the more complex case of Deena the stripping chimpanzee. For $100, Deena and her trainer would appear at a social gathering, during which Deena would perform a striptease act for the partygoers.[70] Is this animal sexual assault? Clearly, this case is one that combines commodification with aspects of sexual objectification. The chimp had been trained to perform *like* a human female stripper—a marketable action that it could not have freely chosen to do and the social context of which it probably could not have properly understood. Although it is true that sexual abuse does not necessarily involve actual physical contact, perhaps this particular act should be understood less as sexual assault than, as Adams suggests, a violation of an animal's right to dignity.

ADOLESCENT SEXUAL EXPERIMENTATION. This is arguably one of the most prevalent forms of animal sexual assault. Precisely what the practice of adolescent sexual experimentation with animals represents symbolically and culturally and how it contributes to gender socialization surely varies from one social context to another. It can be performed either alone or with other adolescents who either watch or else participate. In a group context, some boys of necessity teach how it is done, while others learn. It can be performed for a variety of reasons, including mere curiosity, cruelty, showing off for other boys, or acquiring the techniques of intercourse for later use on girls. An anonymous colleague has told me, for example, that when she was doing her anthropological fieldwork in rural Algeria, she and a coworker witnessed a very nervous young male—on the night before his wedding—"practicing" sexual intercourse with a donkey for the explicit purpose of not appearing hopelessly unskilled with his wife the following night. Presumably, too, there is some point toward the end of their adolescence when some young males desist from experimental sexual activities with animals because such practices are regarded as unmanly or, perhaps, as perverse. But some, presumably, continue and may perhaps begin to regard themselves as "zoophiles."

AGGRAVATED CRUELTY. It is reasonable to suppose, given their great predominance in sexual experimentation with animals, that young males also disproportionately engage in aggravated cruelty during acts of animal sexual assault ("aggravated cruelty" here refers to a level of cruelty over and above that already presented in most such acts of animal sexual assault).

Quite apart from the occurrence of cruelty during adolescent sexual experimentation, aggravated cruelty can be a major element in animal sexual assault in other ways. In mid-nineteenth-century England, for example, one case was reported where knotted sticks two feet in length were thrust into mares' wombs, which were then vigorously rented. In another instance, donkeys and horses used to pull carts had their penises cut off.[71] Multiple cases of such atrocities were confirmed in several English counties in the 1990s.[72] Similarly, in New Bedford, Massachusetts, a deer was found at a zoo with fatal wounds that included a fractured jaw and extensive rectal and vaginal bleeding.[73] Sometimes, aggravated cruelty against animals takes place in conjunction with the humiliation of women. This has been documented both in Nazi concentration camps and in the course of partner abuse.[74] In the latter, it can take the form of battering, which involves the use of animals for humiliation and sexual exploitation by batterers and/or marital rapists. Recent reports from Los Angeles "tell of a man who, after fights with his girlfriend, sought revenge by raping her pet chicken."[75] Moreover, if one allows that, like humans, animals are capable of experiencing non-physical pain, then aggravated cruelty also occurs whenever animal sexual assault produces emotional or psychological pain and suffering.

ZOOPHILIA. This is the form of animal sexual assault that occurs when animals are the preferred sexual objects of human desires.[76] There are three chief views of zoophilia, offered, respectively, by zoophiles themselves ("zoos"), by psychiatry, and by sexology.

Zoophilia is the discourse used to justify their assaultive behavior by those who sexually abuse animals ("zoos"). The vocabulary of this discourse is identical to that used to justify other forms of intrafamilial sexual assault: "I love X and she loves me," and therefore "she consents" and "she enjoys it." Like the practitioners of pedophilia and incest as well, zoophiles and their supporters invoke those cultural rights allegedly inhering in private property and family privacy to justify their assaultive behavior and to deflect moral condemnation of it. Their most common technique of neutralizing condemnation is the claim that theirs is a legitimate gender preference and that, as a minority, they are discriminated against by the straight community.

Following Richard von Krafft-Ebing's foundational text *Psychopathia Sexualis* of 1886, psychiatrists have tried to extrapolate from individual case histories to comments about the causes of bestiality in general, among which the most prominent are psychopathological defects, including zoophilia.[77] Recent psychiatric studies tend to regard zoophilia as a sexual perversion that is practiced largely by young males who are often simpletons or imbeciles with psychopathic personalities and who sometimes also have aggressive and sadistic tendencies. It has even been suggested that zoophilia represents reaction against castration anxiety, that it might involve schizophrenia, and that childhood traumas associated with it can lead to multiple personality disorder. More than one study has tried to explain zoophilia as a heterosexual surrogate experience, as vested sadism, and as a reenactment of primal scenes. According to the National Institute of Neurological Disorders and Stroke, inappropriate sexual behavior with animals may sometimes be caused by a rare neurological disorder known as Klüver–Bucy syndrome.[78] In 2008, the American Psychiatric Association classified zoophilia as a form of paraphilic disorder.[79]

However, in claiming that zoophiles are diseased and defective individuals, psychiatric studies are vulnerable to a number of methodological and theoretical objections. These include a tendency to begin their investigations with a population that is already institutionalized, a failure to compare their subjects with adequate control groups, and, sometimes, quite a crude essentialism. As such, psychiatric findings are highly vulnerable to falsification by counterfactual cases.[80]

Psychiatric pronouncements about the supposed abnormality of zoophilia have been contradicted, in particular, by sexology. Where psychiatry proclaims the abnormality of zoophilia, sexologists implicitly find it to be a relatively normal phenomenon—"normal," that is, in the Durkheimian sense that its absence or presence varies with the intensity of relevant aspects of a given social structure. Sexology thus typically depicts zoophiles as male victims of deficient social structures. On this view, bestiality is posited as an outlet for the satisfaction of biological sexual urges and, despite its posture of methodological and ethical neutrality, as an effect of low morality, great sexual desire, and lack of opportunity for natural (i.e., intraspecies and heterosexual) indulgence.[81] Especially in early studies, these so-called causes tend then to be attached to survey findings that bestiality is engaged in mainly by poor and often relatively uneducated young males in rural areas with nothing better to do.

In recent years, sexologists have turned to the Internet for sources of confidential information about zoophilia and zoophiles.[82] They have uncovered poignant information about the loneliness of zoophiles' lives and about the often hideous social discrimination to which they are exposed if "out of the closet."

There are inevitable methodological limitations associated with the collection of data through self-administered questionnaires distributed on the Internet, foremost among which is the absence of random sampling and of rigorously constituted control groups. Methodological considerations aside, however, it must be said that there is another problem with recent sexological surveys of zoophiles and of similar surveys undertaken in queer studies, for example. This lies in their appreciative position toward the human subjects who are their focus. Their appreciative stance entirely avoids—and avoids the problems generated by—the fact that any given case of animal sexual assault—"bestiality" in these studies—necessarily involves not one but *two* parties, namely, a human and an animal. Yet the respective situation of both these beings merit attention. Who is dominated, and by whom?[83]

FURTHER DEFINITION. This fourfold typology of animal sexual assault is quite provisional and clearly needs further elaboration. Key problems remain. For example, between the categories of aggravated cruelty and adolescent sexual experimentation, especially, there is obvious overlap. One must be able to distinguish, too, not only between the malicious masculinity behind aggravated cruelty and other situations of adolescent sexual experimentation and exploration but also between the latter and innocent and affective fondling. Some difficulties seem to resist a clear answer—for example, is electronically induced ejaculation for insemination a form of animal sexual assault, and, if so, is it an instance of commodification, aggravated cruelty, or both?

Consider, also, that in 2007, Michael Vick, the star football quarterback, was convicted of dogfighting by a federal court in Richmond, Virginia. The widely reported allegations against Vick included his illegal involvement with dogfighting, gambling on fights' outcomes, and executions of dogs by drowning, electrocution, hanging, and shooting. At one of Vick's houses, in Smithfield, Virginia, federal officials found evidence of a variety of dogfighting paraphernalia, including "rape," "mounting," or "breedings" stands. Such stands are

> legitimate dog training tools for the most part, but ones that come in handy for turning pit bulls into vicious fighters. Pooches die so often in fights that owners always need new dogs. This is where the rape stand, also called a breeding stand, comes in. It consists of two steel poles mounted to the ends of a platform that's often made of wood. U-shaped pieces of curved metal sit atop each pole; one goes around the belly of a female pit bull and the other around her neck. The stand isn't illegal, but dog breeders don't normally use it; after all, female dogs in heat aren't so particular. And most people wouldn't want to breed poorly socialized dogs that must be strapped down to mate. But breeders of attack dogs place special value on females that are so mean they might bite any male dogs that get too close.[84]

Is this an instance of animal sexual assault? If it is, does it involve both commodification and aggravated cruelty?

The Prevalence of Animal Sexual Assault

Empirical evidence about the prevalence of animal sexual assault in any given human population is scanty and unreliable. Sexual experimentation with animals has been said by Alfred Kinsey and his colleagues to occur disproportionately among adolescent and preadolescent boys. In fact, the

Kinsey Institute researchers claimed, about 8 percent of males have had some sexual experience with animals. Moreover, they continued, a minimum of 40 to 50 percent of all "American farm boys" experience some form of sexual contact with animals, either with (17 percent) or without orgasm in their preadolescent, adolescent, and/or later histories, as do 5.1 percent of American females.[85] Accompanying these figures is the claim that

> such data begin to show what the significance of animal intercourse might be if conditions were more favorable for such activity . . . in certain Western areas of the United States, where animals are most readily available and social restraints on this matter are less stringent, we have secured incidence figures of as high as 65 percent in some communities, and there are indications of still higher incidences in some other areas.[86]

However, because Kinsey's research entirely lacked probability sampling, it erred in thinking that valid generalizations about the prevalence of stigmatized sexual practices, including bestiality, could be made from the responses of the volunteers recruited to his survey. Kinsey's aggressive personal interviewing techniques ensured, moreover, elevated levels of disclosure and reporting.[87] Additionally, there is little or no hard evidence with which to test in other agrarian and stock-farming societies his claim that bestiality is to a large extent a function of rural life's proximity to and familiarity with animals. In most Western societies—where the ownership of companion animals has dramatically increased since 1900 and where, with the rise of agribusiness, there has been a steady decline in the percentage of the human population living in agricultural areas or sharing their homes with farm animals—it is not even certain that it is animals used to farm who are today the most common objects of adolescent experimentation.[88]

If sexological surveys have thrown little or no light on the prevalence of animal sexual assault, can anything be learned about it from studies of criminal justice processes (crime reports, prosecutions, and convictions)? It so happens that in the past three decades or so, a small but very fruitful literature has developed at the intersection of historical criminology and animal studies. These studies have no obvious common theoretical agenda, but they have effectively proceeded from a social constructionist perspective on judicial records to examine the diverse historical censures of bestiality, masturbation, and homosexuality.

Piecing together relevant aspects of this literature, it appears, first, that defendants in bestiality trials have overwhelmingly been young males from rural areas. The vast majority of these youths seems to have been drawn from already marginalized populations, namely, the poor, nonnatives, and heretics.[89] In other words, the social composition of bestiality defendants is probably very similar to that of those typically charged with other crimes against public order or involving moral turpitude.

It emerges, too, that criminal prosecutions of bestiality have been very rare events,[90] with the prominent exception of prosecutions in Sweden. This has been demonstrated not only in France, Denmark, and the Netherlands but also, perhaps surprisingly, both in seventeenth-century England and in colonial America. The historian J. A. Sharpe, for example, concludes that because of the rarity of bestiality prosecutions in seventeenth-century England and also because of the infrequent and stray nature of the references to the offense at that time, there was not a widespread indulgence of bestiality that failed to be reported there.[91] Drawing a different conclusion from the same sparsity of prosecutions, Bradley Chapin briefly touches on the extent of bestiality in colonial America. He surmises that because of opportunities in such a rural society, "the act must have been common enough."[92] With a somewhat larger compass, Roger Thompson has found that because seventeenth-century cases of homosexuality, bestiality, and pedophilia in court records in England and New England are "so uncommon as to be statistically insignificant"; therefore, "apart from masturbation, deviant sexual activity was exceedingly rare."[93]

Some indication of the prevalence of adolescent sexual experimentation with animals is provided by Jonas Liliequist's study of bestiality in seventeenth- and eighteenth-century Sweden. Liliequist has suggested that the unparalleled indictment rate in Sweden from 1635 to 1754—in some provinces it was as high as five to six per 100,000—implies not only a very intolerant society but also one in which bestiality was widely practiced. These figures are even more puzzling because there was an almost total silence (and lack of indictments) with respect to homosexual acts. Between 1635 and 1754, there were 1,500 trials for bestiality yet only eight for homosexuality.

Liliequist argues that the frequency of indictments in Sweden indicated, on the one hand, "a social network of control over and suspicion of male sexuality, a willingness and eagerness on the part of neighbors, masters, servants, and even family members to maintain the sanctions. On the other hand, there were persons who continued to find sexual gratification in bestiality in spite of the attitudes of disgust and repugnance and the risks of infamy, execution, or eternal damnation and association with the devil."[94]

Liliequist identifies in Sweden a remarkable occurrence of young boys, aged less than fifteen, who had been charged with bestiality. Many were nine to thirteen years old, some even younger. He suggests that at this time, Sweden was a bestiality-prone society, the social, cultural, and psychological basis of which was the socialization of boys.[95] While men oversaw horses and stables and girls and women were responsible for milking and for looking after animals in the cowshed and the farmyard, boys were responsible for herding them to and from pasture. Boyhood in seventeenth- and eighteenth-century Sweden thus entailed very close relationships with farm animals. These animals offered the first view and knowledge of sexual relations as one animal mounted another. "The herdsboys," Liliequist found, were "curious and excited explorers, eager to find out the secrets of sexuality belonging to adult and married life but present and visible in the life of farm animals."[96]

In Switzerland, somewhat by way of contrast, religious zealotry is the key explanatory variable in the historian William Monter's account of sodomy trials (i.e., for homosexuality and bestiality) in two parts of seventeenth-century Switzerland—one Protestant, the other Catholic— each of which recorded several dozen such trials. Monter stresses that the most important conclusion to emerge from Geneva's sodomy trials was the very strong link between religious zeal and the persecution of sexual deviance.[97]

Monter's research was able to draw on the relatively well-preserved criminal archives of early modern Switzerland and to juxtapose a Protestant urban area with a Catholic rural one. In both places, sodomy, including bestiality, was punished with greater intensity than any other form of sexual deviance, possibly excluding infanticide. Both were punished at the respective heights of the Protestant and Catholic Reformations at a time when, like witchcraft, sodomy was treated as a form of heresy.

Monter's wise conclusion is that the evidence about men charged with offenses such as homosexuality and bestiality by the Aragonese Inquisitions "tells us not who was doing such things, but rather whom the Holy Office was able to catch and willing to convict."[98]

One must wonder, given the absence of methodological artifacts like self-report data (possible) and victimization surveys (impossible), whether, from data on bestiality prosecutions, anything meaningful can be inferred about the prevalence of bestiality in a given culture. The hardship of answering this question is compounded by the historical fact that political, judicial, and religious authorities have exhibited a complex assortment of responses when confronted with bestiality. At a minimum, these include prosecuting it to the maximum, ignoring it altogether, and even suppressing all mention of it.

One would expect to find similar difficulties with reporting practices. If bestiality/animal sexual assault is witnessed by someone (other than the offender), then, like many other offenses, whether it is reported to authorities will depend on a variety of factors, including how it is problematized by social control agencies—as bestiality, as animal sexual assault, as a serious social problem, as hilarity (e.g., engaged in by "people up north"), as a private matter, and so on. It does not seem possible to unpack court records in such a way that we can detect the extent to which the social control of bestiality and the practice of it existed independently of each other. Although court records are often prisms through which we can apprehend the development of power relations and although they might yield insight about particular histories of social control and about sexual tolerance or moral panics around bestiality, they cannot reflect the prevalence of bestiality with any accuracy. Rather, they reflect the bureaucratic outcome of the interplay between some unknown volume of the population that engages in illegalities and the reporting, charging, and prosecuting of those unfortunates who have been caught.

Quite independently of the prevalence of bestiality, the volume of formal complaints about it clearly depends on such factors as the power of religious zeal; the precariousness of political authority; whether the complainant has something to gain from the accused, like the recovery of despoiled or stolen property; the level of animosity between complainant and offender; and the perceived likelihood that a complaint will be acted on by political authorities. Moreover, the social control of bestiality has typically occurred through less formal processes, such as moral persuasion from the pulpit and socialization within the family. At a popular level, these mechanisms have no doubt been supplemented by tactics like derisive and hateful attacks on an offender voiced in the rhetoric of affronted manhood. How these various tactics do or do not result in formal complaints by the citizenry to the authorities has yet to be investigated.

Complaints of bestiality are presumably more likely to be made when complainants have something to gain from legal proceedings. Thus, in her study of criminal dispositions for bestiality in Queensland, Australia, between 1870 and 1949, Anne-Marie Collins suggests that the volume of complaints may vary with the perception that bestiality is a property crime more than anything else.[99] In other words, owners of animal companions or of animals used in agriculture are more likely to complain not because the alleged offender has violated Judeo-Christian precepts about the natural order of the universe but because their property has been spoiled or damaged.

Consider the nature of bestiality accusations among the Kaguru, a tribe of matrilineal Bantu cultivators living in a highland area of east-central Africa. Prior to the 1950s, accusations of bestiality would have invited the serious charge of witchcraft. After that time, they led only to laughter and derision. To the Kaguru, a public complaint was justified only when bestiality involved violation of a rule of property. This was so because the Kaguru considered the practice of sexual intercourse with another person's livestock—sheep and cows especially—as an example of inappropriate use of personal property. Thus, in one case, the local Kaguru court was told that a young male who attempted to mount his friend's sheep had enjoyed his friend's property without permission. The court found that had the youth enjoyed his own sheep, there would have been no case at all.[100]

Accusations of bestiality are also more likely to be made the greater the animosity between complainant and offender, such as when an informal complaint is used as an insult arising from an already existing feud. Thus, Scandinavian societies have a long history of using attributions of bestiality as insults, as in *Njal's Saga* when Skarp-Hedin accused Thorkel of sexual contact with a mare: "You would be better employed picking out of your teeth the bits of mare's arse you ate before you came here—your shepherd saw you at it, and was amazed at such disgusting behavior."[101] Personal animosity is also the obvious motive in a case reported in the ancient saga of *Ale-Hood*: "You didn't notice the fat stallion that Steingrim had till it was up your backside. That skinny mare you were on faltered under you . . . and I've never been able to make up my mind whether it was you or the mare that got it. Everybody could see how long you were stuck there, the stallion's legs had got such a grip on your cloak."[102]

Even after complaints of bestiality are brought before authorities, not all of them enter judicial records. Sometimes, allegations of bestiality are hard to prove. In some jurisdictions, charges of bestiality have been allowed to proceed only if penetration of the animal by the male organ could be proved. For example, in England, Coke was adamant that penetration had to occur for a charge of buggery to be successful.[103] This requirement must often have been a difficult one to satisfy, as is demonstrated in the case of William Spiller in seventeenth-century Essex, where the accused was apparently saved by the jury's strict adherence to this rule: "William Spiller, a yeoman's son of Hatfield Broad Oak, was seen following a bullock in a close, having 'his yarde in his hand stiffe standing,' but his explanation that he was prevented from committing buggery because 'the Bullocke would not stand still' apparently succeeded in obtaining an *ignoramus* for his indictment."[104]

Consider, too, the problem of witnessing such an extremely private act. In some jurisdictions, at least two witnesses have been required for conviction, one of which may include a confession by the accused. Suppose a confession is made under torture and then retracted. In 1673, during examination before his trial, one Benjamin Goad of Roxbury, Massachusetts, admitted that he had committed "the unnatural and horrid act of bestiality" on a mare.[105] Goad then retracted his admission, and the court was forced to consider whether the prisoner's "confession against himself" was sufficient to convict him. The court answered in the affirmative, and, the mare having first been "knocked on the head" in front of him, Goad was duly hanged. Indeed, of the four bestiality indictments in the Massachusetts Colony during the period 1673–1692, two resulted in acquittals, one may not even have gone to trial, and only one resulted in a guilty verdict.

In summary, it is fair to say that the prospects for estimating the prevalence of bestiality from data lodged in court records are not auspicious. The various subjective biases behind complaints to the authorities of cases of bestiality mean that, in principle, the skewed recording of bestiality is no different from that of all other crimes. Indeed, as is the case in so many areas where official justifications and popular practices intersect, there is no necessary identity between the justifications for the censure of bestiality, however articulated, and the actual reasons why cases of bestiality are reported to the authorities.

Notes

1. William Bradford (1650), *History of Plymouth Plantation*, p. 320.

2. Bradford, *History of Plymouth Plantation*, p. 321.

3. Bradford, *History of Plymouth Plantation*, p. 321.

4. Except in the case of biblical quotations from other sources, all excerpts from the Bible are from the authorized King James version.

5. On those rare occasions when the topic of bestiality enters the literature of sociology and criminology, it tends to do so either to ask "how much bestiality is there?" or in a purely formal and shallow way that is ancillary to other concerns. Typical of these latter is commentary on a seventeenth-century New Haven case involving a certain Thomas Hogg and a sow by the historian Lawrence Friedman (1993), *Crime and Punishment in American History*. Rather than using this case to explore deviant human–animal relationships, Friedman employs it only as a rhetorical device to deny the uniqueness of "somewhat exotic or notorious or outrageous examples of criminal behavior" (p. 1).

Although accessible descriptions of bestiality are produced ad nauseam by libertine presses and Internet cinematographers as erotic commodities for consumption by a popular audience, fictional and quasi-autobiographical accounts of bestiality sometimes appear in serious works of literature and in plays. Among the former, see William Tester's (1991) *Darling*, Peter Høeg's (1996) *The Woman and the Ape*, and Michael Ryan's (1995) autobiographical *Secret Life*. See also the explicit attraction staged between horses and humans in Peter Shaffer's (1973) award-winning play *Equus* and, in a more muted way, in JoAnna Mendl Shaw's (2005) *Rules of Engagement*. In May 2008, a one-hour television documentary (*Zoo*) aired on the Sundance channel. It was a rather staid "real-life" story about a Washington State aircraft engineer who died after "a sexual encounter" with a stallion.

However, see also the U.K. Channel 4 documentary *Animal Passions* (1999; sequel, 2004). This includes a filmed segment of the *Jerry Springer Show* ("I Married a Horse") that was not actually aired on television because the event—involving a man who genuinely regarded himself as married to his horse—was deemed too outrageous for public consumption. The zoophile, the late Mark Matthews, published an autobiography in 1994 (*The Horseman: Obsessions of a Zoophile*) that was presented as an account of "Jim's" at-first shocked recoil and then gradual and, finally, explosive realization of his sexual attraction to pony mares.

6. In her classic study of the varieties of sexual deviance in 110 early societies, Julia Brown (1952) "A Comparative Study of Deviations from Sexual Mores," found that bestiality was taboo and punished in all societies (93 percent) with information available on it.

7. Hittite Laws, pp. 53–55.

8. Hittite Laws, p. 57.

9. John T. McNeill and Helena M. Gamer (1938), *Medieval Handbooks of Penance*, pp. 4–6.

10. Jacob Milgrom (2000), *Leviticus 17–22*, p. 1523. Milgrom's is the authoritative translation of Leviticus, as is his introduction and commentary.

11. Milgrom, *Leviticus 17–22*, p. 1530.

12. Milgrom, *Leviticus 17–22*, p. 1531.

13. See also Milgrom, *Leviticus 17–22*, p. 1751.

14. Cited in McNeill and Gamer, *Medieval Handbooks of Penance*, p. 313.

15. Early censures of sexual offenses had two chief forms. The concilar decrees, first, originated in the East, especially in the Byzantine Empire and in the Holy Land. Their punishment for bestiality violations was quite strict. The *libri poenitentiales* (penitential handbooks), second, typically consisted of fasting, self-scourging, and vigils that caused acute discomfort by loss of sleep. Originating in sixth-century Wales and Ireland, they spread to France, England, Italy, Spain, and Iceland. See Joyce Salisbury (1994), *The Beast Within: Animals in the Middle Ages*, pp. 84–121.

16. Mary Douglas (1984), *Purity and Danger: An Analysis of the Concepts of Pollution and Taboo*, pp. 53–54.

17. Bradford, *History of Plymouth Plantation*, pp. 404–12. Even Coke (1628), *The Third Part of the Institutes of the Laws of England*, stated that "a great Lady hath committed buggery with a Baboon, and conceived by it" (p. 59).

18. Capel, quoted in Keith Thomas (1983), *Man and the Natural World*, p. 39.

19. Arnold J. Davidson (1991), "The Horror of Monsters," pp. 41–43. On noble families who have traced their descent from wild animals and on early modern missing links, half man and half animal, see Keith Thomas, *Man and the Natural World*, pp. 134–35. See also the Foucauldian-inspired argument in Andrew N. Sharpe (2007), "Structured Like a Monster: Understanding Human Difference through a Legal Category."

20. Aelian (ca. 210), *On the Characteristics of Animals*, 3, p. 305. Elsewhere, Aelian recorded that "I am told that a dog fell in love with Glauce the harpist. Some however assert that it was not a dog but a ram, while others say it was a goose. And at Soli in Cilicia a dog loved a boy of the name of Xenophon; at Sparta another boy in the prime of life by reason of his beauty caused a jackdaw to fall sick of love" (p. 21).

21. Giraldus Cambrensis (1176–1199), *The History and Topography of Ireland*, p. 110 (see also chap. 3). Some of these fabled practices are repeated in Edmunde Campion's (1633) work of the early 1570s, *Two Bokes of the Histories of Ireland*, pp. 21ff. It is also worth noting that punishment for bestiality was usually milder in Ireland, where the penitentials tended to view bestiality as a minor offense linked to masturbation. Elsewhere, particularly in later collections on the Continent, bestiality was linked with homosexuality and punished more severely (James A. Brundage [1987], *Law, Sex, and Christian Society in Medieval Europe*, p. 168).

22. Cambrensis, *The History and Topography of Ireland*, p. 85.

23. Cambrensis, *The History and Topography of Ireland*, p. 85.

24. In the 1641 New Haven case of George Spencer, the litter of John Wakeman's sow contained a deformed piglet that Wakeman brought to the court for its consideration. According to the trial record (*Records of the Colony and Plantation of New Haven* [1641]), "The monster was come to the full growth as the other pigs . . . but brought forth dead. It had no hair on the whole body, the skin was very tender, and of a white colour like a child's; the head was most strange, it had but one eye in the middle of the face, and that large and open, like some blemished eye of man; over the eye, in the bottom of the forehead which was like a child's, a thing of flesh grew forth and hung down, it was a hollow, and like a man's instrument of generation. A nose, mouth and chin deformed, but not much unlike a child's, the neck and ears had also such resemblance. . . . Some hand of God appeared in an impression upon Goodwife Wakeman's spirit, sadly expecting, though she knew not why, some strange accident in that sow's pigging, and a strange impression was also upon many that saw the monster (therein guided by the near resemblance of the eye), that one George Spencer . . . had been actor in unnatural and abominable filthiness with the sow" (pp. 62–63).

25. Thomas, *Man and the Natural World*, pp. 38–41; see also John Canup (1988), "'The Cry of Sodom Enquired Into': Bestiality and the Wilderness of Human Nature in Seventeenth-Century New England." According to the Records of the Court of Assistants, on January 7, 1642, a certain T[eagu] OCrimi was sentenced in Boston "for a foule, & devilish attempt to bugger a cow of Mr. Makepeaces" and "was censured to bee carried to the place of execution, and there to stand with an halter about his ncke, & to bee severely whipped" (p. xxxi).

26. The belief in monstrous offspring did not altogether disappear with the rise of science and empiricism in the early modern era. For example, a French book (ca. 1600) depicted on its cover an ape-child born to a chambermaid, and "Drummond of Hawthornden recounted how a Scot had sex with an ape 'not of any evil intention, but only to create a monster,' which he planned to show around the country and so earn his living" (James Knowles [2004], "Can Ye Not Yet Tell a Man from a Marmoset?," pp. 141–42). On the changing fortunes of monsters in popular culture and on the influence of religion—especially Protestantism—and science in their rise and decline, see Paul Semonin (1996), "Monsters in the Marketplace: The Exhibition of Human Oddities in Early Modern England." On the nineteenth-century argument against vaccination that inoculation with fluid from cows would result in the "animalization" of human beings, see Thomas, *Man and the Natural World*, p. 39.

27. Jeffrey Burton Russell (1982), *A History of Witchcraft*, p. 63.

28. Gaston Dubois-Desaulle (1933), *Bestiality: An Historical, Medical, Legal and Literary Study*, p. 58.

29. See, respectively, J. A. Sharpe (1983), *Crime in Seventeenth-Century England*, pp. 65–66, and Bradley Chapin (1983), *Criminal Justice in Colonial America, 1606–1660*, pp. 127–29.

30. Jonas Liliequist (1991), "Peasants against Nature: Crossing the Boundaries between Man and Animal in Seventeenth- and Eighteenth-Century Sweden."

31. Michael Goodich (1979), *The Unmentionable Vice: Homosexuality in the Later Medieval Period*, pp. 66–67.

32. Brundage, *Law, Sex, and Christian Society in Medieval Europe*, p. 493.

33. Statements of the preeminent influence of Leviticus have been made by Milgrom, *Leviticus 17–22*, p. 1523, and Calum M. Carmichael (2006), *Law, Legend and Incest in the Bible: Leviticus 18–20*, pp. 1–3. The latter notes, for example, that the Table of Levitical Degrees set out by the Church of England in 1563 was in force until 1907.

34. On this early legal history, see Laurence M. Larson, ed. (1886), *The Earliest Norwegian Laws*, pp. 374–81.

35. Brundage, *Law, Sex, and Christian Society in Medieval Europe*, pp. 213–14.

36. Cited in Brundage, *Law, Sex, and Christian Society in Medieval Europe*, p. 400.

37. *An Act for the Punysshement of the Vice of Buggerie* (1533–1534), 25 Hen. VIII, c. 6. The act referred to "buggerie committed with mankynde or beast."

Bestiality remained a capital offense, except for one brief spell, until 1861 (24 & 25 Vic., c. 100).

38. William Blackstone (1769), *Commentaries on the Laws of England*, 4, p. 215.

39. Coke, *The Third Part of the Institutes of the Laws of England*, p. 59. See also Vern L. Bullough and Bonnie Bullough (1977), *Sin, Sickness, and Sanity*, p. 32.

40. Aquinas wrote that bestiality, like other acts not in accord with nature, such as "cannabilism and copulation with members of their own sex," was indulged in habitually only by men "who ail psychologically" (Thomas Aquinas [1265–1274], *Summa Theologica*, vol. 20, p. 25).

41. On the respective merits of these competing histories, see John Boswell (1980), *Christianity, Social Tolerance, and Homosexuality*, p. 323, n. 69, and Andrée Collard (1989), *Rape of the Wild*, p. 24.

42. There is no federal bestiality statute in the United States, and only about half of the fifty states now have such a statute. Most of these statutes focus on penetration; some distinguish among animals, birds, and fowl; and the language of several continues to describe the forbidden act as "an abominable and detestable crime against nature." Today, a defendant will probably be charged with a misdemeanor like public indecency, a breach of the peace, or cruelty to animals.

43. In the course of his support of the decriminalization of sodomy, Jeremy Bentham (1785), "Essay on 'Paederasty,' Part 2," attacked the prosecution and punishment of acts of bestiality, arguing that the more they are permitted, the more scope is allowed for malice or extortion to make use of them to effect its purpose on the innocent. Under the *Sexual Offences Act* (2003), sec. 69, in England, the punishment for sexual intercourse with an animal, either vaginal or anal, was reduced to six months in jail or a fine. The act failed to criminalize oral sex or sex between an animal and a human if the human was a woman.

44. Dekkers's (1994) *Dearest Pet* was originally published in Holland in 1992, then translated into English by Paul Vincent and published in London in 1994 by Verso. Singer's review "Heavy Petting" appeared on March 2 in the March/April 2001 issue of *Nerve* magazine and online at http://www.nerve.com/Opinions/Singer/heavyPetting. It was then published in hard copy by the *San Francisco Chronicle*.

45. Singer, "Heavy Petting," p. 2.

46. Singer, "Heavy Petting," p. 3. When Singer wields Dekkers's references to Kinsey as supporting evidence, he, like Dekkers, seems curiously unaware of the gross methodological defects of Kinsey's sexological surveys. Kinsey's data on the prevalence of bestiality are so unreliable that it would be wrong to use them to champion a probestiality stance (or any other sort of cause).

47. Singer, "Heavy Petting," p. 4.

48. Singer, "Heavy Petting," p. 4.

49. Singer, "Heavy Petting," p. 4.

50. Singer, "Heavy Petting," p. 4.

51. Singer, "Heavy Petting," p. 5.

52. Francione, quoted in Boxer (2001), "Op-Ed," p. A19. See also Piers Beirne (2001), "Peter Singer's 'Heavy Petting' and the Politics of Animal Sexual Assault." In response, Professor Singer sent me a very polite letter stating he "did not say that there is nothing wrong with sex with animals except where it involves cruelty. . . . I wanted to raise that question, but I did not answer it. Apart from that, I think you are taking the review—a brief work, written to be amusing and provocative for a forum that is not scholarly, but encourages frank discussion of matters relating to sex—a bit too seriously" (Peter Singer to the author, April 10, 2001, personal communication).

53. Presumably stung by numerous criticisms (motivated by "hysterical abuse") from members of the animal rights movement that he was a zoophile and that he stand down as president of the Great Ape Project International, Singer released a statement for "fellow activists" in which he claimed that he agreed "to review Midas Dekkers' scholarly study of sexual interaction between humans and animals not because I support such practices, but because I wanted to reflect on what such sexual behavior tells us about the way in which we are like animals, and at the same time seek to draw such sharp lines between ourselves and other species. I also wanted to suggest that, if our concern is for the welfare of animals, it is only too easy to find practices on every modern factory farm that are a great deal worse, for the animal, than some forms of sexual contact between humans and animals" (Singer [2001a], "Clarification [of] the Circumstances and Intent of [My] Review of Midas Dekkers' Book *Dearest Pet*").

54. Cited in Dekkers, *Dearest Pet*, pp. 137, 143.

55. Singer, "Heavy Petting," p. 3.

56. Singer, "Heavy Petting," p. 3.

57. These are exactly the worries raised in Melissa Holbrook Pierson (2000), *Dark Horses and Black Beauties*, p. 38.

58. Pierson, *Dark Horses and Black Beauties*, p. 38.

59. One of the best reasons we should not police human–animal sexual relations can be derived from a section of Tom Regan's (1983) book *The Case for Animal Rights*. In discussing the many implications of his well-known theory of animal rights, Regan argues about wildlife management that, being neither the accountants nor the managers of felicity in nature, we "should be principally concerned with *letting animals be*, keeping human predators out of their affairs, allowing these "other nations" to carve out their own destiny" (p. 357, emphasis in the original).

60. Thus, in the course of his work on the medieval prosecution and capital punishment of animals, the historian E. P. Evans (1906), *The Criminal Prosecution and Capital Punishment of Animals*, gruffly dismissed bestiality as "this disgusting crime" (p. 148). In this regard, Evans was probably expressing not an idiosyncratic prejudice but an enduring sentiment that he shared with the great majority of his colleagues.

61. A good example of the comedic spin given to bestiality in the legal literature and among lawyers is the possibly apocryphal examination-in-chief in the
English case of *R v. Cozins* (1834, 6 C. & P. 351); on the exchange between the
prosecutor and agricultural laborer Albert Harris, see Graham Parker (1986), "Is
a Duck an Animal? An Exploration of Bestiality as a Crime," p. 96. In this case,
George Gilbert was charged with bestiality with a sheep. The act had been witnessed by Albert Harris, who had been called as a witness for the Crown:

Prosecutor: Mr. Harris, on the day in question, were you proceeding along a line adjacent to the farm of Mr. Clarke?

A.H.: I was.

Prosecutor: Would you describe for His Lordship what you saw.

A.H.: Well, George Gilbert was standing in the doorway of the barn with a sheep.

Prosecutor: Yes, and what was he doing?

A.H.: Well, he was messing around with the sheep.

Prosecutor: By that statement, are we to understand that the accused was having sexual
intercourse with the sheep?

A.H.: Er, yes.

Prosecutor: Mr Harris, what did you do when you observed this shocking spectacle?

A.H.: I said, "Morning, George."

62. A rare study of harms to animals is H. M. C. Munro and M. V. Thrusfield
(2005), "'Battered Pets': Sexual Abuse." This Scottish study documents severe
physical injuries to the sexual organs, anus, and rectum, including death, sustained
by dogs and cats after humans had sexually assaulted them.

63. See Carol J. Adams (1995a), "Bestiality: The Unmentioned Abuse," and
Carol J. Adams (1995b), "Woman-Battering and Harm to Animals," pp. 65–69.
See also the fleeting references to sexual assault against nonhumans in Joan Du-
nayer (2004), *Speciesism*, pp. 142, 158.

64. On the importance of these qualities to genuine consent, see Steven Box
(1983), *Power, Crime, and Mystification*, p. 124. For some difficulties in opposing
bestiality from a consensualist position, see Neil Levy (2003), "What (if Anything) Is Wrong with Bestiality?" In his book *The Logic of Consent*, Peter Westen
(2004) tackles head-on the problem with rape laws that were first identified and
then grappled with by feminists in the 1980s. If rape is sexual intercourse with a
woman obtained *by force* (or the threat of force) and *without her consent*, then what
do we actually mean when we try to define terms like "force," "consent," and
"nonconsent"? While Westen himself does not discuss these terms with respect
to human–animal sex, he approaches such an analysis in a discussion of prescrip-
tive attitudinal consent and young children. He argues that young children "are

too young to be able to assess their long-term interests. The same thing is true of persons whose judgement is impaired by intoxicants, or mental disorders, and persons who are manipulated by subtle forms of conditioning, such as patients in psychotherapy relationships."

65. Personal communication to Piers Beirne, September 20, 1996.

66. See also Dunayer, *Speciesism*, esp. chap. 1.

67. Linda Lovelace, with Mike McGrady (1980), *Ordeal*, pp. 107–14. See also Xaviera Hollander (1972), *The Happy Hooker*, p. 35.

68. Accessed September 6, 2006, from http://www.chloecreations.com/cart/cricketcrunch2.htm

69. The listserv e-mail was forwarded to me on March 10, 2002, by the organization ASAIRS (EndAnimalAbuse@aol.com).

70. Carol J. Adams (1990), "Deena—The World's Only Stripping Chimp." Switzerland has recently enacted legislation to protect animals from sexual assault by declaring that it is a violation of their dignity. See also G. Bolliger and A. F. Goetschel (2005), "Sexual Relations with Animals (Zoophilia): An Unrecognized Problem in Animal Welfare Legislation," p. 38.

71. Archer (1985), "A Fiendish Outrage? A Study of Animal Maiming in East Anglia: 1830–1870," *Agricultural History Review* 33 (II): 147–157.

72. See chapter 5 of this book. More empirical examples of aggravated sexual assault are provided in Frank Ascione (2005), *Children and Animals: Exploring the Roots of Kindness and Cruelty*, and esp. pp. 121–26.

73. *Standard Times*, July 26, 1991.

74. See, respectively, Sigmund Fleismann (1968), *Bestiality: Sexual Intercourse between Men and Women and Animals*, pp. 50–71, and Adams, "Woman-Battering and Harm to Animals," pp. 65–69.

75. Quoted in Holmes (1991), *Sex Crimes*, p. 27.

76. An expansive typology of zoophilia is provided by Andrea M. Beetz (2005), "New Insights into Bestiality and Zoophilia." Beetz lists nine basic forms of zoophilia. Only one of these appears to be based on the understanding that zoophilia is a form of animal sexual assault, namely, when an animal is a surrogate object for a behavioral fetishism (such as sadomasochistic practices, sexual murder, and so on).

77. For an early description, see Richard von Krafft-Ebing (1886), *Psychopathia Sexualis*, pp. 376–77. Krafft-Ebing's view that zoophilia is based on a natural preference has echoed strongly in subsequent studies. Looked at from a somewhat different perspective, this was presumably also true in eighteenth-century Sweden for those persons who, despite the very hostile and punitive social attitudes toward it, continued to find sexual gratification in bestiality (see Liliequist, "Peasants against Nature," p. 410). In twentieth-century Australia, too, one study has found that from the male participant's viewpoint, bestiality is often not a "replacement object" deriving from heterosexual starvation but rather a sexual practice sought after, often at great length, in its own right. On this, see Anne-Marie Collins (1991), "Woman or Beast? Bestiality in Queensland, 1870–1949," pp. 40–41.

78. National Institute of Neurological Disorders and Stroke (2006), *Klüver-Bucy Syndrome Information*, p. 1. This incurable syndrome is said to cause individuals to place foreign objects in their mouths and even to engage in sexual behavior with animals. It is sometimes associated with herpes encephalitis and brain-damaging trauma. Accessed July 29, 2006, from http://www.ninds.nih.gov/disorders/kluver_bucy/kluver_bucy.htm.

79. The American Psychiatric Association (2000), *Diagnostic and Statistical Manual of Mental Disorders*, listed zoophilia in the category "Paraphilia—Not Otherwise Specified."

80. Liliequist's large-scale study of eighteenth-century bestiality prosecutions in Sweden, for example, found that some of the defendants there "were idiots or not completely sensible, *but not very many*" ("Peasants against Nature," p. 410, emphasis added).

81. However, using twentieth-century data from Queensland, Australia, Collins, "Woman or Beast?", suggests that urban men choose animals for sexual gratification and that bestiality cannot be explained by the sexological explanation of heterosexual sexual starvation.

82. See Hani Miletski (2001), "Zoophilia—Implications for Therapy." See also Colin J. Williams and Martin S. Weinberg (2003), "Zoophilia in Men: A Study of Sexual Interest in Animals," and Alvin Cooper, Coralie R. Scherer, Sylvain C. Boies, and Barry L. Gordon (1999), "Sexuality on the Internet: From Sexual Exploration to Pathological Expression."

83. In queer studies, see, for example, Jens Rydström (2003), *Sinners and Citizens: Bestiality and Homosexuality in Sweden, 1880–1950*. Rydström's approach to the intertwined histories of bestiality and social control (e.g., police practices) is a self-conscious "position of, and loyal to, the dominated"—where "the dominated" are seen exclusively as humans.

84. See, for example, Mark Maske (July 18, 2007), "Falcons' Vick Indicted in Dogfighting Case," *Washington Post*, p. EO1. This particular description of a "rape stand" is available at http://www.slate.com/id/2170734.

85. Respectively, see Alfred C. Kinsey, Wardell B. Pomeroy, and Clyde E. Martin (1948), *Sexual Behavior in the Human Male*, p. 671, and Alfred C. Kinsey, Wardell B. Pomeroy, Clyde E. Martin, and Paul H. Gebhard (1953), *Sexual Behavior in the Human Female*. p. 505. However, see also a study comparing the sexual outlet experiences of 100 single Iowan male and female college students in 1974 and 1980 (M. D. Story [1982], "A Comparison of University Student Experience with Various Sexual Outlets in 1974 and 1980"). This found that while the number of students who reported having had sexual contact with an animal was very small, there was virtually no difference in incidence for males and females.

86. Kinsey et al., *Sexual Behavior in the Human Male*, p. 671.

87. For example, in Kinsey et al., *Sexual Behavior in the Human Male*, survey interviewers were explicitly warned to place the burden of denial on the respondent or "subject": "The interviewer should not make it easy for a subject to deny his

participation in any form of sexual activity. It is too easy to say no if he is simply asked whether he has ever engaged in any particular activity. We always assume that everyone has engaged in every type of activity. Consequently, we always begin by asking *when* they first engaged in such activity" (p. 53).

88. Dekkers, *Dearest Pet*, estimates that the extent of humans who have sex exclusively with animals is "far below" 1 percent (p. 149). But this altogether lacks proper evidence. Another study (J. Nagaraja [1983], "Sexual Problems in Adolescence") found that "only 1%" of Indian youths engage in zoophilia and that these are mainly from rural areas (p. 17). But it is unknown if Nagaraja's figure refers to youths who actually have sexual relations with animals or to those who experience sexual excitement while looking at animals engaging in sex. Rurality is also a focus in Gerald Cerrone (1991), "Zoophilia in a Rural Population: Two Case Studies," who interviewed twenty female undergraduate psychology students from rural areas about their knowledge of zoophilia. These women reported information provided by brothers, husbands, and former high school peers revealing that human–animal sexual intercourse with sheep, dogs, goats, and chickens "is more common than clinically reported" (p. 31A).

Two studies of inmates have, or at least seem to have, rather different findings. A study of 561 sex offenders in Memphis and New York City reported that only 1.1 percent of completed paraphilias involved bestiality (Gene G. Abel, Judith V. Becker, Mary Mittelman, Jerry Cunningham-Rathner, Joanne L. Rouleau, and William D. Murphy [1987], "Self-Reported Sex Crimes of Nonincarcerated Paraphiliacs," p. 19; Karla Miller and John Knutson (1997), "Reports of Severe Physical Punishment and Exposure to Animal Cruelty by Inmates Convicted of Felonies and by University Students," report that about 11 percent of a large sample of inmates in the Iowa Department of Corrections admitted either to having touched an animal sexually or to having had intercourse with an animal or to having watched someone else do one of these. A reanalysis of the data of Kathleen Gerbasi (2004), "Gender and Nonhuman Animal Cruelty Convictions: Data from Pet-Abuse.com," on 720 cases of animal cruelty shows that 2.8 percent were of bestiality and 85 percent by males.

89. In seventeenth-century Switzerland and Spain, for example, those indicted were often Protestant heretics, the victims of Catholic zeal, and vice versa. In Spanish Aragon, between 1570 and 1630, the accused were usually foreigners, particularly French men and African slaves (Monter [1980], "Sodomy and Heresy in Early Modern Switzerland"; Monter [1990], *Frontiers of Heresy: The Spanish Inquisition from the Basque Lands to Sicily*). In Sweden, almost all those indicted and executed were either very young boys or else ordinary peasants, farm servants, soldiers, boatswains, craftsmen, and apprentices (Liliequist, "Peasants against Nature"). Moreover, a study of Swedish court records up to 1950 has found that, with few exceptions, all those accused of bestiality were poor and male (Rydström [2000], "'Sodomitical Sins Are Threefold': Typologies of Bestiality, Masturbation and Homosexuality in Sweden, 1880–1950"). So, too, from 1740 to 1850 in

Somerset, England, of twenty-five bestiality defendants, eighteen were identified as laborers, one as a mason, and another as a carpenter (Morris [1989], "Sodomy and Male Honor: The Case of Somerset, 1740–1850"). Similarly, in Queensland, Australia, of fifty-three criminal dispositions for bestiality between 1870 and 1949, defendants were very largely European laborers, though Chinese and aboriginal men were also accused (Collins, "Woman or Beast?"). Similarly, almost all defendants in lycanthropy cases in sixteenth-century France were of the lowest social status—vagrants, beggars, shepherds, and peasants; some of them were not natives, and many were women (Caroline Oates [1989], "Metamorphosis and Lycanthropy in Franche-Comté, 1521–1643").

90. Sharpe, *Crime in Seventeenth-Century England* (see also Thomas, *Man and the Natural World*) documents that of nine persons indicted for bestiality between 1620 and 1680 in Essex, England, two were acquitted, four had their bills found *ignoramus,* and only three were hanged; Kent had ten cases, Sussex five, Hertfordshire four, and Surrey three. Thus, despite the horror with which it was viewed by commentators such as Coke and Blackstone, bestiality was therefore rarely indicted and not unduly likely to result in a conviction.

91. Sharpe, *Crime in Seventeenth-Century England*, pp. 65–66, and Morris, "Sodomy and Male Honor."

92. Bradley Chapin (1983), *Criminal Justice in Colonial America, 1606–1660,* p. 128. Yet Chapin documents that between 1606 and 1660, very few men were arraigned for bestiality and that, perhaps because common folk regarded it as a victimless crime, only four or five were actually hanged for it. In fact, only two men were executed for bestiality in seventeenth-century Massachusetts and none for sodomy (Roger Thompson [1986], *Sex in Middlesex: Popular Mores in a Massachusetts County, 1649–1699*).

93. Thompson, *Sex in Middlesex*, pp. 74–75.

94. Thompson, *Sex in Middlesex*, p. 410. An interesting twist on this masculinity thesis is given by Rydström, "'Sodomitical Sins Are Threefold.'" He is adamant that the discourse around bestiality in Sweden was so imbued with masculinity that the masculinity of the bestialist was never questioned and was actually enhanced by his sexual activities with animals. Moreover, "perhaps this was one reason why the [bestialist] was so highly stigmatised: his actions threatened the honor and respectability of male sexuality by stripping it of all finesse and reducing it to a dirty, animal act. No women were prosecuted for bestiality in twentieth-century Sweden, and the discourse at play here suggests why: its masculinity made it inconceivable that a woman could even be accused of such activities" (p. 250).

95. Liliequist, "Peasants against Nature," p. 414.

96. Liliequist, "Peasants against Nature," p. 413.

97. Monter, "Sodomy and Heresy in Early Modern Switzerland," p. 45.

98. Monter, "Sodomy and Heresy in Early Modern Switzerland," p. 293.

99. Collins, "Woman or Beast?," p. 39.

100. T. O. Beidelman (1961), "Kaguru Justice and the Concept of Legal Fictions," pp. 12–13.

101. Salisbury, *The Beast Within*, p. 94.

102. Salisbury, *The Beast Within*, p. 95.

103. Coke, *The Third Part of the Institutes of the Laws of England*, p. 58.

104. Sharpe, *Crime in Seventeenth-Century England*, pp. 65–66.

105. *Records of the Court of Assistants of the Massachusetts Bay 1630–1692, 1*, pp. 10–11. In seventeenth-century Scotland, also, some cases could not be pursued because, for whatever reason, witnesses sometimes fled or else simply disappeared. On this, see P. G. Maxwell-Stuart, 2002, "'Wild, Filthie, Execrabill, Detestabill, and Unnatural Sin': Bestiality in Early Modern Scotland," pp. 84–85.

Horse Maiming and the Sport of Kings

4

T HE PREVIOUS CHAPTER OUTLINED various views of human–animal sexual relations. I suggested that there is good reason to view as assaultive what has traditionally been seen either as a serious violation of religious commandments or else as harmless and humorous and as more or less socially acceptable activity. Animal sexual assault ("bestiality"), it was argued, is abusive for the very same reasons that sexual assault of one human by another is abusive.

Animal sexual assault is, of course, but one of the many ways in which humans can and do assault animals. However, just as it is with one human's abuse of another, so it is with cases of animal assault: sometimes they are seen as assaultive and condemned as such, and at other times, for a whole host of possible reasons, they are not. The source of this variation remains something of a mystery. At times, certain forms of human–animal relationships are seen as assaultive, and knowledge and condemnation of them travels across national and continental boundaries. Sometimes the process of condemnation even results in a reduction in the prevalence of animal assault. Arguably, this positive effect has happened with trafficking in animal body parts, with experimentation on nonhuman primates in laboratories, with whale and seal hunting, with the raising and fattening of geese to make pâté de foie gras, with battery farming, and with the rearing and transport of calves (for consumption of "veal").

Sometimes knowledge and condemnation of animal assaults does not extend beyond the relatively small-scale areas where they actually occurred. In the past decade or so, this has probably been the case with pigeons poisoned in Central Park in New York City,[1] with cattle defaced and otherwise mutilated in Montana,[2] with dogs poisoned in Hong Kong[3] and in Italy,[4] and with horses poisoned in Kentucky.[5] For the pigeons, cattle, dogs, and horses assaulted in these locales, the situation is not especially auspicious.

Now consider, for a moment, the life and death of Barbaro, a famous colt used in the racing industry in the United States. Barbaro was the revered winner of the Kentucky Derby and the odds-on favorite to win the second stage of the Triple Crown, the Preakness Stakes. However, on the evening of May 20, 2006, Barbaro collapsed just after the start of the Preakness, seriously injuring his lower hind right leg and breaking it above and below the ankle in three places. Ambulances sped to the scene. With Barbaro's euthanasia imminent, the packed stadium was hushed. Many fans had tears in their eyes. This "horrific scene" and "devastating development" ended with Barbaro being transported, X-rayed, and driven to the University of Pennsylvania's New Bolton Center, a state-of-the-art veterinary hospital.[6] During the night, Barbaro was operated on by two residents, an intern, two anaesthesiologists, and three nurses. To repair Barbaro's ankle, the surgeons fused it with a locking compression plate with twenty-three screws; his leg was then put in a cast.

The American nation waited, breathlessly, for the results of the surgery. By the next morning, well-wishers had already tacked up hundreds of messages saying "Thank You, Barbaro" and "We Love You Barbaro!"[7] For several days thereafter, Barbaro and his life-threatening injuries continued to be front-page news (he was finally euthanized, eight months later, on January 29, 2007).

Barbaro's story raises the interesting problem of how injuries to some horses are matters of great concern to many people and yet the question of assault or wrongdoing never arises there. To pose this problem slightly differently, why are some human-perpetrated injuries to horses regarded as assaults and others are not? When are horses seen as victims? When are humans seen as offenders? The focus of what follows here is the vociferous public outcry that arose against certain horse assaults ("maimings") in England in the 1990s.

Moral Panics and Horse Maiming in the English Countryside, 1991–1993

Very few of the diverse social practices investigated by criminologists and sociologists of deviance have attracted as much attention as those designated by the concept of moral panic. Although it is unclear quite why moral panics arise when and as they do, it is nevertheless true that every so often a society becomes engrossed in a process of public frenzy directed to certain forms of crime and deviance. Well-documented examples of moral panics include those associated with the McCarthyite communist scare of the 1950s, dope fiends in the 1960s, youth gangs and serial killers in the 1980s, child molesters and high school murderers in the 1990s, and sexual predators and immigrants in the first decade of the new millennium.

Although any given moral panic has its own dramatic idiosyncrasies, each also shares with other such panics certain sociological properties. Among these properties are (1) a point of inception at which, for whatever reason, certain social practices or events are identified as a social problem in need of a solution; (2) the emergence of a vanguard of moral entrepreneurs whose stated purpose is leadership in attacking the problem; (3) the formulation of the vanguard's message about the seriousness of the problem and about attributions of blameworthiness and victimhood, which is most effectively disseminated to a concerned social audience by the mass media; and (4) a demand for the deployment of agents of social control to identify and apprehend appropriate offenders and thereby to reaffirm the moral values of the community.

This chapter investigates certain aspects of the moral panic associated with a series of horse assaults that occurred in England in the early 1990s. For nearly a decade, some unknown number of horse assaults occurred in fields and stables. Mainly but not exclusively, these took place in southern England, especially in the counties of Hampshire and Surrey. Although the empirical focus of this chapter is confined to the moral panic that occurred in rural Hampshire from June 1991 to February 1993 (see figure 4.1), horse assaults were also reported from 1993 to 1997 in Oxfordshire, Buckinghamshire, Cleveland and Hull,[8] Dorset,[9] Greater Manchester,[10] Swindon to North Yorkshire ("100 attacks in 12 months"), and Wiltshire.[11]

The assaults were extensively reported in the national and local tabloid and broadsheet press. One national tabloid, the *Daily Mail*, added a reward of 10,000 pounds to the 8,000 pounds already pledged by organizations such as the International League for the Protection of Horses, Naturewatch Trust, and the equestrian magazine *Horse & Hound* for information leading to the conviction of those responsible.[12] When a mare named Mountbatten was found dead in her stable with cuts to her genitals, a meeting of concerned citizens in the small village of Four Marks in rural Hampshire set up the Horsewatch organization in early February 1993; this organization was the first of eighty-five such groups formed within eighteen months.[13]

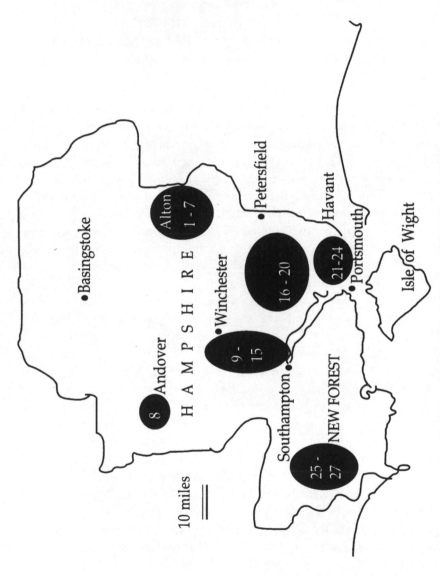

Figure 4.1.   Media-Identified Horse Assaults in Hampshire, June 1991–February 1993

Key

Alton:
1. May 4, 1992. Pony mare assaulted in stable—internal injuries from blunt instrument.
2. June 22, 1992. Thoroughbred cross gelding stabbed in a stable—cuts to shoulder.
3. June 31, 1992. Hack gelding cut on the shoulder while standing in a field.
4. July 16, 1992. Hack gelding cut with sharp instrument.
5. January 7, 1993. Pony mare found bleeding from the rear.
6. January 7, 1993. Gelding taken from stable and "covered in mud."
7. January 22 1993. Mountbatten found dead.

Andover:
8. July 16, 1992. New Forest mare—internal bruising and lashed with barbed wire.

Between Winchester and Southampton:
Chilworth:
9. August 4, 1991. Palomino pony assaulted.
10. August 28, 1991. Welsh cob mare cut on legs and flanks.

Romsey:
11. March 17, 1992. Arab gelding cut on head.
12. March 19, 1992. Internal cuts to pony in field.

Southampton:
13. October 15, 1992. Four horses attacked—slashed with sharp instrument; one had spike stuck in chest.

Winchester:
14. June 13, 1991. Pony mare burnt with rope.
15. August 13, 1992. Hack gelding attacked—rope burns on legs.

Between Southampton and Petersfield:
Botley:
16. July 13, 1992. Shetland gelding slashed.
Bursledon:
17. February 28, 1991. Pony attacked in field—internal bruising and swelling, external cuts.
Droxford:
18. July 13, 1992. Mare attacked in a field—internal bruising.
Durley:
19. September 2, 1991. Palamino mare attacked—beaten with a blunt instrument.
Kilmeston:
20. January 6, 1993. Mare attacked.

Havant and Portsmouth area:
Havant:
21. July 26, 1992. Riding pony mare slashed four times under the tail.
Meon:
22. June 13, 1992. Shetland pony mare assaulted—lacerations internally and externally.
Portsmouth:
23. June 14, 1992. Welsh cob mare—wounds to hind legs and internal bruising.
Upham:
24. February 3, 1993. Pregnant mare assaulted.

New Forest area:
Fordingbridge:
25. November 23, 1992. Pregnant brood mare assaulted internally—lost her foal.
New Forest:
26. September 14, 1992. Mare burnt with caustic substance.
27. September 17, 1992. Gelding cut deeply on the nose.

Source: Adapted from *The Times*, February 6, 1993.

The police then established the Mountbatten Operation, with twelve officers attached to it. Some police officers were designated as wildlife liaison officers in police stations located in the relevant areas.

This chapter does not actually examine such questions as "Who committed the Hampshire horse assaults?" and "Why did they commit them?" These are important questions, needless to say, but they require the demonstration of additional evidence that is, quite frankly, still not available. Rather, what is examined here is the problem of how various individuals, ad hoc groups, and social organizations tried to make sense of events that to them seemed deviant, irrational, and/or criminal to an outraged Hampshire citizenry. It is hoped, moreover, that some aspects of the nature of human–animal relationships can be revealed through authoritative utterances on the Hampshire horse assaults by the media, the police, and the humans who felt they had a stake in the horses' well-being.

Two preliminary points must be made about the Hampshire horse assaults and the attendant moral panic in Hampshire. First, in England and elsewhere, not only horses but also many other animals have been assaulted for centuries, sometimes systematically and routinely so. For example, a large number of related maimings of cattle and horses occurred 150 years ago in Norfolk, Suffolk, and parts of Cambridgeshire. Contrary to the traditional view that animal maiming was simply a vicious form of rebellion by rural laborers against the landed gentry, John Archer has shown in his book *By a Flash and a Scare* how in practice it was a peculiar, complex, and quite varied activity.[14] Animal maiming was sometimes undoubtedly a form of social rebellion, as in the maiming of their masters' horses by horsekeepers. Typically, however, it was a form of psychological terror, of symbolic murder, that resulted from personal feuds between members of the same social class. Thus, the maiming of donkeys and asses tended to indicate a dispute between one craftsperson and another—such as blacksmiths, cordwainers, butchers, and laborers—since they were the main owners of such animals. But the poisoning of cats and dogs, for example, suggests a conflict between farmers and gamekeepers over the rearing of game birds.[15]

However, the social situation and significance of these earlier maimings differed profoundly from the ones addressed in this chapter. Information about these earlier assaults does not seem to have been widely circulated at the time, while the horse assaults of the 1990s were extensively publicized. In addition, whereas the earlier animal maimings led to several convictions, no one has ever been convicted of the Hampshire assaults of the 1990s (at least as of this writing in 2008). The discourse of the 1990s moral panic was thus highly speculative about such key questions as the offender's identity and characteristics.

Second, the moral panic about horse assaults in 1990s rural England differed from nearly all other moral panics in that many of its central characters were animals rather than humans. This is to say not that animals have never been visible in other moral panics but that, if present, their roles tend to be passive, their voices peripheral to the main script. This typically secondary and socially unproblematic role of animals is evident in dramatic events as diverse as witchcraft crazes, bestiality trials, nineteenth-century agrarian "outrages" in Ireland, and mad cow disease (bovine spongiform encephalopathy).

In the case at hand, within the framework of a moral panic, horses and their plight occupied or seemed to occupy the central role of victim. An analysis of the circumstances in which victimhood was or might be ascribed to horses is therefore the focus of what follows now.

Horse-Maiming Matters

It is impossible to speculate with much confidence about whether, before the emergence of the moral panic that brought them widespread attention in the early 1990s, horse assaults in Hampshire were very rare phenomena or, instead, quite common. Indeed, because an isolated incident can be easily denied or declared relatively unimportant, the primary definers in this moral panic were consistently at pains to claim that the horse assaults were not isolated incidents but sequential events with an observable pattern. One cannot therefore identify the precise conjuncture of time, place. and assault in Hampshire such that it can in retrospect be identified as the first case in a series of horse assaults that occurred there during the 1990s. According to one account, the series of horse assaults in question started in Hampshire at some time before 1983,[16] although a Horsewatch official claimed that horses had been mutilated there as far back as 1966.[17] Another claimed that "the 'horse rippers' first came to public attention during the Eighties, though attacks had occurred before that."[18] In 1993, *The Times* felt able to identify twenty-seven horse assaults in Hampshire. Basing its figures on comments from a police spokesperson, *The Times* referred to "scores of reports" that it had received about the assaults.[19]

Whatever the reasons, the Hampshire horse assaults were portrayed as newsworthy and serious events. The notion of seriousness and its differing degrees may, of course, be understood in several ways, one of which is through straightforward descriptions of the physical injuries sustained by the horses. Reports in *The Times*, for example, refer to the following cases:

1. A pregnant Welsh cob mare named Daphne who was attacked with a Stanley knife strapped to a pole[20]
2. A twenty-three-year-old mare named Chiltern Hills who had her genitals mutilated[21]
3. A thirty-one-year-old mare named Gay Minstrel who was slashed across the quarters and had her genitals mutilated[22]
4. An eleven-year-old thoroughbred named Kerry who was stabbed in the genitals[23]
5. A twenty-year-old mare cut into by a five-inch knife[24]
6. A four-year-old "working horse" stabbed in the shoulder[25]
7. A mare named Chrissie who had her genitals slashed and a fencepost driven inside her[26]
8. Ponies burned with caustic soda[27]
9. An Irish hunter mare named Mountbatten who was found dead in her stable with cuts to her genitals[28]

Despite routine media dramatization and hyperbole, which are hardly conducive to reliable estimates of incidence, some unknown number of horses unquestionably experienced pain, sexual assault, and even, in one or two cases, death. Yet not all such harms inflicted on animals are taken seriously. Why did the Hampshire assaults reported here matter? To whom? How should they be understood?

An obvious feature of the societal reaction to the Hampshire horse assaults is that they were universally regarded as reprehensible. The public condemnation of the nameless and faceless horse maimers was just as unequivocal as it was later to be for the "Yorkshire Ripper," the serial murderer Peter Sutcliffe, and the notorious murderers Thomas Hamilton and Fred West. No one publicly tried to justify the horse assaults. Was this simply because the British are a nation of animal lovers? Clearly, the assaults prompted a line of questioning intended to understand events that, though known by all as abhorrent and aberrant, were seen mainly as senseless.[29] As ethnomethodologists and others have observed, those who initially regard an event as senseless are liable—if it concerns them enough—to spend a great deal of time and energy trying to make sense of it. But the question must again be asked: why did anyone care about these assaults? The Hampshire citizenry was invited to care because the media simultaneously described the assaults as both systematic and random. They were described as systematic because it appeared that each of the horse assaults was one act in a whole series of assaults and as random because no one had any idea when or where the perpetrator would strike next.

But we aren't horses, are we, so why should the citizenry (and we) care? One reason we should care is that the media conveyed the message that horse assaults are a serious matter. They are serious because very many people seem to think them serious. Certainly, important sections of the local community in Four Marks seemed to take them seriously. The local paper, the *Alton Herald*, informed its readers that at the inaugural Horsewatch meeting, "hundreds of people crowded into Four Marks village hall, whilst others were forced to stand outside straining to hear through open windows."[30] Moreover, some residents started to employ private security companies, while others blocked the police switchboard in search of advice. The horsekeeping community was understandably most anxious and insisted that the police apprehend the culprit. Horse owners expressed their feelings of loss and fear, resolutely unwilling to suffer a similar experience again.

The police certainly took the horse assaults seriously, and it was indeed they who established the Mountbatten Operation. Of course, regardless of any given officer's feelings for and about horses, these events provided the police with a heaven-sent opportunity to be seen to be responding to demands placed on them by the national and local press and by significant members of the local community. Referring to the "overwhelming response" from the public, the police spoke of a general need for the police and the public to bond together. As crime prevention officer Bill Slater told horsekeepers, "The police are the professionals in detecting crime, but you are our eyes and ears of the equestrian community."[31] In response, the Horsewatch coordinator declared, "Hopefully, by all of us being a bit more vigilant, we can start to make a hole in the crime rates of Hampshire."[32]

The respective interests and concerns of each of the main protagonists in this drama coalesced around the numerous sound bytes and column inches devoted to one key question: what sort of person could assault horses? As Fiona Broderick, daughter of Mountbatten's owner, Robert Broderick, asked, what "drive[s] people to do this to an animal?"[33] This is a valid and meaningful question. It remains so. Yet no one was ever convicted of these horse assaults or even prosecuted for them. Public discourse about such key questions as the assailants' identity, characteristics, and motives therefore tended to be highly speculative, its protagonists almost off guard, one might say, when giving voice to their opinions or vent to their prejudices.

As will soon become clear, behind this sometimes frenzied rhetoric lie hidden quite strongly held beliefs about the nature of criminality and of how and under what circumstances victimhood may be ascribed to animals. In the specific cultural context of racialization, for example, it has been argued that "animals and their bodies appear to be one site of struggle over the protection of national identity and the production of cultural difference."[34] Indeed, the whys, the hows, and the whens of the processes of victim construction occupy an often hotly contested cultural landscape at the nexus of struggles that may involve kaleidoscopic issues of class, gender, race, and age.

Offenders

As soon as the horse assaults were constituted as a series of serious deviant events, questions were inevitably raised about the identity and motivation of the offender(s). Among the many motives, qualities, and characters attributed to the offenders were mental illness, sadism, pedophilia, Satanism, fertility and other cults, fundamentalist Christianity, imitative copycats, vengeful unemployed horse-industry workers (e.g., stableboys), and rival horse owners. Some even claimed that the horses' wounds were self-inflicted.

The key voices that speculated in public and in the media on these questions were those of the horse owners, henceforth often self-identified victims ("owner-victims"); the police; and various experts attached to the investigation or consulted by the media.

The great majority of those who claimed to have authoritative knowledge of the horse assaults immediately assumed, albeit with varying degrees of sophistication, that the offenders had a pathological character. This assumption, when voiced from the dominant perspective of owner-victims, tended to be articulated in statements such as the following:

> It would have taken two strong men, one to hold Daphne, the other to cut the terrified horse. What kind of person would do that? . . . Sick. They are sick.[35]

Perhaps this pathological male—all seemed to have assumed the horse assailant was male—came from that pathological world beyond the normal and pleasant world of village halls and country fetes. The police warned the public to be on the lookout for "shady-looking characters," and they were reportedly seeking information on "unfamiliar cars" parked in the "wrong place."[36] As the mother of owner-victim Anna Sheldon commented, "It is a sick society we live in today"[37]—from whose ailments, presumably, even Four Marks, the small Hampshire village in which the ten-year-old Irish mare Mountbatten was killed, and similar places were not immune.

One interpretation of these events is that they were a metaphor: the evil world of shady characters was insinuating itself into the hitherto solid and respectable world of Middle England. There was a fear of the enemy without, among whom were "New Age Travellers," "Hunt Saboteurs," "Eco-Warriors," "Refugees," and "Asylum Seekers." However, alongside this fear was something even more worrisome—might the enemy be from within? One frightened resident of Four Marks speculated that perhaps "somebody could be living next door to this person or just down the road from them."[38] Moreover, a speaker at Four Marks' village hall put it in a classic Agatha Christie vein: "The person carrying out these attacks could be anyone. They could even be in this room tonight."[39]

The openly stated consensus view about the offender's identity, though, was clearly the pathological one. The designation of offenders as pathological, moreover, served to preclude further consideration as to the conceivable rationality of their actions. Certainly, for those who are neither professionally nor personally involved in any specific case, it is fairly simple to dismiss some acts as purely pathological, especially when their perpetrators remain at large and unknown. Moreover, a descriptive term that was often attached to the as-yet-unknown assailants—"horse rippers"[40]— invoked not only the dubious skills of an amateur, if wayward, surgeon (a medical student, perhaps, or a crazed aristocrat?) but also a bygone era in London's East End when another Ripper reigned with similarly unpredictable psychological terror. Thus, in the course of a conversation that could flow smoothly into a discussion of the state of world soccer or the latest Hollywood blockbuster, the horse assaults could easily be dismissed as the work of a "maniac,"[41] a "psychopath,"[42] a "lunatic,"[43] a "pervert,"[44] or a "disturbed"[45] or "sick"[46] person who "needs help."[47] We raise our eyebrows in horror and express our contempt for those whom the *Sunday Times* termed a "madman or madmen . . . the most hated men in Britain. . . . Mention that there are at present more than 100 unsolved prostitute murders in Britain, and few people will register much outrage."[48] How easily we pass on to other, less serious matters.

The closer a given person was to the horse assaults, the greater was the need to reflect on the meaning of it all. At the very least, a concerned local citizenry wanted some understanding of the precise nature of the pathology. Such reflection tends to evince a simple polar dichotomy of sane/ insane. But this polarity is clearly only a starting point. Thus, one horse owner spoke of the perpetrator as "dreadfully sick mentally."[49] A spokesperson for the Royal Society for the Prevention of Cruelty to Animals reflected that "whoever is doing this must have a sick, disturbed mind."[50] Obviously, the sane/insane dichotomy is altogether too neat and tidy in the sense that, in practice, people offer viewpoints that allude to their awareness of the kernels of rationality that might lie within the pathology. Given an individual's "crazed assumptions," a sort of reason might well be exercised in order to guide crazed actions. If one insanely believes "x," then the flow of thought that leads to insane action "y" might internally be quite rational. Moreover, when confronted by an insane act, personally motivated and professional investigators of truth may seek to pursue the insane beliefs that are held to explain that act. Thus, with regard to the horse maiming cases, Dr. Tony Black, a retired chief psychologist at Broadmoor Hospital, speculated that the offender was a person who suffered from "bizarre mental delusions" and who, furthermore, "saw horses as devil-carriers."[51] In other words, the delusional belief that horses were devil carriers led to a somewhat rational wish to destroy them. From the offender's perspective, Black seemed to imply, it was not really the horses that were victimized but the Devil.

There was an alternative and contradictory version of this sort of symbolic hypothesization. One Horsewatch official noted that many local residents believed the attacks might be the work of Satanic cults hell bent on sacrificing innocent horse victims to the Devil.[52] Such sacrifices might of course make sense to believers in Satan. A police officer suggested that perhaps the perpetrator was a hunt saboteur (presumably, for antihunting fanatics it would be quite rational to leave a series of animals dead and maimed around the countryside of southern England).[53] This brings us to rather less publicly voiced suspicions held by some owner-victims as to the meaning of these crimes. This was the notion that horse owners rather than the horses were the real targets. An interview conducted with a Horsewatch representative indicated that, while uniformly rejecting any idea that they had done anything that might somehow justify revenge attacks, several people were worried that the perpetrator's real target was their way of life. Such anxieties are a manifestation of the "respectable fears" that are an endemic feature of middle- and upper-middle-class life in contemporary rural England. Commonsense theory on deviance takes an act and then pursues assumptions about the actor's characteristics. The ideological function of the process is to render those sections of the population who seem to have those characteristics highly suspicious. In the case at hand, this may have interesting negative implications not only for Satanists but also, rather more seriously perhaps, for those opposed to the norms, values, and practices of rural England's upper-middle classes.

Victims

The problem of the victims' identity and status is one issue arising from these cases. Victim identification should never be assumed. To be a victim requires the ability to be successfully constituted as such. Victimhood is therefore not an objective juridical or sociological condition. It is an ascribed social status. But because victimhood can be instigated by effective claims making, some sections of society have acquired the ability to establish that their suffering is unnecessary, serious, and caused by dangerous criminals. This process of victimhood in the making is both quickened and intensified if the innocence of the would-be victims can be dramatically contrasted with the malevolence of their assailants. Put bluntly, some victims are worthy, while others are not. Moreover, the worthier the victim, the more reprehensible the offender.

With regard to humans, modern law assumes a principle of individual worth and rights, even if political and sociological factors routinely amplify the worthiness of some claims and render invisible that of others. However, if as a matter of principle and legal parchment all humans have legal rights, what of animals in general and of horses in particular? Can a horse be a victim? Why should we care about a horse's suffering? Certainly, in the sense of animal welfare legislation, it is illegal to cause horses unnecessary suffering. However, the master status of horses is that of humans' property. As such, in practice, the horse assaults were interpreted by the police as constituting acts of "criminal damage"[54] (i.e., property offenses), and victimhood was legally ascribed to the property owners. It is very likely that the horse owners in question tended to come from the higher—if not the highest—echelons of their communities and that they had very comfortable levels of income, status, and social influence. They were well situated in terms of the local hierarchy of credibility. It is *their* victimhood that in one sense enables the horse assaults to be treated seriously. This is quite logical. After all, it is not the horses themselves that can and do complain but humans. Yet on whose behalf do humans complain?

Clearly, malicious injury to a horse is not usually regarded as equivalent to the intentional infliction of damage on other forms of fast transport, such as cars and motorcycles. Yet why not? Car and motorcycle owners invest much time and money in their machines and arguably obtain emotional satisfaction from them. Indeed, some very similar and easily transferable phrases might be used by their respective owners to describe the purely instrumental qualities of horses and cars. Some statements by horse owners included, for example, the following: "Last season, he did well in dressage. . . . Obviously, this is going to slow things down a bit";[55] "[He was] a very expensive show jumper";[56] "a well-bred potential superstar";[57] and "wonderful to ride."[58] However, often combined with such transferable observations by horse owners are utterances that, if used by car owners to refer to their cars, would sound absurd. Would people comment tearfully about a damaged or wrecked car that "Her death left a great gap in my life" or "I'd owned her since she was a yearling" or "She was almost a member of the family"? Even if such comments might conceivably be made about cars, they surely would involve additional claims making on the behalf of owner-victims. On the surface, at least, they also therefore create doubt about whether the horse assaults were in fact only about property.

To understand the importance of this ambiguity, we must return to the meaning of English animal welfare legislation, which contains an explicit acknowledgment of animal sentiency.[59] As noted, this legislation is based on the concept of "unnecessary suffering" (and before that on the notion that other animals could not be "cruelly" treated). English law does seem to recognize, therefore, that animals can be victims of suffering and cruelty or, at least, recipients of them. It may posit that animals are sentient beings, yet it remains true that harming an animal puts one at no greater legal risk than of being charged with minor damage to property. With regard to assaults on animals, it is possible in law to violate the property rights of persons whether or not unnecessary suffering is caused to the property in question. In this sense, any suffering inflicted on an animal becomes a matter separate from the original property offense and secondary to it. Like human slaves before them, animals are afforded in law the strange status of sentient property.

How far does this status help us explain the situation of police officers who stress the property nature of the offenses or of owners who emphasize the noninstrumental qualities or characteristics of *their* horses? Why else does Mountbatten's owner bother to tell reporters, "I hate the thought that a helpless animal, who has grown to trust and love in their own little way, could suffer at the hands of a human like this?"[60] Why does another owner-victim tell journalists, "He was a nice horse"?[61]

Perhaps, after all, the horse is the victim. Certainly, the detective superintendent investigating the assaults implied just this very thing with his observation that "the victims can't talk to you."[62] Yet human murder victims can't talk, either. Their victimhood is socially recognized and usually extended and transported beyond themselves. Their family and friends suffer. So, too, might their "community," and indeed, on occasions, we are told that "the nation grieves." It has also been argued that the whole world—at least the decent bit of it—shares the pain of the Kosovan dead and the innocents massacred in Rwanda and Somalia. In theory, we recognize the right of people to draw attention to others' victimhood; in practice, we usually depend on their doing so. With regard to the Hampshire horse assaults, there was considerable ambiguity about the victim's identity. This ambiguity, in practical terms, is partially smoothed over by a consensus that something very wrong had occurred, but it also indicates the unsettled nature of the relationship between horses and humans and also between the latter and all other animals. As Keith Thomas has put it, "If we look below the surface we shall find many traces of guilt, unease and defensiveness about the treatment of animals."[63]

There is yet another way in which we are invited to take the horse assaults seriously. This lies in the popular belief that an assault on a horse might be a precursor to an assault on a human (see also chapter 5). Thus, just after a local girl had been stabbed, one media commentator mused that "it was only a matter of time before these attacks turned from horses on to people."[64] Another noted that

> the attacks against the horses were, in themselves, sinister enough; but from the beginning police were predicting that horse rippers might also turn on children. Could that now have happened?[65]

This view might be credible regardless of whether the perpetrator is perceived as "purely pathological" or as "pathologically rational." A psychopath sufficiently deranged as to seek to assault horses might well be inclined to turn his attention to humans. Or had he already assaulted humans before turning to animals? Alternatively, a resentment of privileged people might mean that the "real" victims would likely be targeted next time around, not just *their* horses as property or indeed *their* proxy. This sort of ad hoc theorizing implies that the meaning of the horse assaults needed to be taken even more seriously than the assaults themselves. Because a killer is a killer is a killer—so goes the logic—strident warnings were given to vulnerable young and especially female owners not to take risks by watching over their horses and ponies during the night.[66] If seriousness cannot be accorded on a principled basis, perhaps it can be on the basis of pragmatic self-interest.

Clearly, this sort of projection functions to sharpen broader perceptions and intensify the magnitude of the sense of threat and anxiety. At the same time, it dulls our ability to see assaults on horses as serious in their own right. From a speciesist perspective, "it's all about us."

Extending the Circle of Concern: A Note on Horse Assaults and the Sport of Kings

Thus far, this chapter has identified some of the key themes of the moral panic associated with a series of horse assaults in rural Hampshire during the early 1990s. These events marked a rare example of a moral panic about crime and deviance in which animals other than humans occupied or seemed to occupy the central role of victim. Just as moral entrepreneurs and the media invoke categories of crime and deviance in all other moral panics, so the horse assaults in Hampshire involved fundamental claims about wrongness: claims about the *wrong* person, the *wrong* place, the *wrong* reasons/intentions, the *wrong* methods, the *wrong* time, and the *wrong* targets.

For all the confusion that surrounds them, both the horse assaults and the moral panic described here belie the fact that humans are sometimes allowed to assault, injure, and kill horses and that for doing so they are rewarded with financial gain, with personal satisfaction, and with social prestige. It is true that the moral panic surrounding the Hampshire horse assaults went beyond such lawful or socially acceptable situations. It is also true that the hand-wringing that accompanies popular explanations of such deviance might lead to broader inquiry into the ways in which humans use and abuse animals, though in practice it tends precisely to distract us from further exploration.

It must be stressed that there is a variety of institutionalized social practices in which horses are routinely and systematically assaulted but that are not generally viewed as unlawful and socially unacceptable behavior. These other locations of horse assaults include laboratories, farms, racetracks, and abattoirs. About the perpetrators of harm and injury in these other places, it somehow seems much harder and much less appropriate to invoke notions of wrongful actions and pathological character. It therefore appears ethically and ontologically incorrect, also, to ask, What drives the humans involved to do what they do? or Who could do such an awful thing? It even seems to cast a shadow on the putative logic within the claim that a killer is a killer is a killer.

Why are some horse assaults condemned but others condoned? This thorny question has no simple answer, of course. But it can be said that during the Hampshire horse assaults, members of the public, the police, criminal psychologists, and animal welfare officials admitted only particular sorts of abused horses into their circle of concern. The focus of their concern, of their analyses, and of their utterances was not harm done to horses in general but, rather, assaults against individual horses, against individual acts of horse abuse, and against individual perpetrators of horse assaults.

Roughly the same sort of individualist prejudice dominates much recent thinking about the relationships between society and animal abuse. In the same way that in this discourse "society" has tended to be conceived of as an amalgam of atomized individuals apart from questions of race, gender, social class, and, especially, speciesism, so too the animals whose lives are admitted to the acceptable circle of concern tend only to be those who are considered as individuals with, as Geertrui Cazaux rightly points out, "a visible and acknowledged personality and biography."[67] In contrast, she argues, millions of other animals are exploited in large-scale commercial processes in which individual animals are lost in production quotas and mortality rates.

It is now worth returning to a point of entry into this chapter, namely, the problem of the social visibility of injuries sustained in the Preakness by Barbaro, the famous colt used in the racing industry. It must be said that the awesome gravity and shock of the scene at Barbaro's injury and possible euthanasia was in stark contrast to the almost invisible death a few days later of a four-year-old filly named Lauren's Charm, who collapsed and died in the home stretch of a race at Belmont Park racetrack. Except for Lauren Charm's owner, her jockey, two veterinarians, and one New York Times sports reporter, no one seemed to notice her death or even to care about it. Her carcass was pushed unceremoniously against a concrete wall by a mechanical earthmover.[68]

At least two reasonable inferences can be made from the respective fates of Barbaro and Lauren's Charm after each had been injured. The first is that of the unknown number of horses that suffer physical injuries when they are used in the horse-racing industry, a few horses are treated much better than others. Of course, neither owners not jockeys nor the public wishes to see horses injured, yet some horses, when they are injured, are the objects of intense concern to humans, receiving great affection and lavish medical care. Other horses and their injuries are of little or no concern at all. The contrasting fates of Barbaro and Lauren's Charm surely illustrate this difference.

The second, less straightforward inference from the respective circumstances of the deaths of Barbaro and Lauren's Charm is that horses are not
treated equally because, when they are injured, the level of concern that
they attract in part hinges on how extensively their cases are publicized.
In any given case, the greater the publicity, probably the greater the ensuing concern, including medical attention. I write *probably* here because,
of course, even if correct, this reasoning is dangerously close to a vicious
circle: some injured horses attract concern because their cases are more
publicized, and, conversely, because their cases are more publicized the
greater the concern and care that they attract. But in this quagmire, a vital
question still remains: why, when they suffer harm, do some horses receive
greater publicity and concern than others? Is it simply that the fortunate
few whose cases are publicized happen to be more financially valuable to
their human owners, as in Barbaro's case? It is very likely, for example, that
if Barbaro had not been a Kentucky Derby winner with future stud fees
amounting to an estimated $30 million to $40 million, then he also would
have been killed, unceremoniously and out of sight, immediately after he
received his injury at the racetrack.

In Britain, horse racing is a very large, multi-billion-pound industry,
with fifty-nine racetracks and approximately 1 billion pounds generated in
annual profits for bookmakers. The number of horses and ponies in the
United Kingdom is usually put at about 1 million, with 17,000 to 20,000
of these involved in horse racing. About 5,000 thoroughbred foals are
raised each year for the purpose of racing.[69]

The racing industry is a social institution in which horses are subjected
to widespread, endemic commercial exploitation. For humans' business and
pleasure, horses used in the racing industry are routinely devalued, harmed,
and assaulted. Estimates of how many horses die annually in British racing
vary considerably. One estimate, made in 1995, is that 200 horses die on
racetracks in Britain annually.[70] Another estimate, made in 2007 by the
same organization, Animal Aid, in its "Racehorse Deathwatch" campaign,
claims that currently 375 horses die each year on racetracks in Britain.[71]
According to Dr. David Nunamaker, a University of Pennsylvania professor of orthopedic surgery, in 2006 fatal muscle and bone injuries occurred
in racehorses 0.65 times per 1,000 starts in England (the horse fatality rates
in England may be contrasted with 1.5 fatalities per 1,000 starts in the
United States and 0.58 per 1,000 in Hong Kong).[72]

It is not only deaths that deserve mention but also nonfatal injuries suffered by horses. According to a recurring estimate from several sources, for
each horse that dies on a racetrack, two other horses die from injuries sus-

tained either on racetracks or in training. In flat racing, for example, great pressure is placed on the developing limbs of young (two-year-old) horses, and the racing of horses at a young age results in a high burnout rate and "near epidemics of tendon and ligament damage."[73] According to data released at a conference organized by the racing industry itself (stated conference goal: "to see that racehorses receive all the help we can give them *to do their job* as safely as possible"), 80 percent of fractures in British flat racehorses occur during training, and more than half of all fractures are stress fractures.[74] The scar tissue formed by the common practice of firing horses' tendons with red-hot irons is intended to act as an adequate support to permit racing, but sometimes the horses break down—and they are then destroyed.[75] Some horses destined for competition in steeplechase (horses raced over fences) or dressage events have sensitivity-increasing chemical substances applied to their legs, with the result that that they experience great pain should they touch a fence or a pole. This is to say nothing of the widespread injection of anabolic steroids into horses before races and jockeys' use of whips during them. In steeplechases, the chance of injury is heightened because the horses used here run longer races and can suffer many falls. It is rare even for showpiece events such as Liverpool's annual Grand National—where standards are closely monitored and enforced because of the attention of the media and the animal protection movement—to pass without fatalities. At the prestigious Cheltenham meeting, as many as ten horse deaths have occurred in a single week.[76]

In order to decrease the number of horse deaths and injuries, the racing industry's Horserace Betting Levy Board commissions vivisection experiments—to put it plainly, it kills horses—on lesser-valued horses. For example, at the Animal Health Trust in Newmarket (the site of the famous English racetrack) in 1993—the very same year that the Hampshire horse assaults reportedly reached their peak—twelve pregnant Welsh mountain ponies were injected with equine herpes, a practice that resulted in aborted pregnancies and paralysis. Following the experiments, the ponies were killed so that postmortem examinations could be performed on them. The researcher who performed these experiments—who was not, note, constructed as insane or perverse or at risk of committing other violent or harmful actions—explained that they were conducted for economic reasons, namely, that "equine herpes is an important source of loss to the horse industry."[77] "Loss" here, of course, refers to horse owners' financial losses—no less, no more. Further experiments are carried out on horses to study their reproductive processes and to investigate the treatment of racing-induced injuries.[78]

Each year, between 4,000 and 5,000 horses are withdrawn ("retired") from the horseracing industry.[79] The plight of ex-racehorses may be "a debilitating downward spiral of sale, resale and neglect."[80] Some unknown number of these horses is sent to one of the three British abattoirs licensed to slaughter horses or else sold to overseas slaughterhouses. Although legislation stipulates that horses worth less than 175 pounds cannot be exported, dealers in horse meat are able to avoid this restriction by claiming that horses are being sent overseas to race. Once abroad, they are diverted to abattoirs.

Notes

1. Jeff Morris (1999), "Serial Pigeon Killer on the Loose in NYC! Public Menace or Service?," *Whoa!,* August 24, pp. 1–3. See also Andrew D. Blechman (2006), *Pigeons: The Fascinating Saga of the World's Most Revered and Reviled Bird.*

2. Jim Robbins (2001), "Unsolved Mystery Resurfaces in Montana: Who's Killing Cows?" *New York Times*, September 17, p. C1.

3. See Kate Linebaugh (2005), "On a Hong Kong Trail, A Serial Dog Slayer Terrorizes Pet Owners," *New York Times*, p. A1; Mary Ann Benitez (2002), "Search for Dog Poisoner Widens," *South China Morning Post*, January 4, p. 6; and Neil Gough (2002), "The Killer among Us," *Time Asia Magazine*, March 25, p. 4. In a probably unrelated assault, Hong Kong police have reported that someone had placed under the turf of a local horse-racing track a device that could fire liquid-filled darts into the stomachs of horses as they waited at the starting gate. See Keither Bradsher (2007), "Reward Offered," *New York Times*, March 28, p. C18.

4. Celestine Bohlen (1997), "Citta di Castello: White Truffles Are to Die for, but Not Like This," *New York Times*, December 18, p. A4.

5. Several horses used competitively and with great acclaim for show ("show horses") were reported to have been poisoned near Lexington, Kentucky, in 2003. Although no perpetrator or motive has been discovered, three of the horses died several days after having had an unidentified agent injected into the hind side of their left forelegs. See Bill Mooney (2003), "Mystery in the Bluegrass: Who Poisoned the Horses?," *New York Times*, July 21, p. A10.

6. Anonymous (2006a), "Barbaro Breaks Down with Life-Threatening Injury in Preakness," Associated Press.

7. Anonymous (2006b), "Barbaro Faces Long Road to Recovery," Associated Press.

8. See *The Times*, February 6, 1993.

9. *The Times*, June 23, 1997.

10. *Daily Telegraph*, September 19, 1997.

11. *Observer*, October 12, 1997.

12. *Alton Herald*, January 29, 1993; *The Times*, January 6, 1993. Numerous animal maimings of sheep, cows, and horses, in particular, have since continued to be reported in Devon, Cornwall, Derbyshire, Scotland, and elsewhere. See, for example, Simon de Bruxelles (2006), "Sheep Are Mutilated 'in Satanic Rituals,'" September 25, available at http://www.timesonline.co.uk/article/0,,2-2369783,,00.html.

13. *Alton Herald*, February 4, 1993; see also *The Times,* April 9, 1993.

14. On these nineteenth-century animal assaults, see John Archer (1990), *By a Flash and a Scare: Incendiarism, Animal Maiming and Poaching in East Anglia 1815–1870*, pp. 152–53. For his comments on the 1990s horse maimings discussed in this chapter, see John Archer (1993), "Breaking the Last Taboo," *Guardian*, March 2, p. 19.

15. Archer, *By a Flash and a Scare*, p. 211.

16. *The Times*, January 5, 1993.

17. *Sunday Times*, October 31, 1993.

18. *Observer*, October 12, 1997.

19. *The Times*, February 6, 1993.

20. *Sunday Times*, November 28, 1993.

21. *The Times*, January 5, 1993.

22. *The Times*, May 23, 1997.

23. *The Times*, May 23, 1997.

24. *The Times*, May 23, 1997.

25. *Alton Herald*, July 10, 1992.

26. *Observer*, November 12, 1997.

27. *Borden Times & Mail*, February 2, 1993.

28. *The Times*, January 25, 1993; *Alton Herald*, January 29, 1993.

29. Perhaps senselessness was one of the main reactions to Peter Shaffer's famous play *Equus* of 1973, in which there are not only strong suggestions of heavy petting between the play's human protagonists and its horses but also admissions of horses blinded with metal spikes.

30. *Alton Herald*, February 4, 1993.

31. *Alton Herald*, February 4, 1993.

32. *Alton Herald*, February 4, 1993.

33. *Daily Telegraph*, March 6, 1993.

34. Glen Elder, Jennifer Wolch, and Jody Emel (1998), "Race, Place and the Bounds of Humanity," pp. 188–89.

35. *Sunday Times*, November 28, 1993.

36. *Alton Herald*, January 29, 1993.

37. *The Times*, June 23, 1997.

38. *Alton Herald*, January 29, 1993.

39. *Alton Herald*, February 4, 1993.

40. For example, see "Horse Rippers Run to Ground," *Observer*, November 12, 1997.

41. "Horse Hit by Attack," *Alton Herald*, March 7, 1992; *The Times*, January 5, 1993.

42. *The Times*, February 6, 1993.

43. *Observer*, November 12, 1997.

44. *Alton Herald*, January 29, 1993.

45. *Alton Herald*, January 29, 1993.

46. *Daily Telegraph*, March 6, 1993.

47. *The Times*, February 6, 1993.

48. *Sunday Times*, February 6, 1993.

49. *Alton Herald*, January 29, 1993, p. 1.

50. *Alton Herald*, January 29, 1993, p. 2.

51. *The Times*, January 25, 1993.

52. *Sunday Times*, November 28, 1993.

53. *The Times*, February 6, 1993.

54. *Sunday Times,* January 31, 1993, p. 31. In a case of sexual assault, for example, the victim is sometimes seen as an abused woman's spouse. However, this shared victimhood is often derived not from a male's assumed empathy toward a woman's suffering but from how his property has been damaged or polluted by sexual assault, thereby depicting him—the property owner—as the real victim.

55. *Alton Herald*, July 10, 1992.

56. *Alton Herald*, July 3, 1992.

57. *Alton Herald*, July 3, 1992.

58. *Alton Herald*, January 29, 1993.

59. Mike Radford (2005), *Animal Welfare Law in Britain*, pp. 198–201.

60. *Alton Herald*, January 29, 1993.

61. Personal interview of a Horsewatch representative by Chris Powell, July 30, 1998.

62. *Borden Times & Mail*, February 2, 1993.

63. Keith Thomas (1983), *Man and the Natural World: Changing Attitudes in England 1500–1800*, p. 50.

64. *The Times*, February 6, 1993.

65. *Sunday Times*, November 3, 1993.

66. For example, see the front-page report "Home Counties Horse Owners Mount a 24hr Guard against Attackers," *The Times*, February 6, 1993.

67. Geertrui Cazaux (1999), "Beauty and the Beast: Animal Abuse from a Nonspeciesist Criminological Perspective," p. 21.

68. Just after Barbaro's collapse, George Vecsey, a well-known sportswriter, wrote about the humane destruction of horses ("as the saying goes") that in his occasional forays to the track he had "seen this all too frequently. . . . I wonder how long it will be before the animal-rights people take a look at racing" (George Vecsey [2006], "The Psychic Pull of an Injured Racehorse," *New York Times*, May 24, p. C16). On the almost unnoticed demise of Lauren's Charm, see William C.

Rhoden (2006), "Witnessing an Unknown Filly's Death," *New York Times*, May 25, p. C16.

69. These figures are taken from the *Guardian*, accessed January 20, 2008, from http://sport.guardian.co.uk/horseracing/theobserver/story.

70. Mark Gold (1995), *Animal Rights: Extending the Circle of Compassion*, p. 115.

71. Animal Aid, accessed December 17, 2007, from http://www.animalaid .org.uk/h/n/NEWS/pr_horse/ALL/1713.

72. These data have been taken from interviews with Nunamaker in Joe Drape (2006), "Now Is a Time for Healing, for Barbaro and for Matz," *New York Times*, p. C16, and in Gina Rarick (2007), "I'm Not Barbaro, for Lots of Reasons," *Boston Globe*, p. 3.

73. Drape, "Now Is a Time for Healing, for Barbaro and for Matz," and Rarick, "I'm Not Barbaro, for Lots of Reasons."

74. "National Conference Report: Seminar on Preventing Racehorse Injuries" (November 15, 2001), *Hoofcare & Lameness Magazine* (emphasis added), accessed January 20, 2008, from http://www.hoofcare.com/archives/uk_racing_injuries_ report2001.html.

75. Christine Davies (1998), "They Save Horses, Don't They?," *The Big Issue, Cymru*, p. 9.

76. This was reported in K. Saunders (1996), "What's So Grand about the National?," p. 8.

77. Quoted in Mark Gold (1993), "Straight from the Horse's Mouth," *Animal Aid Report*, p. 2.

78. Mark Gold (1996), "Racing's Dead End," p. 11. According to the Department for Environment, Food and Rural Affairs, between 6,000 and 10,000 horses are slaughtered every year in Britain for horse meat, the vast bulk of which are killed for consumption abroad. For estimates of the number of horses slaughtered annually, see http://sport.guardian.co.uk/horseracing/theobserver/story.

79. These figures are taken from the *Guardian*, accessed January 20, 2008, from http://sport.guardian.co.uk/horseracing/theobserver/story.

80. Mark Gold (1995), *Animal Rights: Extending the Circle of Compassion*, p. 115.

Is There a Progression from Animal Abuse to Interhuman Violence?   **5**

IN 1836, PIERRE RIVIÈRE, a Normandy peasant aged about twenty, was tried by a French court for the crime of parricide, convicted, and sentenced to death. According to the diverse historical records collected and analyzed by Michel Foucault and his colleagues and published in the book *I, Pierre Rivière*, the accused openly admitted that he had brutally murdered his pregnant mother, his sister (aged eighteen) and brother (aged seven) with a pruning hook.[1]

At Rivière's trial, the court was presented with a convincing array of exhibits of his guilt. The evidence dossier contained numerous descriptions of how, from the period of his youth up to and including the time just before and just after the murders, Rivière had behaved in bizarre, sinister, and threatening ways. From these accumulated descriptions there emerged the unusual profile of a sullen and unsociable young man who shunned the company of persons of his own age, who detested his mother for having routinely mistreated his father, and who lived a strange and at times wild and beastly existence. The diverse evidence that Rivière had intentionally planned the murder of half his family was based on medical and judicial reports, on testimony from the peasant inhabitants of Rivière's Normandy village, and, perhaps most damning of all, on a self-incriminating memoir of which the accused himself was the proud author. Even though among his fellow peasants and between lawyers and medical doctors there was considerable debate at the time of his trial and afterward about whether and, if so, to what degree and for how long his actions were those of a madman or an idiot, the evidence of Rivière's premeditated guilt was, in short, utterly convincing.

There was no doubt whatsoever that under the French law of homicide, Rivière was guilty of murder. Notwithstanding Rivière's legal guilt, it is also clear that the precise meaning and importance of some of the details of the events *leading up to* the murders are sometimes ambiguous. Moreover, in this contested terrain there lurks evidence of animal cruelty. Court records and newspaper reports reveal that Pierre Rivière had a great aversion not only to women but also to all female animals. They also indicate that Rivière confessed to having enjoyed torturing animals and that he had gone so far as to have constructed a special instrument for the killing of birds. Indeed, in his memoir of the murders, Rivière wrote,

> I crucified frogs and birds, I had also invented another torture to put them to death. It was to attach them to a tree with three sharp nails through the belly. I called that enceepharating them. I took the children with me to do it sometimes and sometimes I did it all by myself.[2]

At Rivière's trial, prosecutor and presiding judge alike pointedly invoked his repeated acts of cruelty to animals as exemplars or signs of an inexorable logic that led more or less directly to his brutal slaughter of three members of his own family. However, this sort of explanation is perhaps not a very satisfying one and even then only in some convoluted and retrospective way. Thus,

> [Rivière] laughed interminably, with a terrible laughter, if asked the reason for his bizarre behavior. After his arrest his fellow peasants spoke of his laughter as of the intolerable accompaniment of morbid symptoms. Only the parish priest thought to minimize them: "Certainly no one would have thought anything more of it had it not been for the murders he has committed," he said. . . . What peasant did not remember taking pleasure in such acts of cruelty to children and animals? . . . But once Pierre Rivière killed, all his games became signs of madness.[3]

To be explicit, *certainly no one would have thought anything more of Rivière's animal cruelty had it not been for the murders he had committed*. It is a very fair question, therefore, whether the details of Rivière's life had an inner logic such that, as they unfolded, their ghastly conclusion was arrived at in a progression that was inexorable and unalterable. The question of whether animal abuse leads to subsequent violence between humans is also the focus of this chapter.

The Progression Thesis

That there is a significant relationship between animal abuse and interhuman violence is a claim with a lengthy and impressive pedigree. Impas-

Figure 5.1.   "First Stage of Cruelty" (William Hogarth, 1751).

sioned assertions about its veracity can be found in utterances by such diverse thinkers as Pythagoras, Thomas Aquinas, Montaigne, Kant, Mary Wollstonecraft, Gandhi, and Margaret Mead. Espoused by its holders at a high level of abstraction, it is today often disseminated in the mantralike catchphrase "the link." It is most prominently advanced by feminists and by members of state agencies and philanthropic organizations who work with at-risk families. It also implicitly appears in the writings of moral philosophers about animal welfare and animal rights.

By the mass media and by numerous practitioners and activists in the animal protection community, moreover, the obviousness and the acute importance of this claim are sometimes held to be indisputable scientific revelations with policy ramifications of the utmost urgency. Sometimes, the causal chain of the link is quite specific, with a particular form of animal abuse (e.g., animal sexual assault) held appropriately to presage a corresponding form of interhuman violence (e.g., rape). Thus, a casework division manager of People for the Ethical Treatment of Animals (PETA), intervening against a sixty-three-year-old male prosecuted in March 2005, for multiple rapes of calves in Neillsville, Wisconsin, asked the judge vigorously to prosecute the defendant because "studies show that offenders who commit bestiality often go on to commit sex crimes against humans."[4]

I do not wish to imply here that animal abuse and interhuman violence are not linked. To the contrary, I will suggest that they are often intimately intertwined and that they may be linked not in one but in a variety of ways. In what follows, I focus on just one aspect of this web of entanglement, namely, the claim that there is a causal relationship between animal abuse and interhuman violence. This claim I term "the progression thesis." When it first appeared in sociological research of the 1960s and 1970s, the term the "progression thesis" referred to apparent relationships of cause and effect in the nonmedical use of drugs and alcohol, though its basic causal formula was also denominated as "escalation," "graduation," "predisposition," and the "stepping-stone theory."[5] As a more or less focused object of study, the progression thesis has been applied to human–animal interaction only from the 1990s to the present.[6]

Especially in popular discourse, the lack of subtlety with which the complex relationship between animal abuse and interhuman violence is sometimes asserted tends to make the link appear, however well intentioned, more the brittle product of sloganeering than of hard evidence and logic. Indeed, before it can confidently be said that a pattern of progression from animal abuse to interhuman violence really exists—and, if so, then of what sort—several quite thorny evidentiary problems must first be explored. In particular, it is not fully appreciated that demonstration of the truth of the progression thesis ultimately depends on the successful combination by its proponents of two quite separate propositions. Chronologically and causally, one of these propositions looks forward, the other backward. In the one, it is proposed that those who abuse animals are more likely than those who do not subsequently to act violently toward humans. In the other, it is held that those who act violently toward humans are more likely than those who do not to have previously abused animals. Clearly, the logical associations embedded in these propositions need not be ones of strict Humean causality but rather ones of robust and persistent statistical association. The question is, How strong and robust is the association? If there is a persistent association between animal abuse and interhuman violence, then how is this to be explained?

While these two propositions—one prospective, the other retrospective—are the necessary twin pillars of the progression thesis, the originating site of the thesis is commonly lodged in the social dynamics of families in crisis. Among the main dysfunctional qualities of these families is their propensity for interpersonal violence, to whose stated links with animal abuse I now turn.

Family Violence and Companion Animal Abuse

It is well established that different forms of family violence tend to coexist.[7] If a male is battering his spouse, for example, then it is more likely that children in that household are also being abused or neglected there. Households where women are being abused by men—and also, no doubt, where men are abused by women—are more likely to have not only children who are being abused but also one child who is abusing a sibling.

Is this also the case with animal abuse? If in a household one human is abusing another, then is it more likely that companion animals are also being abused there? In trying to answer these questions, it must first be said, on the one hand, that empirical data on intrafamilial animal abuse are woefully thin. Thus, in none of the technologically advanced societies do there exist any large-scale, police-based data on animal abuse. In its compilation of the crime data for 17,000 police departments across the United States, for example, the Federal Bureau of Investigation's annual *Crime in America: The Uniform Crime Reports* has no entries whatsoever on crimes involving animal abuse—though it does refer, next to "office equipment" and "televisions," to the proprietary items of "livestock" and "clothing and furs." There are no large-scale household victimization surveys that seek information on the incidence and prevalence of animal abuse, including the U.S. Department of Justice's annual *National Crime Victimization Survey*. There are not even any well-publicized local surveys of animal abuse.

Sparse though they might be, existing data do suggest that, in situations of intrafamilial conflict, animals are often used as instruments of psychological and physical terror by one human against another or as objects against which humans vent their aggression, whether pent up, learned, or random. Precisely because the several forms of family violence tend to cluster and because companion animals are usually regarded as family members, we should expect to find that in families where any given form of family violence exists, animal abuse is also more likely to exist there. Empirical evidence does indeed indicate that companion animal abuse often occurs disproportionately in a variety of situations of family violence. Schematically, these include the following:

- Heterosexual partner abuse[8]
- Lesbian partner abuse[9]
- Child physical abuse[10]
- Child sexual abuse at home[11] and in day care centers[12]
- Sibling abuse[13]
- Multiple abuse[14]

One study of families where children have been abused, for example, has found that the abuse of household pets by a family member had occurred in 60 percent of the families; two-thirds of the animals had been abused by fathers, the remainder by children.[15] In another study, this one of lesbian partner abuse, 38 percent of the respondents who had companion animals reported that their partners had abused their pets.[16] Such findings have also been supported by research on battered women who had sought refuge in shelters. For example, 71 percent of pet-owning women in a Utah shelter reported that their partners had killed or mistreated one or more of their pets or that they had threatened to do so; 32 percent of women with children reported that one or more of their children had abused or killed companion animals.[17] Moreover, in a study of battered women in a South Carolina shelter, of forty-three women with pets, twenty (46.5 percent) reported that their male abusers had threatened to harm or actually did harm their pets.[18] Taking these findings one step further, another study has revealed that women residing in domestic violence shelters are much more likely to report having their pets hurt or killed by their abusing partner than a comparison group of women who had not experienced intimate violence.[19]

Diversity in the sites of its empirical support is an undoubted strength of the finding that companion animal abuse is more likely to exist with other forms of family violence. These include not only structured interviews with battered women and abused children but also reports of animal abuse in self-report studies and made to veterinarians, animal control officers, animal shelters, women's shelters, and police. Clearly, family violence, including animal abuse, is a multifaceted phenomenon in which various forms of abuse often occur together and in which the presence of one form might signify the existence of others. It is likely, too, that some of the key sociological dimensions of animal abuse mirror those of interhuman violence. For example, in addition to the predominance of males in the commission of animal abuse by adults, all indications are that among children and adolescents, it is also young males who commit animal abuse far more frequently than young females. Moreover, when young males engage in animal abuse, their abuse is often considerably more egregious.

But there are annoying gaps and inconsistencies in existing research. While it is very plausible that households with animal abuse are more likely also to be households suffering from interhuman violence, nothing very precise is known about the prevalence of animal abuse among young males and young females, just to mention one area of uncertainty. Karla Miller and John Knutson found that 20.5 percent of 308 Iowan undergraduate psychology students (with a small overrepresentation of females) reported that they had actually engaged in one or more acts of animal cruelty.[20] But Clifton Flynn found that from a sample of undergraduate psychology and sociology students at a southeastern university in the United States, 34.5 percent of males and 9.3 percent of female admitted that during childhood they had abused animals.[21] However, much higher rates of animal abuse than these have been identified by Anna Baldry. In her study of animal abuse and exposure to interparental violence among Italian youth aged nine to seventeen, she found that 50.8 percent of the 1,392 youth taking part in her study had abused animals at least once; 66.5 percent of these were committed by boys.[22]

How do we account for why these findings are so widely discrepant? Do they really mean that Italian youth are more abusive than American youth? Surely not, though in the absence of other information this possibility cannot be ruled out. Are the discrepancies purely random? With so few studies available, there is no way of really knowing. But the discrepancy might simply be a function of various methodological factors, such as the influence of the different levels of willingness of subjects to report that they have abused animals and of the nature and sensitivity of the survey instrument.

Regarding this last possibility, for example, most studies have tended to focus on relatively extreme forms of animal abuse. Baldry's operationalization of the concept of animal abuse, rather, is much broader and includes any form of hitting, tormenting, bothering, harming, or being cruel to them. It is not altogether surprising, therefore, that her more sensitive definition of animal abuse would result in the discovery of greater prevalence among the youth in her study.

Baldry also persuasively shows how, in trying to discover the factors that might precipitate animal abuse by children, it is important to examine the particular form of violence to which children have been exposed in households. For example, a significant positive correlation has since been determined for adolescents between the witnessing of animal abuse and subsequent animal cruelty.[23] It might also be usefully asked whether this correlation is of the same magnitude as that for those children who have themselves been direct victims of family violence or of bullying. Whichever is the case, were the offenders male or female, and were the victims humans or animals?

Examination of such questions is important for a variety of reasons. Quite apart from the harm done to animals, for example, juvenile victims of interhuman violence are known to be at risk for developing a variety of psychological difficulties in interpersonal relationships, and within one year they are more likely to engage in violence against humans, including against themselves.[24]

By way of summary thus far, it may be said that existing research on how often, how seriously, and in what ways companion animal abuse exists with other forms of family violence tends neither to confirm nor to disconfirm the progression thesis. While there is no good reason to suppose that the etiology of companion animal abuse differs markedly from that of the abuse of human family members (animals are likely abused by humans for many of the same dominionistic reasons that all subordinate populations are abused by more powerful ones),[25] nothing systematic is known about the direction of abuse. It is true that animal abuse and interhuman violence are linked in the sense that they tend to occur in the same household disproportionately, but this tendency does not necessarily mean that a developmental relationship exists from one to the other. For example, it is unknown whether men who currently batter their spouses previously tended to have abused animals. Do these men perhaps begin a cycle of violence by concurrently abusing animals and their partners? Perhaps, instead, they first abuse their partners and later abuse animals.

The (mis)behavior of children can be questioned in the same way. Do young boys typically witness their father abusing their mother, for example, and then afterward abuse an animal? Or are they more likely to do this if, rather than witnessing violence, they are the direct victims of it? Thus, Clifton Flynn has found that boys who commit animal cruelty are more likely, for example, to have had corporal punishment inflicted on them.[26] Is this process one of social learning motivated by anger? What of older siblings—do they abuse their younger siblings first and later abuse animals, or do they begin by abusing animals?

These and other important questions must be addressed before the un-doubted propensity of animal abuse to coexist with other forms of family violence can be inserted into a full assessment of the merits of the progres-sion thesis. At present, therefore, this segment of the evidence about the progression thesis is inconclusive.

Animal Abuse and the Futures of Assaultive Children

The first proposition embedded in the progression thesis is that those who abuse animals are more likely than those who do not subsequently to act violently toward humans. Mass-media reports have suggested, for example, that some young male animal abusers have later committed interhuman mass murders. Thus, it was reported that prior to the Satanic cult killing of two schoolgirls and the wounding of seven others by an armed teenager in a Mississippi school in 1997, the alleged (now convicted) teenage murderer, Luke Woodham, had engaged with a friend in the gruesome torture of his own dog, named Sparkle. According to police, the two teenagers "repeat-edly beat the dog with a club." Woodham later wrote about this: "I'll never forget the sound of her breaking under my might. I hit her so hard I knocked the fur off her neck." "He then wrapped Sparkle in garbage bags, torched it with a lighter and flammable fluid, listened to it whimper and tossed it in a pond."[27] After describing the sight of the dog sinking beneath the surface of the pond, Woodham added, "It was true beauty."[28]

Supported by similarly sensational cases,[29] some observers have of-fered mathematically precise generalizations about the relationships among animal abusers and other types of offender. Thus, Arnold Arluke and his colleagues have reported in their study of police records and files of the Massachusetts Society for the Prevention of Cruelty to Animals (MSPCA) that animal abusers were 5.3 times more likely to have a violent criminal record.[30] They were also four times more likely than nonabusers to be arrested for property crimes and three and a half times more likely to be arrested for drug-related offenses and disorderly conduct.

Yet how might one test whether those who abuse animals are more likely than those who do not subsequently to act violently toward humans? Every methodology from cross-sectional analysis to life histories has its own specific advantages and limitations, but longitudinal analysis is the best way to test the chronological causal sequence embedded in the progression thesis.[31] With the cautious use of both self-report studies and official crime records, a longitudinal study of a random sample of the youth population could be done that measured animal abuse and interhuman violence at two or more points in time. The effect of prior animal abuse on subsequent interhuman violence could then be estimated, with controls for prior interhuman violence and other variables known or thought to be correlated with animal abuse and interhuman violence, like gender, race and ethnicity, social class, age, opportunity, urban/rural location, and access to animals. How, too, might opportunity be influenced by varying degrees of urbanization and rurality?[32]

However, such a study could not prove conclusively that the commission of animal abuse causes animal abusers to subsequently engage in human violence. Problematically, moreover, it would be comparing the subsequent interhuman violence of individuals who had different degrees of prior animal abuse. For more conclusive proof, a randomized experiment is needed, though for ethical and other reasons it would be extraordinarily difficult to carry out. But it would substantially increase our confidence that engaging in animal abuse exerts an independent causal effect on interhuman violence.

Because no longitudinal analysis has ever been applied to the progression thesis, any current assessment of the status of this thesis must settle for a reworking of cross-sectional research on children and adolescents that has been generated in a hodgepodge of intellectual and social contexts.

In this regard, three main claims have been advanced about children ("assaultive children") who abuse animals. The first involves the claim that assaultive children are likely to have mental and characterological defects. Assaultive children are sometimes described as having multiple personality and dissociative disorder, for example.[33] Inadequate role models, peer influences, posttraumatic play, hostility displacement, and suicidal tendencies have all been variously associated with or described as the personality characteristics of assaultive children. Besides these personality characteristics, second, it has sometimes been asserted that assaultive children have other antisocial tendencies. These include nonproductive firesetting and enuresis, though the empirical evidence for these tendencies has been quite mixed. About assaultive children it has also been variously said, third, that they are overwhelmingly young, male, and of normal intelligence; often sexually abused at home or physically abused and neglected there; and, as was discussed earlier, often live in a situation of family violence.

These findings portend little, however, about the chain of causation from animal abuse to interhuman violence. Actually, they serve mainly to open up an array of other, equally unresolved questions. For example, why are assaultive children overwhelmingly male, if this is so? After polite nods to concepts like the socialization process, existing commentary on this question is either too individualistic in its explanatory basis or else prone to degenerate into hollow biological assertions about innate male aggressiveness. In abusing the most available living beings that are unable to offer resistance to them—dogs, cats, fish, birds, and reptiles—young boys are perhaps mimicking their fathers' violence against their mothers and sisters. But does this mean that their witnessing of others' interhuman violence precedes some children's animal abuse? Is this progression necessarily, inexorably so? Moreover, if the original tendencies that propel some children to abuse animals are so ironclad, then why do some young males eventually desist from abusing animals and others not?

Given the importance of these unanswered questions, existing research on the futures of assaultive children cannot even with generosity be regarded as a functional, if lesser, equivalent of the would-be findings of longitudinal studies. Even if it is true that youthful animal abusers tend to have more psychosocial health problems than nonabusers and also to engage in other antisocial acts, these facts alone shed no light on the question of whether they are more likely subsequently to engage in interhuman violence.

Animal Abuse and the Histories of Violent Adults

The second proposition embedded in the progression thesis is that those who act violently toward humans are more likely than those who do not to have previously abused animals. In this regard and with varying degrees of methodological sophistication, most research has proceeded with the use of questionnaires and/or structured interviews that ask violent adults to recall the frequency and intensity of their childhood violence against animals. Among the findings that tend to support the progression thesis are the following:

- In-depth interviews with seven female serial killers reveal that all of them suffered abuse, abandonment, and instability as children and that each of them tortured or killed animals, especially cats.[34]
- In a case study of the respective social situations of five serial murderers and 354 convicted serial murderers, 21 percent had previously committed acts of animal cruelty.[35]

- A comparison of fifty violent and fifty nonviolent inmates at a maximum-security prison in Florida found that the proportion of the former who had committed acts of cruelty to animals (56 percent) was significantly higher than that of the latter (20 percent).[36]
- A comparison of the frequency of animal abuse by (1) aggressive and nonaggressive male inmates in federal penitentiaries in Connecticut and Kansas and (2) a control group of randomly selected noncriminals in New Haven and Topeka found that 25 percent of the aggressive group reported having abused animals five or more times during childhood, compared with only 5.8 percent of the nonaggressive group and 0 percent of the noncriminals.[37]
- In a study of convicted psychiatric patients, murderers were found more likely than nonviolent offenders to have abused animals.[38]

Each of these findings is gleaned from information provided by convicted criminals or by psychiatric patients who, when they were interviewed, were serving time of one sort or another in a carceral institution. However, comparisons between incarcerated populations and nonincarcerated populations should be viewed with great caution. For one thing, it is an error to suppose that comparisons of the behavior and characteristics of those who are incarcerated with those who are not incarcerated will enable us confidently to identify differences between those who commit crimes and those who do not commit them. Rather, because incarcerated populations by definition comprise those unfortunates who have been charged with crimes and convicted, they are not and can never be representative of all those who commit crime. By the same token, moreover, those who are not or who never have been incarcerated cannot represent the law-abiding citizenry. Among those who have never been incarcerated, for example, are numerous citizens who have committed crimes and who, for one reason or another, have avoided detection, arrest, conviction, and incarceration.[39]

This segment of the progression thesis must also confront the inconvenience that several studies are said by their authors to provide, at best, nonconfirming arguments and, at worst, counterfactual arguments to the claim that adults who act violently toward humans are more likely than those who do not to have previously abused animals.[40] Consider two of these:

- Miller and Knutson's study compared the responses to self-report questionnaires of 314 inmates in the Iowa Department of Corrections with those of 308 college students. The study found either a modest association or none at all among abusive childhood environments, witnessing or committing animal cruelty, and subsequent violent behavior.[41]

- In a second study conducted in Massachusetts by Arluke and his colleagues, the criminal records of 153 animal abusers were compared with those of 153 neighborhood control participants. It was found that although animal abusers were also more likely to commit a range of offenses, including those associated with property, drugs, and public disorder, there existed no progression from animal abuse to interhuman violence. While it would therefore seem that this finding tends to disconfirm the progression thesis, the authors suggest instead that it reveals the presence of "deviance generalization."[42]

However, the degree to which the progression thesis is weakened by these counterfactual cases is unclear. This is so neither because the counterfactual cases might or might not damage the thesis nor because philosophers of science cannot agree on how many counterfactual cases are required to disconfirm a given hypothesis or theory. It is because both of these studies have methodological difficulties impairing their ability adequately to test the progression thesis. The methodology in the first study does not permit a determination of the key question of whether those particular felons who as children or youth frequently either engaged in acts of animal abuse or witnessed such acts subsequently committed violent acts against humans.[43] Indeed, the authors themselves caution that their data allow no inference whatsoever about a causal or temporal sequence between animal cruelty and interhuman violence.[44] In other words, their methodology permits findings about animal abuse and interhuman violence that are, at their closest, only tangential to the progression thesis.

Now consider the second study mentioned here, which was devised as a direct test of the progression or "violence graduation" thesis. This study concluded that no graduation existed from animal abuse to interhuman violence. For at least two reasons, however, this conclusion should be treated with caution. On the one hand, because the authors were legally barred from obtaining any criminal records in Massachusetts for those aged sixteen years and younger, the study was unable to test whether there is a progression from animal abuse to interhuman violence during the period from childhood to adulthood. Yet it is precisely this lengthier age span that is commonly asserted to lie at the heart of the progression thesis—and probably rightly so.[45]

On the other hand, in self-consciously trying to avoid the methodological problems associated with self-report data, the authors' solution necessarily falls prey to a different set of methodological and, even, conceptual difficulties. In their study, they rely on official crime data that derive from reports of animal abuse to the MSPCA and from reports of adult crime to state and local police. This is not the place to rehearse all the problems with the use of official crime data as a measure of the amount or the serious or the frequency of crime, but it must be said, whatever animal abuse data are lodged in official MSPCA and police records, that they are social constructions rather than a measure of some objective social reality. As such, their meaning is problematic and entirely open to question. Each act of animal abuse in official MSPCA records is the result of complicated social processes that include (1) a potential complainant who must perceive an animal that is capable of being abused, (2) a potential complainant who must perceive an act of commission or of omission as animal abuse, (3) a perceived case of animal abuse that must somehow come to the attention of MSPCA officers, (4) formal recognition by an MSPCA official that a report of animal abuse has correctly identified an illegal act of animal abuse and that the act is worthy of their attention, and (5) a given case of animal abuse that has negotiated steps 1 to 4 then being accurately entered into official MSPCA records. Official records of animal abuse, in other words, do not speak for themselves. Another way of putting this is to say that only a tiny minority of cases of animal abuse is recorded in official data.

Social constructivist objections to the meaning and accuracy of official crime data have been universally understood in sociology and criminology since the early 1960s. We are indeed still disadvantaged by not knowing quite what can properly be inferred from official records of animal abuse. Are those animal abusers whose acts eventually enter official records typical of animal abusers as a whole? Not necessarily because perhaps they are less adept at avoiding detection. Perhaps the acts of those who commit greater abuse or who commit it more regularly are somehow less likely to be recognized, detected, and recorded. Or, for a whole host of reasons, the lives of those whose acts enter official records might be vulnerable to more surveillance than those of other citizens.

Just as it is important to understand who enters official records of animal abuse and why, so too we need to know whether the cases of animal abuse that enter official records are representative of animal abuse as a whole. On this note, it should therefore be stressed that the detection of acts of animal abuse by scholars, by police, and by members of the public very much hinges on how animal abuse is defined. "More" animal abuse undoubtedly would have been detected in the Massachusetts study, for example, if the authors' concept of abuse had been broader than "*cruelty*"—which was operationalized as any investigated case where an animal had been intentionally harmed physically (e.g., "beaten, stabbed, shot, hanged, drowned stoned, poisoned, burned, strangled, driven over, or thrown").[46] Acts of animal cruelty like those in this definition are actually more extreme than everyday cases of animal abuse, roughly half of which are acts of neglect and some unknown amount of which involves verbal and emotional abuse.[47]

It seems, therefore, that in trying to assess the merits of the progression thesis, it is at present prudent not to rely too much on the two counterfactual cases mentioned previously. Indeed, such cases very usefully underline the pressing need for careful investigation of the relationship between official data on animal abuse and the unrecorded, otherwise socially invisible character of much animal abuse.

A second avenue of potential support for the progression thesis lies in numerous anecdotal accounts of multiple murder presented in the mass media. These anecdotes suggest that those who commit multiple murders—that is, mass murder or serial murder—tend as children disproportionately to have engaged in serious animal abuse. Consider, for example, the case of serial murderer James Hicks, who, aged forty-eight, was convicted in 2000 of killing three women in Maine between 1977 and 1996. Although the voices of both Hicks's victims and Hicks himself were conspicuously absent from contemporary media accounts of the murders, the following excerpt from a lengthy newspaper account of Hicks's life well illustrates the genre's explanatory structure. In the excerpt, an investigative journalist recounts his interview with Denise Clark (Hicks's childhood friend and the sister of one of the murdered women) as follows:[48]

> The saga of Jimmy Hicks can begin almost 30 years ago with four cold words that haunt Denise Clark still. "I killed your cat," she said Hicks, then 18, told her in a calm voice, a few days after she'd said something that he didn't like. Clark, 15 at the time, told him she didn't believe him. But Hicks insisted, explaining that he had wrapped a wire around the cat's neck, hooked it to his bumper, and dragged the helpless animal along the roadway. "He didn't blink an eye," she recalled. Clark and a friend later found the cat, dead, with a wire still around its neck.

This journalistic narrative invites its audience to ponder how and why local boy Jimmy Hicks could have become a serial murderer. It does so by leading its readers to believe that this process of becoming a serial murderer

("The saga of . . .") was a more or less straightforward series of salient events that logically preceded and prepared the way for Hicks to commit multiple murders. Readers are informed that the relevant events in this chain of causation "can begin" thirty years earlier, when Hicks calmly told his friend Denise Clark that he had tortured and killed her cat.

Consider, also, the following reports:

- Patrick Sherrill, a postal worker who killed fourteen coworkers in 1986, is said to have stolen local companion animals and then to have allowed his own dog to mutilate them.[49]
- Ted Bundy, executed in 1989 for one of perhaps fifty murders, reportedly spent much of his childhood torturing animals with his grandfather.[50]
- It was reported in Ohio that alleged serial killer Thomas Lee Dillon was known to neighbors and coworkers for having "stabbed, stomped and shot 1,000 cats and dogs."[51]
- Alberto DeSalvo, the "Boston Strangler," is said to have shot arrows at trapped dogs and cats.
- It was reported that as a young man, Jeffrey Dahmer kept the bones of chipmunks, squirrels, dogs, cats, groundhogs, and raccoons inside formaldehyde-filled pickle jars that lined his neighborhood clubhouse. He roamed the neighborhood for roadkill and had a little graveyard with animals buried in it.[52] A school friend of Dahmer's recalled that Dahmer also collected stuffed rabbits, owls, and small birds and that, when asked about taxidermy, Dahmer had told him that "I always wanted to do that to a human."[53]

How much weight should be attached to such anecdotal evidence? It's hard to say. The narrative of an anecdote tends to be prised from a specific cultural context in order to illuminate with dramatic effect and in a trivial and often distorting way some aspect of a larger and more complex story. Clearly, anecdotes are not generated systematically. Rather, they are flimsy constructions the narrative truth of which is far less important than either the discursive functions they are asked to serve or the interests of those who wield them. Consider, for example, the problems posed for the progression thesis by Lionel Dahmer's reflection on the childhood of his son Jeffrey:

> [A] sense of something dark and shadowy, of a malicious force growing in my son, now colors almost every memory I have of his childhood. In a sense, his childhood no longer exists. Everything is now a part of what he

did as a man. Because of that, I can no longer distinguish the ordinary from the forbidding—trivial events from ones loaded with foreboding.[54]

Predictably, the would-be generalization that multiple murderers tend as adolescents to have disproportionately engaged in animal abuse is vulnerable to simple counterfactual cases. For example, its applicability in her own case has been strenuously and credibly denied by the notorious English "Moor's murderess," serial murderer Myra Hindley.[55] Counterfactual cases where animal abuse does not seem to be in the background of recent mass murderers include the twenty-three-year-old Virginia Tech shooter Seung-Hui Cho, who, in the worst non–war-related murder spree in U.S. history, killed thirty-two and wounded many more (April 16, 2007); an eighteen-year-old student, Pekka-Eric Auvinen, who, at his Tuusula high school in Finland, killed eight people before shooting himself (November 8, 2007), and Robert Hawkins, who, at an Omaha shopping mall, shot nine persons to death, including himself (December 6, 2007).

The generalization also faces the thorny problem that some mass murderers have regarded themselves as longstanding "animal lovers" and even, in the case of some leading Nazis in 1940s Germany, as champions of animal rights.[56] If the possibly relevant facts in the prior histories of serial murderers are to include anecdotes, then one anecdote may of course be legitimately countered with another. Thus, an acquaintance recently confided in me that as a young teenager, she used to collect roadkill. She told me that for about three years she had been fascinated with death and, walking back home from her school in Florida, had carefully collected dead squirrels, birds, frogs, and lizards, which she would place in a plastic bag, take home, and preserve in formaldehyde jars. The chances are good that this young teenager, who has grown into a career probation worker in her thirties, is not a serial killer and is most unlikely ever to become one.

Moreover, at least some aspects of the anecdotal evidence presented here are clearly more complex than their dramatic presentation indicates. Consider, for example, the previously mentioned report of Patrick Sherrill. Suppose it is true that at some point in time before he killed fourteen co-workers, Sherrill had allowed his dog to mutilate neighborhood companion animals. From this, it would by no means follow that those who allow their dogs to mutilate such animals have a greater propensity subsequently to engage in interhuman violence. Even if these facts had been true in Sherrill's case, we would also need to inquire of Sherrill's life history not only how the earlier form of violence led to the later one but also whether other aspects of his life might have been even more proximate or more influential. Did Sherrill commit other forms of violence before his mass-murder spree? Had he been abused at work? Passed over for promotion? Was he suicidal, and, if so, why? Consider, also, Dvorchak's account of Dahmer mentioned previously and add, for good measure, Goleman's report that Dahmer had impaled or staked frogs and cats to trees.[57] Nothing in either of these descriptions suggests that Dahmer himself ever tortured or killed live animals, and Dahmer's father has stated that his adolescent son even rescued several at-risk animals.[58] Were we to learn that any given adolescent is fascinated with dead animals, why should we infer that he is a serial killer in the making rather than a budding zoologist or forensic scientist?

Expanding the Scope of the Progression Thesis: From Individual Animal Cruelty to Institutionalized Animal Abuse

Thus far, I have tried to identify some worrisome evidentiary weaknesses in knowledge claims about the progression thesis. Chief among these weaknesses are the paucity of empirical data, the absence of longitudinal studies and, as I have hinted, the uncritical constitution and employment of such concepts as "animal abuse" and "cruelty." In concert, these weaknesses suggest that current generalizations about a progression from animal abuse to interhuman violence are, at best, premature. Indeed, rather than comprising a convincing body of focused research, support for the progression thesis currently amounts to little more than hastily scribbled, pro-animal sloganeering. Unfortunately, among the undesirable consequences of such slogans is their tendency to undermine confidence in other aspects of their authors' agenda.

While the several forms of family violence are undoubtedly strongly associated, existing knowledge of how and how often companion animal abuse exists with other forms of family violence tends neither to confirm nor to disconfirm the progression thesis. Crucially, it is not known whether animal abuse precedes and signifies other forms of violence or whether it follows them. Whichever is the case, we need additionally to know under what circumstances it is so and why. What is currently known about their futures actually sheds little light on the likelihood that assaultive children will subsequently engage in interhuman violence. To complicate matters further, there is even some "reverse" evidence to do with serial theriocide by adult humans. In the lengthy and unsolved series of grisly mutilations of horses in England and Wales in the 1990s, discussed in chapter 4, there was intense public speculation, if not direct evidence, that the sadistic the-riocides might soon be progressing to the committing of homicide.

Suppose it is actually confirmed that assaultive children really are more likely later to act violently toward humans—we would then need to in-quire whether this heightened disposition derives from assaultive children's prior animal abuse and, if so, why. Are there factors other than animal abuse in the lives of assaultive children that influence them later on to act violently toward humans? What might be the bearing of gender, age, and other variables on subsequent interhuman violence by assaultive children? Moreover, given the largely anecdotal and somewhat contradictory nature of the evidence in this regard, it is not yet known if those who act violently toward humans are more likely than those who do not to have previously abused animals.

But it is not only suitable empirical evidence that the progression thesis lacks. Reconsider, for a moment, the Foucauldian analysis of the "facts" of the case against Pierre Rivière, the French peasant convicted of parricide in 1836. This chapter began with a particular question about the necessary explanatory logic of linking cruelty to animals with subsequent interhuman violence. Were the details of Rivière's life, including his self-confessed propensity to torture and to kill animals, "microscopic seeds"[59] such that their murderous conclusion was reached according to some inexorable and immutable logic? Rivière's dossier suggests that the answer to this question can only be *only in retrospect*. In dissecting the respective powers of law, medicine, gossip, and newspaper and broadsheet reportage to structure the evidentiary facts in Pierre Rivière's case, the Foucauldian analysis is broad and diverse in its grasping of emerging practices to do with madness, idi-ocy, and extenuating circumstances. For present purposes, another crucial question emerges from that analysis. This has to do with the definition and meaning of murder itself. Why was Pierre Rivière's slaughter of members of his family defined as murder?

This question has no simple or straightforward answer. Of course, Riv-ière's slaughter of three family members was considered murderous because, with their respective and combined authorities, criminal law and medicine defined the gruesome killings as such. It is also the case that Rivière engaged in the everyday sort of killing—albeit of an unusually dramatic sort—that. was and is typically thought of and defined as murder. However, much larger slaughter lay in the mass killings of foreign soldiers and civilians— and, yes, of nonhuman animals—premeditated, coordinated, and ordered by certain European governments on adjacent soil and in empires across the seas. This slaughter resulted in more numerous dead bodies—*many times more numerous.* These killings committed for love of God, country, and empire and, at the time of Rivière's birth, for Bonaparte, were not considered as murderous illegalities. Not at all. By ideological sleight of hand and eye and law book, these killings were deemed nothing less than manly and courageous.

Similarly, and returning to the main task at hand, not nearly enough attention has been paid to the adequacy of concepts like "animal abuse" and "animal cruelty." Neither of these concepts has been properly scrutinized, yet the content of each is hugely contentious. For example, at what level in hierarchies of consciousness and sentience must animals be positioned for them to be included in the concept of animal abuse? If I swatted the mosquito that is sucking blood from my arm, for example, would that be animal abuse? Similarly, what should count as abuse? Should the concept of animal abuse be expanded from the purely physical domain to include emotional and psychological dimensions as well? Should it include neglect? Why are most existing studies limited to one-on-one or face-to-face situations of "intentional cruelty" to companion animals? Should these situations include abuse to feral animals or to animals used in agribusiness and in research laboratories? Surely, there is no warrant to base studies of animal abuse on societal definitions of acceptable and unacceptable behavior—ways of seeing that are often anthropocentric, arbitrary, and capricious.

As such, the current emphasis on the link between those harms that are regarded as socially unacceptable, one-on-one cases of cruelty to companion animals has tended to close off exploration of less obvious yet even more pervasive ways in which the abusive situation of one type of being might lead to a situation of violence against another. The link between animal abuse and interhuman violence must surely be sought not only in the personal biographies of those individuals who abuse or neglect animals but also in those institutionalized social practices where animal abuse is routine, widespread, and often defined as socially acceptable.

Among these social practices, consider, for example, the multiple forms of violence perpetrated in slaughterhouses. There is, first, the grotesque animal abuse that inheres in the painful carnage wrought annually on billions of terrified animals. In 2007, according to the U.S. Department of Agriculture (USDA), there were approximately 34.3 million cattle killed in slaughterhouses in the United States, 109.2 million pigs, 2.69 million sheep and lambs, and 758,100 calves. To these official USDA counts for "red meat" slaughtered in 2007 must be added 9.4 billion chickens, 316.7 million turkeys, and 27.8 million ducks.[60]

PLEASE DO NOT ANNOY, TORMENT, PESTER, PLAGUE, MOLEST, WORRY, BADGER, HARRY, HARASS, HECKLE, PERSECUTE, IRK, BULLYRAG, VEX, DISQUIET, GRATE, BESET, BOTHER, TEASE, NETTLE, TANTALIZE, OR RUFFLE THE ANIMALS

SAN DIEGO ZOO

SAN DIEGO WILD ANIMAL PARK

Figure 5.2. "Please Do Not Annoy, Torment, Pester . . . The Animals" (San Diego Zoo, San Diego Wild Animal Park, 2008).

Less well known is the physical and psychological toll that is wreaked on slaughterhouse workers. Among all private-sector industries in the United States, U.S. Department of Labor data show that year after year workers in slaughterhouses suffer among the very highest rates of nonfatal injuries and illnesses and of disorders associated with repeated trauma. Although these injuries are less dramatic than those recorded in industries like construction, mining, fishing, and logging, they tend to occur cumulatively over time, and, partly because of changes in the methodology of reporting practices since 2002 and partly because of a decline in levels of unionization, workers' injuries sustained in slaughterhouses are today less likely to be reported than those in some other dangerous workplaces.[61] Even less well known and only rarely recorded is the violence visited on those beings with whom slaughterhouse workers interact outside their places of work. The toll on this group of victims is graphically uncovered in Gail Eisnitz's *Slaughterhouse*, an important book of investigative journalism. A slaughterhouse worker interviewed by Eisnitz—Van Winkle—believed that "it was not uncommon" for slaughterhouse workers to be arrested for having assaulted humans. Describing the mental attitude developed from "sticking" hogs (i.e., slitting hogs' throats in the often-botched attempt to kill them), he divulged that

> the worst thing, worse than the physical danger, is the emotional toll. If you work in that stick pit for any period of time, you develop an attitude that lets you kill things but doesn't let you care. You may look a hog in the eye that's walking around down in the blood pit with you and think, God, that really isn't a bad-looking animal. You may want to pet it. Pigs down on the kill floor have come up and nuzzled me like a puppy. Two minutes later I had to kill them—beat them to death with a pipe. I can't care.[62]

"My attitude was," Van Winkle continued, "its only an animal. Kill it."[63]

Surely, wherever and whenever relationships between humans and animals are marked by authority and power and thus by institutionalized social distance, the possibility of further, extrainstitutional violence is actively encouraged. Thus, as Van Winkle admitted,

> I've had ideas of hanging my foreman upside down on the line and sticking him. I remember going into the office and telling the personnel man I have no problem pulling the trigger on a person—if you get in my face I'll blow you away. Every sticker I know carries a gun, and every one of them would shoot you. Most stickers I know have been arrested for assault. A lot of them have problems with alcohol. They *have* to drink, they have no other way of killing live, kicking animals all day long.[64]

Moreover, Van Winkle added that when he was working in a Morrell's slaughterhouse, alcohol abuse was not the only outlet for stickers:

> [A] lot of guys at Morrell just drink and drug their problems away. Some of them end up abusing their spouses because they can't get rid of the feelings. They leave work with this attitude and they go down to the bar to forget. Only problem is, even if you try to drink those feelings away, they're still there when you sober up.[65]

If some version of the progression thesis eventually turns out to be true, then this will not be altogether surprising. But for it to be intelligible, animal abuse as a complex of social practices must be properly understood and explained. Some explanatory power can be afforded by existing sociological theories of violence that are mindful of the role of subjective states such as empathy, caring, and compassion. If compassion involves an understanding of others' and Others' suffering and the desire to ameliorate it, then compassion for animals and for humans, respectively, is probably strongly linked. Thus, whatever their social situation and motivation, assaultive children are perhaps so desensitized by the act of animal abuse that they subsequently have reduced compassion for the suffering and welfare of many other beings (including humans). In reducing abusers' compassion, animal abuse might be found to increase tolerance or acceptance of proviolent attitudes and, thereby, to foster interhuman violence.[66] Indeed, a plausible corollary of the progression thesis, especially were it found to be true, is that children who have or who are taught to have compassion for animals might be more likely to become adults who act more sensitively and more gently toward humans.[67]

Notes

1. Michel Foucault, ed. (1975), *I, Pierre Rivière, Having Slaughtered My Mother, My Sister, and My Brother* . . .

2. Pierre Rivière (1835), "The Memoir," p.104. Oddly enough, Rivière penned his memoir of the events that preceded the murders *before* he had committed them. Perhaps this was an attempt to feign madness.

3. Rivière, "The Memoir," p. 196.

4. PETA's correspondence about this case is available at the Animal Sexual Abuse Information Resource Site, http://www.animalrights.net/archives/year/2005/000149.html (accessed January 2, 2008).

5. For the use of all these terms in a single book, see Michael Schofield (1971), *The Strange Case of Pot*, chap. 9.

6. Studies of the progression thesis include Suzanne R. Goodney Lea (2007), *Delinquency and Animal Cruelty*; Marie Louise Petersen and David P. Farrington

(2007), "Cruelty to Animals and Violence to People"; Christopher Hensley, Suzanne E. Tallichet, and Stephen D. Singer (2006), "Exploring the Possible Link between Childhood and Adolescent Bestiality and Interpersonal Violence"; Anna Baldry (2003), "Animal Abuse and Exposure to Interparental Violence in Italian Youth"; Mark R. Dadds, Cynthia M. Turner, and John McAloon (2002), "Developmental Links between Cruelty to Animals and Human Violence"; Geertrui Cazaux (2002), "Anthropocentrism and Speciesism regarding Animals Other Than Human Animals in Contemporary Criminology"; Frank R. Ascione (2001), *Animal Abuse and Youth Violence*; Lorna Bell (2001), "Abusing Animals, Abusing Children"; Helen Munro and M. V. Thrusfield (2001), "Battered Pets: Features That Raise Suspicion of Non-Accidental Injury"; Linda Merz-Perez, Kathleen M. Heide, and Ira J. Silverman (2001), "Childhood Cruelty to Animals and Subsequent Violence against Humans"; Arnold Arluke, Jack Levin, Carter Luke, and Frank Ascione (1999), "The Relationship of Animal Abuse to Violence and Other Forms of Antisocial Behavior"; Clifton P. Flynn (1999), "Animal Abuse in Childhood and Later Support for Interpersonal Violence in Families"; Karla S. Miller and John F. Knutson (1997), "Reports of Severe Physical Punishment and Exposure to Animal Cruelty by Inmates Convicted of Felonies and by University Students"; and Dorian Solot (1997), "Untangling the Animal Abuse Web."

7. See, for example, Kathleen J. Ferraro (2006), *Neither Angels nor Demons: Women, Crime, and Victimization*, esp. pp. 32–33.

8. Baldry, "Animal Abuse and Exposure to Interparental Violence in Italian Youth"; Clifton P. Flynn (2000a), "Battered Women and Their Animal Companions: Symbolic Interaction between Human and Nonhuman Animals"; Clifton P. Flynn (2000b), "Woman's Best Friend"; Frank R. Ascione (1998), "Battered Women's Reports of Their Partners' and Their Children's Cruelty to Animals"; Frank R. Ascione, Claudia V. Weber, and David S. Wood (1997), "The Abuse of Animals and Domestic Violence: A National Survey of Shelters for Women Who Are Battered."

9. Claire Renzetti (1992), *Violent Betrayal: Partner Abuse in Lesbian Relationships*, p. 21.

10. E. C. Guymer, D. Mellor, E. S. L. Luk, and V. Pearse (2001), "The Development of a Screening Questionnaire for Childhood Cruelty to Animals"; Munro and Thrusfield, "Battered Pets."

11. William N. Friedrich, Anthony J. Urquiza, and Robert L. Beilke (1986), "Behavior Problems in Sexually Abused Young Children"; Mic Hunter (1990), *Abused Boys: The Neglected Victims of Sexual Abuse*, pp. 214–216; Barbara Boat (1999), "Abuse of Children and Abuse of Animals," pp. 83–100.

12. David Finkelhor and Linda Meyer Williams with Nanci Burns (1988), *Nursery Crimes: Sexual Abuse in Day Care*; Susan J. Kelley (1989), "Stress Responses of Children to Sexual Abuse and Ritualistic Abuse in Day Care Centers," p. 508; Kathleen Coulborn Falle (1990), *Understanding Child Sexual Maltreatment*, pp. 199–201; see also Hunter, *Abused Boys*, pp. 19–20.

13. Vernon R. Wiehe (1990), *Sibling Abuse*, pp. 44–45.

14. Catherine Itzin (1997), "Pornography and the Organization of Intra- and Extrafamilial Child Sexual Abuse," p. 66. This study has uncovered the coexistence in a single family of incest, pornography, sibling abuse, child sexual abuse, and animal sexual assault.

15. Elizabeth Deviney, Jeffery Dickert, and Randall Lockwood (1983), "The Care of Pets within Child Abusing Families." There is also some evidence that children exposed to wartime violence are more prone to animal cruelty. On this, see Jonathan Randal and Nora Boustany (1990), "Children of War in Lebanon," pp. 66–67.

16. Renzetti, *Violent Betrayal*, p. 21.

17. Ascione, "Battered Women's Reports of Their Partners' and Their Children's Cruelty to Animals."

18. Flynn, "Woman's Best Friend."

19. Frank R. Ascione, Claudia V. Weber, Teresa M. Thompson, John Heath, Mika Maruyama, and Kentaro Hayashi (2007), "Battered Pets and Domestic Violence: Animal Abuse Reported by Women Experiencing Intimate Violence and by Nonabused Women."

20. Miller and Knutson, "Reports of Severe Physical Punishment and Exposure to Animal Cruelty by Inmates Convicted of Felonies and by University Students," p. 77.

21. Flynn, "Animal Abuse in Childhood and Later Support for Interpersonal Violence in Families," pp. 165–66.

22. Baldry, "Animal Abuse and Exposure to Interparental Violence in Italian Youth," p. 272.

23. Kelly L. Thompson and Eleonora Gullone (2006), "An Investigation into the Association between the Witnessing of Animal Abuse and Adolescents' Behavior toward Animals." In their study, Thompson and Gullone also found that adolescents were more likely subsequently to be cruel to animals if they had witnessed an animal being abused by a friend, relative, parent, or sibling rather than by a stranger.

24. See, for example, Jennifer N. Shaffer and R. Barry Ruback (2002), *Violent Victimization as a Risk Factor for Violent Offending among Juveniles.*

25. Animal abuse is one among many battering strategies whereby men, for example, try to achieve control over women. On this, see Carol J. Adams (1995b), "Woman-Battering and Harm to Animals," pp. 71–73, and Robert Agnew (1998), "The Causes of Animal Abuse: A Social Psychological Analysis," p. 187. The success of this male strategy is documented in Angela Browne's (1987) *When Battered Women Kill*, a study of the respective social situations of battered women who do and who do not kill their spouses: 62 percent of the former and 37 percent of the latter confided that their mates had forced or urged them to perform various sex acts, including sex with animals.

26. Flynn, "Animal Abuse in Childhood and Later Support for Interpersonal Violence in Families," p. 261.

27. Kevin Sack (1997), "Grim Details Emerge in Teen-Age Slaying Case," p. A10.

28. Sack, "Grim Details Emerge in Teen-Age Slaying Case," p. A10.

29. In another report of mass murder, in 1998 in Springfield, Oregon, it was revealed that prior to killing two classmates and both his parents, fifteen-year-old Kip Kinkel had enjoyed shooting squirrels, setting off firecrackers in cats' mouths, or stuffing them down gopher holes (Associated Press, 1998, May 23).

30. Arluke et al., "The Relationship of Animal Abuse to Violence and Other Forms of Antisocial Behavior," p. 969. See also Joseph Sauder (2000), "Enacting and Enforcing Felony Animal Cruelty Laws to Prevent Violence against Humans," pp.13–14, and Jack Levin and James Alan Fox (2001), *Dead Lines: Essays in Murder and Mayhem*, p. 16.

31. Scott Menard and Delbert Elliott (1990), "Longitudinal and Cross-Sectional Data Collection in the Study of Crime and Delinquency."

32. Although the abuse of animals is not an object of her concern, similar complaints are made about problems with "cycle-of-violence" studies by Ferraro, *Neither Angels nor Demons*, pp. 111–12.

33. In 2008, the American Psychiatric Association identified physical cruelty to animals as a diagnostic criterion for conduct disorder. See American Psychiatric Association (2000), *Diagnostic and Statistical Manual of Mental Disorders* (4th ed.), p. 99.

34. Deborah Schurman-Kauflin (2000), *The New Predator: Women Who Kill*, pp. 119–24.

35. Jeremy Wright and Christopher Hanley (2003), "From Animal Cruelty to Serial Murder: Applying the Graduation Hypothesis."

36. Linda Merz-Perez and Kathleen M. Heide (2004), *Animal Cruelty: Pathway to Violence against People*.

37. David Tingle, George W. Barnard, Lynn Robbins, Gustave Newman, and David Hutchinson (1986), "Childhood and Adolescent Characteristics of Pedophiles and Rapists," p. 113; Pekka Santillo and Jaana Haapasalo (2001), "Neurological and Psychological Risk Factors among Young Homicidal, Violent and Nonviolent Offenders in Finland," p. 247; Merz-Perez et al., "Childhood Cruelty to Animals and Subsequent Violence against Humans." See also Lisa Anne Zilney (2007), *Linking Animal Cruelty and Animal Violence*. Using retrospective telephone questioning of 402 respondents derived from a needs assessment survey in Knox County, Tennessee, Zilney found partial confirmation of the progression thesis ("graduation hypothesis"). However, her methodology is not without difficulty, admittedly skewed as her sample is with an overrepresentation of southerners and those college educated and younger than the general population of Knox County.

38. R. Langevin, D. Paitich, B. Orchard, L. Handy, and A. Russon (1983), "Childhood and Family Background of Killers Seen for Psychiatric Assessment," p. 338.

39. This problem looms ominously and perhaps unrecognized for Merz–Perez and Heide, *Animal Cruelty*, who ask, at the end of their detailed study of the respective prior propensities for childhood animal cruelty of forty-five violent and forty-five nonviolent inmates of a Florida maximum-security prison, "Would the association of animal cruelty and human violence hold up if tested on a noninstitutionalized sample?" (p. 153). Also consider a study by Suzanne Goodney Lea (2007), *Delinquency and Animal Cruelty*, which was generated from a community sample of 570 young people in Bloomington, Indiana. While 14 percent of the sample reported having engaged in acts of animal cruelty when they were children and 25 to 35 percent or more reported having been involved in a range of other deviant acts as children, the study looked for but was unable to find any evidence that childhood animal cruelty is associated with violence during adulthood. Lea's study, however, might have had different results if it had either raised the age of her respondents or broadened the index of a "violent adult" as someone who "fights" or "fights with weapons."

40. Miller and Knutson, "Reports of Severe Physical Punishment and Exposure to Animal Cruelty by Inmates Convicted of Felonies and by University Students." A study of eleven diverse American cities found that in 276 cases of femicide or attempted femicide, the women were not statistically more likely to have had their pets hurt by their male assailants than were a control group of women in the same cities—J. McFarlane, J. Campbell, S. Wilt, C. Sachs, Y. Ulrich, and X. Xu (1999), "Stalking and Intimate Partner Femicide."

41. Arluke et al., "The Relationship of Animal Abuse to Violence and Other Forms of Antisocial Behavior." Similarly, interview data produced in a study of the precursors of late-onset criminality found that in only two of thirteen cases did adults with criminal convictions reveal that as children they were cruel to animals (James Elander, Michael Rutter, Emily Siminoff, and Andrew Pickles [2000], "Explanations for Apparent Late Onset Criminality in a High-Risk Sample of Children Followed Up in Adult Life").

42. Arluke et al., "The Relationship of Animal Abuse to Violence and Other Forms of Antisocial Behavior." This study advances the claim that deviance generalization is a more accurate characterization of animal abuse than the violence graduation hypothesis. The claim is structurally similar to one conclusion of the 1960s and 1970s testing of the progression thesis in the nonmedical use of drugs and alcohol. In that earlier research, some authors found, for example, that a progression did not exist from marijuana use to heroin use. Rather, for a complex variety of reasons, those who used heroin were more likely to have previously used an assortment of drugs, including amphetamines, barbiturates, hallucinogens, alcohol, and marijuana. See, for example, Government of Canada (1972), *Commission of Inquiry into the Non-Medical Use of Drugs*.

43. Some of this study's other difficulties, including its restricted range of forms of violence, are discussed by the authors themselves in Arluke et al., "The Relationship of Animal Abuse to Violence and Other Forms of Antisocial Behavior."

44. Miller and Knutson, "Reports of Severe Physical Punishment and Exposure to Animal Cruelty by Inmates Convicted of Felonies and by University Students," p. 74.

45. Arluke et al., "The Relationship of Animal Abuse to Violence and Other Forms of Antisocial Behavior," write that "we do provide some data indicating that graduation from late adolescence [i.e., from age seventeen and older] through adulthood, does not happen. If graduation does not occur in adulthood, it is reasonable to speculate that it also does not occur in childhood" (p. 970). But no evidence is offered in support of this speculation.

46. Arluke et al., "The Relationship of Animal Abuse to Violence and Other Forms of Antisocial Behavior," p. 966.

47. One study has found that from 200 randomly sampled animal abuse complaints received and investigated by the MSPCA in 1996, almost all involved medical (26 percent) or husbandry-related (62 percent) neglect. See Lori Donley, Gary J. Patronek, and Carter Luke (1999), "Animal Abuse in Massachusetts: A Summary of Case Reports at the MSPCA and Attitudes of Massachusetts Veterinarians."

48. Jason Wolfe (2000), "Suspect's Deal Holds Promise of Closure," p. A12.

49. International Association of Chiefs of Police (1989), "Cruelty to Animals and Human Violence," p. 2.

50. Kenneth White (1992), "The Shape of Cruelty," p. 6.

51. Anonymous (1993), "Alleged Serial Killer Thomas Lee Dillon," p. 17.

52. Robert Dvorchak (1991), "Dahmer's Troubled Childhood Offers Clues but No Simple Answers," p. A8.

53. Dvorchak, "Dahmer's Troubled Childhood Offers Clues but No Simple Answers," p. A8.

54. Lionel Dahmer (1994), A Father's Story, p. 54.

55. Myra Hindley (1995), "The Moors Murderess."

56. Arnold Arluke and Boria Sax (1992), "Understanding Nazi Animal Protection and the Holocaust"; Aleksander Lasik (1998), "Rudolf Höss: Manager of Crime," p. 288.

57. Daniel Goleman (1991), "Clues to a Dark Nurturing Ground for One Serial Killer," p. A8.

58. Dahmer, A Father's Story.

59. Foucault, I, Pierre Rivière, Having Slaughtered My Mother, My Sister, and My Brother . . ., p. 204.

60. USDA (2008), "Livestock Slaughter: 2005 Summary," National Agricultural Statistics Service, pp. 2–3, and USDA (2008), "Poultry Slaughter: 2007 Annual Summary," National Agricultural Statistics Service, pp. 2–3.

61. Injury rates in a variety of workplaces and industries, including those sustained in slaughterhouses ("meatpackers"), may be found in the U.S. Department of Labor's annual "Nonfatal Occupational Injuries and Illnesses." See also Roger Horowitz (2008), "That Was a Dirty Job! Technology and Workplace Hazards in Meatpacking over the Long Twentieth Century."

62. Gail A. Eisnitz (2007), *Slaughterhouse*, p. 87. See also, especially, Amy J. Fitzgerald (2006), "Spillover from 'The Jungle' into the Larger Community: Slaughterhouses and Increased Crime Rates." That slaughterhouses greatly reduce workers' compassion is confronted head-on in Jennifer Dillard (forthcoming), "A Slaughterhouse Nightmare: Psychological Harm Suffered by Slaughterhouse Employees and the Possibility of Redress through Legal Reform."

63. Eisnitz, *Slaughterhouse*, p. 87.

64. Eisnitz, *Slaughterhouse*, pp.87–88.

65. Eisnitz, *Slaughterhouse*, p. 88.

66. Flynn, "Animal Abuse in Childhood and Later Support for Interpersonal Violence in Families," p. 163. Ascione (2005), *Children and Animals: Exploring the Roots of Kindness and Cruelty*, has insightfully written that "if abusing animals both socializes children to engage in violence, and inhibits the development of empathy in children, then not only is animal abuse more likely to lead to interpersonal violence, but also animal abuse may relate to more accepting attitudes toward interpersonal violence." Specifically, he found that respondents who committed animal abuse during childhood were significantly more likely as adults to approve of corporal punishment and of violence against women and children in families (pp. 167–68). This was so even after other potential influences were controlled for, such as the frequency of corporal punishment received from both parents, race, gender, and belief in biblical literalism. See also Lyle Munro (2005), *Confronting Cruelty*, pp. 64–96, on animal rights "insider" accounts of the importance of developing compassion.

67. Although this corollary is probably true, no evidence clearly supports it. According to a postal questionnaire of 514 British adults, though there is a small but significant positive correlation between self-reported scores on human-oriented and animal-oriented emotional empathy, it was not found that the one preceded the other (Elizabeth S. Paul [2000], "Empathy with Animals and with Humans: Are They Linked?"). See also J. A. Serpell and E. S. Paul (1994), "Pets and the Development of Positive Attitudes to Animals." As Paul, "Empathy with Animals and with Humans," summarizes, "Past and present pet owning was associated with higher levels of animal-oriented but not human-oriented empathy, while child rearing was associated with higher levels of human-oriented but not animal-oriented empathy" (p. 199).

Epilogue

OVING BACKWARD IN TIME, for a moment, I wish to record that in the same month that Professor Peter Singer's libertine essay "Heavy Petting" appeared in the online magazine *Nerve*, in March 2001, I was preparing to give oral and written testimony to the Criminal Justice Committee of the Maine state legislature in favor of a bill (LD 1283) that would criminalize bestiality. The committee heard testimony in support of the bill from several groups and individuals. Among its supporters were concerned citizens, a prosecutor, licensed social workers, animal control officers, and a college professor (myself). It is fair to say that at the bill's public hearing testimony in favor of criminalization concentrated on three arguments: bestiality is a form of animal cruelty in and of itself; it is a form of violence linked to other forms of violence, particularly in the family; and it should be named animal sexual assault.

Only two opponents testified against the bill. One represented the Maine Civil Liberties Union. She opposed the bill not on its merits or lack thereof but because of her objection to the fact that prisons in Maine, like everywhere else in the United States, were already bursting at the seams. Her point was greeted with polite silence.

The bill's other opponent was a well-known male, B.P., age forty-four, from Parkman, Maine, who regarded his dog Lady as his spouse and who on his website and elsewhere had been quite candid about his sexual preferences for several years. (B.P. had also been at the center of a minor scandal as a result of an incident that led to his father, who vehemently disapproved of his son's union with his canine spouse, being charged with attempted murder and elevated aggravated assault. He had attacked his son with a crowbar. Following a plea bargain, the father was given an eight-year jail sentence, all but nine months of which were suspended.) In his impassioned testimony, this self-proclaimed zoophile positioned himself as a victim of a Maine citizenry that he alleged to be uneducated, puritanical, and, at root, prejudiced against his sexual preference for animals. According to B.P., unless it involves animal cruelty, there is nothing unnatural or wrong about sex with animals because it has been practiced for millennia, because animals are beloved family members and because, in his own case, he was certain that his dog assented to having sex with him and that she derived as much gratification from it as he did. He therefore insisted that he was a gendered minority whose rights were in need of protection.

None of these sentiments had been given much consideration beforehand by the thirteen members of the Criminal Justice Committee of the Maine legislature. The members' reactions to this event, as I and a bank of television cameras witnessed, were an uncomfortable mix of astonishment, anger, and embarrassment. Some of the committee members tried to shelter from public gaze their hitherto uncharted emotions on this issue by placing the palms of their hands over their faces. Others, at first gently but then with increasing gusto, rocked to and fro in their official, high-backed swivel chairs. This was a not-so-typical afternoon at the legislature. Eventually, Bill LD1283 was passed unanimously in the Maine house, and bestiality was designated a class D offense—those found guilty of violating its provisions would be liable to incarceration for a term of up to one year.

I relate this tale mainly to confess that my testimony against animal sexual assault I presented to the legislative committee with decidedly conflicting emotions. Yes, I oppose animal abuse and regard animal sexual assault as one of its forms. But two things in particular worried me. The first was that I feared that the movement to criminalize animal sexual assault did not have a great deal to do with the entry of some of the concerns of the animal protection community into the mainstream of American society. Rather, I feared that it reflected more a rightward shift in the state regulation of sexual practices between consenting human adults. In fact, in my support of the bill, I seemed to be standing shoulder to shoulder in the corridors of power as much with conservative proponents of family values (read: heterosexual and sex for procreation only) as with animal rights activists. In other words, it was unclear to me whether the forthcoming passage of the bill reflected pro-animal or pro-Christian values. Or was it, instead, a law-and-order attempt to widen the net of incarcerated deviants?

A view that I hope to have encouraged in this book is the simple one that the meaning of animal cruelty or animal rights legislation should never be taken at its self-stated face value. More often than not, humans' concern with animal abuse is motivated by human interests. Although I do not want to enter the debate of animal welfare versus animal rights here (somewhat of a silly polarization that smacks of 1918 Munich or 1968 Berkeley), it does seem pure folly to believe that animals' interests and rights can ever adequately be secured through legislative reform while their master status continues to be that of property. This is so not because, to paraphrase Rosa Luxembourg quite freely, (s)he who chooses the path of animal welfare in place of and in contradistinction to the victory of animal rights actually chooses not a calmer and a surer road to the same aim but a different aim altogether. Much more, it is that seemingly pro-animal regulation is a complex site that, when it is inserted into the legal arena, is capable of serving a multiplicity of human purposes, including notions of humanness, national and cultural chauvinism, and private profit. This more nuanced reading of anticruelty statutes is as true for seventeenth-century England, Ireland, and the Massachusetts Bay Colony as it was for Nazi Germany in the 1930s and 1940s. In the extreme case of the latter, a deeply racist discourse allowed strict laws regulating animal experimentation to exist side by side with a genocide that exterminated many millions of humans.

My first worry, then, about a proposed law to regulate animal sexual assault was the difficulty of deciding whether it was part of a progressive trajectory or a conservative one. In supporting a bill to criminalize a form of animal sexual abuse, I was also concerned, second, that I not contribute to the creation of yet another category of marginalized and incarcerated humans.

As someone who regularly tries to explore the intersection of animal rights, sociology, and green criminology, I am acutely aware that the animal rights movement has paid insufficient attention to the social control of animal abuse. It is true that if animal sexual assault, for example, is a harm that is objectionable for the same reasons as is an assault on one human by another—because it involves coercion, because it produces pain and suffering, and because it violates the rights of another being—then it would seem to constitute a sufficient condition for the censure of the human perpetrator. But the nature of that censure needs to be confronted directly. What sort of censure should it be and of what severity? Should the censure be formal or informal? Should culpability be strict, or should the scales of justice depend on such factors as the moral significance of what was done, the degree of harm, and the species of animal assaulted? Should animal-victims include all animals without exception or only those on the higher levels of the phylogenetic scale?

If the social censure of animal abuse involves incarceration, then should incarceration be part of some utilitarian calculus designed to control the future behavior of those convicted of crimes against animals? Might incarceration's rationale lie more in rehabilitation than in revenge or just deserts and retribution? Or in the get-them-off-the-street-through-incapacitation response? Having deep and longstanding sympathies for penal abolitionism, I am horrified by the fact that with only 5 percent of the world's population, the United States has 25 percent of the world's prison population. Indeed, a decade into the new millennium, the prison population in the United States is the largest it has ever been and the largest in the entire world. In 2008, there were considerably more than 2 million inmates in federal and state penitentiaries and in local jails, at an unprecedented rate of about 750 inmates per 100,0000 citizens. Not surprisingly, this exceptional harm is wrought disproportionately on the poor and on minorities.

So what is to be done? Less formal alternatives to criminalization and incarceration can perhaps be found in humane education and in the processes of conferencing and constructive shaming within the restorative justice movement. The chief stated aim of humane education, first, is the inculcation in children and adolescents of compassion toward animals. However, a serious drawback with the use of humane education as a form of social control of animal abuse is that today, in that majority of places where it is not compulsory, humane education typically begins for students in elementary school and then dies a quick death in secondary schools as it is seen as a luxury and inessential to business-driven curricula. To be successful, humane education would probably have to be universal, compulsory, and sustained over two or more generations.

For those who are not familiar with it, second, constructive shaming is also a type of (re-)education and tends to be the central tactical mechanism in the movement of restorative justice that began in New Zealand and Australia and that is based on directed conferencing with victims and offenders. During conferences, offenders are confronted by their victims and by their victims' friends and families in an effort to help them understand the harm that they have caused others through their wrongful actions or omissions. At the same time, victims are encouraged not to see offenders as vile and fixed objects of punitiveness but rather to understand them as existing somewhere between, on the one hand, authentic beings and, on the other, beings with damaged identities who likely did what they did because of sociological and psychological circumstances over which they had little or no control.

Yet it is hard to imagine how, even with their legendary flexibility and informality, restorative justice conferences could proceed when animals are the primary victims. Assuming that most animals are unlikely to sit, stand, or otherwise be attentive to the niceties of pro-animal arguments raised on their behalf in a conference about why their abuser should desist from abusing them in the future, who would represent animals' interests, and who would confer with whom and about what? Representatives from the Society for the Prevention of Cruelty to Animals? Veterinarians? Animal control officers? PETA? Pillars of the community?

Furthermore, suppose that through educative processes like humane education and constructive shaming, a cultural consensus could be established about the harmfulness of animal sexual assault and other forms of animal abuse. Suppose, in addition, that it was agreed that this principled liberation from human-induced harm was regarded as animals' right. Especially in self-avowed, property-owning democracies and in societies where individualism is energetically cultivated, for those animals who are kept in confinement by humans, the effectiveness of this right would unfortunately tend to be thwarted, if not altogether undermined, by the rival cultural powers associated with the right to enjoy their property and the right to privacy. (Not coincidentally, it is precisely these rival rights that men often invoke when they abuse women and children.) The right to privacy would tend to undermine the detection and prosecution of animal sexual assault. The right to property would be invoked to defend it. As members of the animal rights movement often argue for animals and against the latter, those who wish to ascribe rights to animals, including the right to respectful treatment, would eventually be forced to challenge the very existence of animals as property.

One must wonder, too, whether in the assignation of rights to animals lie some of the same problems as those entailed in human rights. If one thing is known definitively about human rights, it is that law on the books all too often has little bearing on law in action. Among the problems facing animal rights, in particular, are that their claims to universality are vulnerable to objections from cultural relativism and postmodernism—that, once acquired both in principle and in law, they are in practice individualist notions that do little to aid the plight of all their bearers. This book has shown that there is often a great selectivity at work in what species count as worthy of protection, that they are abstract and formal rights with no necessary substantive content, and that, if enacted, they might not be enforced either because violations of them are not reported to lawful authorities or because they are not seen as real harms (or "real crime").

If violations of animals' rights are to be taken seriously, I recommend that activists and scholars could profitably examine why some harms to animals are defined as criminal, others as abusive but not criminal, and still others as neither criminal nor abusive. In exploring these questions, a narrow concept of crimes against animals would necessarily have to be rejected in favor of a more inclusive concept of harm. Without it, the meaning of animal abuse will be overwhelmingly confined to those harms that are regarded as socially unacceptable, one-on-one cases of animal cruelty. Certainly, those cases demand attention. But so, too, do those other and far more numerous institutionalized harms to animals, where abuse is routine, invisible, ubiquitous, and often defined as socially acceptable.

Appendix 1

Act Against Plowing by the Tayle and
Pulling the Wooll off Living Sheep
(Ireland, 1635)

None shall plow or work horses by the tail.

WHEREAS in many places of this kingdome, there hath been a long time used a barbarous custome of ploughing, harrowing, drawing and working with horses, mares, geldings, garrans and colts, by the taile, whereby (besides the cruelty used to the beasts) the breed of horses is much impaired in this kingdome, to the great prejudice thereof:

Barbarity of the custom, a prejudice to the breed of horses.

and whereas also divers have and yet do use the like barbarous custome of pulling off the wool yearly from living sheep in stead of clipping or shearing of them; be it therefore enacted by the Kings's most excellent Majesty, and the lords spirituall and temporall, and

The commons in this present Parliament assembled, that no person or persons whatsoever, shall after one yeare next ensuing the end of this present Parliament, plough, harrow, draw or worke with any horse, gelding, mare, garran or colt, by the taile, nor shall cause, procure or suffer any other to plough up or harrow his ground, or to draw any other carriages with his horses, mares, geldings, garrans or colts, or any of them, by the taile;

None shall instead of shearing or clipping, pull off the wool from living sheep.

and that no person or persons whatsoever, shall, after the end of this present Parliament, pull the wool off any living sheep, or cause or procure to be pulled, instead of shearing or clipping of them;

Justices of assize and of the peace may inquire and punish by fine and imprisonment.

and if any shall doe contrarie to this act, and the intention thereof, that the justices of assize at the generall assizes to be holden before them, and the justices of peace at their quarter-sessions, shall have power by this act to enquire of, heare and determine all and every offence and offences done contrary to this present act, and to punish the offendors which shall do contrary to the same, by fine and imprisonment, as they in their discretion shall think fit.

Source: The Statutes at Large, Passed in the Parliaments held in Ireland, 1310–1761 (1765), vol. 2, pp. 168–69. Dublin: Boulter Grierson.

Appendix 2

Act to prevent the custom of burning of corne in the straw
(Ireland, 1635)

"Bad effects of improvident husbandry"

Whereas there is in the remote parts of the kingdome of Ireland, commonly a great dearth of cattell yearly, which for the most part happened by reason of the ill husbandrie and improvident care of the owners, that neither provide fodder, not stover for them in winter, nor houses to put them in extremitie of stormy cold weather, but a natural lazie disposition possessing them, that will not build barnes to house and thresh their corne in, or houses to keep their cattell from the violence of such weather, but the better to enable them to be flitting from their lands, and to deceive his Majestie of such debts as they may be owing at any time, and their landlords of their rents, doe for a great part instead of threshing burn their corn in the straw, thereby consuming the straw, which might relieve their cattell in winter, and afford materials towards the covering or thatching their houses, and spoiling the corne, making it black, loathsome and filthy . . . (none shall burn corn or grain in the straw), Penalty, ten days imprisonment for first offence and to pay the charges.

Source: The Statutes at Large, Passed in the Parliaments held in Ireland, 1310–1761 (1765), vol. 2, p. 171. Dublin: Boulter Grierson.

Appendix 3

"Of the Bruite Creature"

92 No man shall exercise any Tirranny or Crueltie
towards any bruite Creature which are usuallie
kept for man's use.

93 If any man shall have occasion to leade or drive
Cattel from place to place that is far of, so
That they be weary, or hungry, or fall sick, or
lambe, It shall be lawful to rest or refresh
them, for a competent time, in any open place
that is not Corne, meadow, or inclosed for some peculiar use.

Source: Laws of the Massachusetts Colony, from 1630 to 1686, a Bibliographical Sketch, in Which are Included the Body of Liberties of 1641 (1890), pp. 29–64. Edited by William H. Whitmore. Boston: Rockwell and Churchill.

Bibliography

Statutes and Other Laws

Britain

1533   "Act for the Punysshement of the Vice of Buggerie," 25 Hen. VIII, c.6.

1617   "Proclamation Against Pulling Wool from Sheep Instead of Clipping It." P.285, vol. II, p. 285, in *A Bibliography of Royal Proclamations of the Tudor and Stuart Sovereigns, 1485–1714*. New York: Burt Franklin.

1654   *Ordinance for Prohibiting Cock-matches*. P. 861 in *Acts and Ordinances of the Interregnum, 1642–1660* (1911).

1822   "Act to prevent cruel and improper Treatment of Cattle," 3, Geo IV, c.71.

Ireland

1635   *Act Against Plowing by the Tayle and Pulling the Wooll off Living Sheep*. Pp. 168–69, vol. 2, of *The Statutes at Large, Passed in the Parliaments held in Ireland, 1310–1761* (1765). Dublin: Boulter Grierson.

1635   "Act to prevent the custom of burning of corne in the straw." P. 171, vol. 2, of *The Statutes at Large, Passed in the Parliaments held in Ireland, 1310–1761* (1765). Dublin: Boulter Grierson.

Colonial America

1641   "Body of Liberties of 1641." Pp. 29–64 in *Laws of the Massachusetts Colony, from 1630 to 1686, a Bibliographical Sketch* (1890). Edited by William H. Whitmore. Boston: Rockwell and Churchill.

1641   "Of the Bruite Creature". P. 53 in *Laws of the Massachusetts Colony, from 1630 to 1686, a Bibliographical Sketch* (1890). Edited by William H. Whitmore. Boston: Rockwell and Churchill.

1647   *Providence Colony: The Code of Laws: The Proceedings of the First General Assembly.* (1847). Edited by William R. Staples. Providence: Charles Burnett.

1648   *Charters and General Laws of the Colony and Province of Massachusetts Bay 1648* (1814). Boston: T. B. Wait.

1650   *General Laws and Liberties of Connecticut Colonie.* In vol. 1 of *The Public Records of the Colony of Connecticut, 1636–1665* (1850). Edited by Charles J. Hoadly: Brown and Parsons.

Geneva
1562   *Laws and Statutes of Geneva* (1999). Ann Arbor: University of Michigan Press.

Books and Articles
Abel, Gene G., Judith V. Becker, Mary Mittelman, Jerry Cunningham-Rathner, Joanne L. Rouleau, and William D. Murphy (1987). "Self-Reported Sex Crimes of Nonincarcerated Paraphiliacs." *Journal of Interpersonal Violence* 2(1):3–25.

Adams, Carol J. (1990). "Deena—The World's Only Stripping Chimp." *Animals' Voice Magazine* 3(1):72.

———. (1994). *Neither Man nor Beast: Feminism and the Defense of Animals.* New York: Continuum.

———. (1995a). "Bestiality: the Unmentioned Abuse." *The Animals' Agenda* 15(6):29–31.

———. (1995b). "Woman-Battering and Harm to Animals." Pp. 55–84 in Carol J. Adams and Josephine Donovan (eds.), *Animals and Women: Feminist Theoretical Explorations.* Durham, NC: Duke University Press.

———. (2003). *The Sexual Politics of Meat: A Feminist-Vegetarian Critical Theory.* New York: Continuum.

Adams, Carol J., and Josephine Donovan, eds. (1995). "Introduction." Pp. 1–8 in *Animals and Women: Feminist Theoretical Explorations.* Durham, NC: Duke University Press.

Aelian. [ca. 1840 B.P.] (1958–1959). *On the Characteristics of Animals.* Translated by A. F. Scholfield. Cambridge, MA: Harvard University Press.

Agnew, Robert. (1998). "The Causes of Animal Abuse: A Social Psychological Analysis." *Theoretical Criminology* 2(2):177–210.

Alagappan, Meena. (2003). *Expanding Humane Education: The Development of "Animals and Society" Courses in Liberal Arts Colleges.* M.S. thesis, Tufts University.

American Psychiatric Association. (2000). *Diagnostic and Statistical Manual of Mental Disorders* (4th ed., text revision). Washington, DC: American Psychiatric Association.

Anderson, Virginia DeJohn. (2004). *Creatures of Empire: How Domestic Animals Transformed Early America*. Oxford: Oxford University Press.

Annals of Connacht. [1224–1544] (1996). Edited by A. Martin Freeman. Dublin: Dublin Institute for Advanced Studies.

Anonymous. (1643). "A perfect Diurnal of some Passages of Parliament, and from other Parts of the Kingdom, from Monday July 24th, to Monday July 31st, 1643 (Wednesday July 26th)," Bodleian Library, microfiche, unit 24, reel 1194, p. 26.

———. (1653). "Advertisement from London, last day of February, 1653." Bodleian Library, Carte MSS, 131B, fol. 184v.

———. (1840). "May 21." *Antiquarian Researches*, pp. 634–36.

———. (1993). "Alleged Serial Killer Thomas Lee Dillon." *Animal People* (January/February), p.17.

Aquinas, Thomas. [1265–1274] (1968). *Summa Theologica*. 42 vols. London: Eyre and Spottiswoode.

Archer, John E. (1985). "A Fiendish Outrage? A Study of Animal Maiming in East Anglia: 1830–1870," *Agricultural History Review* 33 (II): 147–157.

———. (1990). *By a Flash and a Scare: Incendiarism, Animal Maiming and Poaching in East Anglia*. Oxford: Clarendon Press.

Arkow, Phil. (1994). "Child Abuse, Animal Abuse, and the Veterinarian." *Journal of the American Veterinary Medical Association* 2047:226–47.

Arluke, Arnold, and Boria Sax. (1992). "Understanding Nazi Animal Protection and the Holocaust." *Anthrozöos* 5(1):6–31.

Arluke, Arnold, Jack Levin, Carter Luke, and Frank Ascione. (1999). "The Relationship of Animal Abuse to Violence and Other Forms of Antisocial Behavior." *Journal of Interpersonal Violence* 14(9):963–75.

Ascione, Frank R. (1998). "Battered Women's Reports of Their Partners' and Their Children's Cruelty to Animals." *Journal of Emotional Abuse* 11:120–33.

———. (2001). *Animal Abuse and Youth Violence*. Washington, DC: U.S. Department of Justice, Office of Juvenile Justice and Delinquency Prevention.

———. (2005). *Children and Animals: Exploring the Roots of Kindness and Cruelty*. West Lafayette, IN: Purdue University Press.

Ascione, Frank R., Claudia V. Weber, Teresa M. Thompson, John Heath, Mika Maruyama, and Kentaro Hayashi. (2007). "Battered Pets and Domestic Violence: Animal Abuse Reported by Women Experiencing Intimate Violence and by Nonabused Women." *Violence Against Women* 13(4):354–73.

Ascione, Frank R., Claudia V. Weber, and David S. Wood. (1997). "The Abuse of Animals and Domestic Violence: A National Survey of Shelters for Women Who Are Battered." *Society & Animals* 5(3):205–18.

Bagwell, Richard. (1909). *Ireland under the Stuarts and during the Interregnum.* 3 vols. London: Longmans, Green.

Balcombe, J. (1999). "Animals and Society Courses: A Growing Trend in Post-Secondary Education." *Society & Animals* 7(3):229–40.

Baldry, Anna. (2003). "Animal Abuse and Exposure to Interparental Violence in Italian Youth." *Journal of Interpersonal Violence* 18(3):258–81.

Beattie, J. M. (1986). *Crime and the Courts in England, 1660–1800.* Princeton: Princeton University Press.

Bede, Cuthbert. (1878). "Note." *Notes and Queries* x(5):503.

Beers, Diane L. (2006). *For the Prevention of Cruelty: The History and Legacy of Animal Rights Activism in the United States.* Athens: Swallow Press/Ohio University Press.

Beetz, Andrea M. (2005). "New Insights into Bestiality and Zoophilia." Pp. 98–119 in Andrea M. Beetz and Anthony L. Podberscek (eds.), *Bestiality and Zoophilia.* West Lafayette, IN: Purdue University Press.

Beidelman, T. O. (1961). "Kaguru Justice and the Concept of Legal Fictions." *Journal of African Law* 5:11–14.

Beirne, Piers. (1993). *Inventing Criminology: The Rise of "Homo Criminalis."* Albany: State University of New York Press.

———. (2001). "Peter Singer's 'Heavy Petting' and the Politics of Animal Sexual Assault." *Journal of Critical Criminology* 10(1):43–55.

———. (2007). "Animal Rights, Animal Abuse and Green Criminology." Pp. 55–83 in Piers Beirne and Nigel South (eds.), *Issues in Green Criminology.* Cullompton: Willan.

Beirne, Piers, and Nigel South. (2007). "Approaching Green Criminology." Pp. xiii–xxii in Piers Beirne and Nigel South (eds.), *Issues in Green Criminology: Confronting Harms against Environments, Humanity and Other Animals.* Cullompton: Willan.

Bell, Jonathan. (1987). "The Improvement of Irish Farming Techniques since 1750: Theory and Practice." Pp. 24–41 in Patrick O'Flanagan, Paul Ferguson, and Kevin Whelan (eds.), *Rural Ireland 1600–1900: Modernisation and Change.* Cork: Cork University Press.

Bell, Lorna. (2001). "Abusing Children—Abusing Animals." *Journal of Social Work* 1(2):223–34.

Bentham, Jeremy. [1785] (1978). "Essay on 'Paederasty,' Part 2." *Journal of Homosexuality* 4(1):91–107.

Benton, Ted. (2007). "Ecology, Community and Justice: The Meaning of Green." Pp. 3–31 in Piers Beirne and Nigel South (eds.), *Issues in Green Criminology: Confronting Harms against Environments, Humanity and Other Animals.* Uffculme: Willan.

Bewick, Thomas. (1885). *A General History of Quadrupeds.* Newcastle-upon-Tyne: R. Ward & Sons.

Blackstone, William. [1769] (1966). *Commentaries on the Laws of England.* 4 vols. New York: Oceana Publications.

Blake, John B. (1959). *Public Health in the Town of Boston, 1630–1822.* Cambridge, MA: Harvard University Press.

Blechman, Andrew D. (2006). *Pigeons: The Fascinating Saga of the World's Most Revered and Reviled Bird.* New York: Grove Press.

Boat, Barbara. (1999). "Abuse of Children and Abuse of Animals." Pp. 83–100 in Frank R. Ascione and Phil Arkow (eds.), *Child Abuse, Domestic Violence, and Animal Abuse.* West Lafayette, IN: Purdue University Press.

Bolliger, G., and A. F. Goetschel. (2005). "Sexual Relations with Animals (Zoophilia): An Unrecognized Problem in Animal Welfare Legislation." Pp. 23–45 in A. M. Beetz and A. L. Podberscek (eds.), *Bestiality and Zoophilia: Sexual Relations with Animals.* West Lafayette, IN: Purdue University Press.

Boswell, John. (1980). *Christianity, Social Tolerance, and Homosexuality.* Chicago: University of Chicago Press.

Box, Steven. (1983). *Power, Crime, and Mystification.* London: Tavistock.

Boxer, Sarah. (2001). "Op-Ed Piece." *New York Times,* June 9, p. A19.

Bozeman, Theodore Dwight. (1988). *To Live Ancient Lives: The Primitivist Dimension in Puritanism.* Chapel Hill: University of North Carolina Press.

Bradford, William. [1650] (1856). *History of Plymouth Plantation.* Boston: Little, Brown.

Breen, T. H. (1980). *Puritans and Adventurers: Change and Persistence in Early America.* New York: Oxford University Press.

Brewer, James Norris. (1826). *The Beauties of Ireland: Being Original Delineations, Topographical, Historical and Biographical, of Each County.* London: Sherwood, Gilbery, & Piper.

Brooman, Simon, and Debbie Legge. (1997). *Law Relating to Animals.* London: Cavendish.

Brown, Julia. (1952). "A Comparative Study of Deviations from Sexual Mores." *American Sociological Review* 17 (2): 135–146.

Browne, Angela. (1987). *When Battered Women Kill.* New York: Free Press.

Brundage, James A. (1987). *Law, Sex, and Christian Society in Medieval Europe.* Chicago: University of Chicago Press.

Bullough, Vern L., and Bonnie Bullough. (1977). *Sin, Sickness, and Sanity.* New York: Garland.

Calendar of State Papers, Ireland 1509–1670 (1860–1912). 24 vols. (1611–1641 vol. edited by C. W. Russell and John Prendergast). London: H.M.S.O.

Calvin, John. [1562] (1999). *The Laws and Statutes of Geneva.* London: Rouland Hall and Thomas Hacket (electronic reproduction, Ann Arbor: University of Michigan Press).

———. [1541–1559] (1960). *Institutes of the Christian Religion.* Edited by John T. McNeill. Translated by Ford Lewis Battles. 2 vols. Philadelphia: Westminster.

———. [n.d.] (1958). *Commentaries.* Translated by Joseph Haroutunian. Philadelphia: Westminster.

Cambrensis, Giraldus. (1863). *Historical Works.* Edited by Thomas Wright. London: H. G. Bohn.

———. [1176–1199] (1982). *The History and Topography of Ireland.* Translated by John J. O'Meara. London: Penguin.

Campion, Edmunde. [1633] (1963). *Two Bookes of the Histories of Ireland.* Amsterdam: Van Gorcum.

Canny, Nicholas. (1976). *The Elizabethan Conquest of Ireland: A Pattern Established, 1565–76.* Hassocks: Harvester Press.

———. (2006). *Making Ireland British 1580–1650.* Oxford: Oxford University Press.

Canny, Nicholas, and Anthony Pagden, eds. (1987). *Colonial Identity in the Atlantic World, 1500–1800.* Princeton, NJ: Princeton University Press.

Canup, John. (1988). "The Cry of Sodom Enquired Into: Bestiality and the Wilderness of Human Nature in Seventeenth-Century New England." *American Antiquarian Society* 98(1):113–31.

———. (1990). *Out of the Wilderness: The Emergence of an American Identity in Colonial New England.* Middletown, CT: Wesleyan University Press.

Carmichael, Calum M. (2006). *Law, Legend and Incest in the Bible: Leviticus 18–20.* Baltimore: Johns Hopkins University Press.

Carrabine, E., P. Iganski, M. Lee, K. Plummer, and N. South. (2004). *Criminology: A Sociological Introduction.* London: Routledge.

Carson, Gerald. (1972). *Men, Beasts, and Gods: A History of Cruelty and Kindness to Animals.* New York: Charles Scribner's Sons.

Cartmill, Matthew. (1993). *A View to a Death in the Morning: Hunting and Nature through History.* Cambridge, MA: Harvard University Press.

Cazaux, Geertrui. (1999). "Beauty and the Beast: Animal Abuse from a Nonspeciesist Criminological Perspective."

———. (1999). "Anthropocentrism and Speciesism regarding Animals Other than Human Animals in Contemporary Criminology." Unpublished PhD diss., Faculty of Law, University of Ghent.

———. (2007). "Labelling Animals: Non-Speciesist Criminology and Techniques to Identify Other Animals." Pp. 87–113 in Piers Beirne and Nigel South (eds.), *Issues in Green Criminology.* Cullompton: Willan.

———, and Piers Beirne. (2001). "Animal Abuse." Pp. 8–10 in E. McLaughlin and J. Muncie (eds.), *Sage Dictionary of Criminology.* London: Sage.

Cerrone, Gerald H. (1991). "Zoophilia in a Rural Population: Two Case Studies." *Journal of Rural Community Psychology* 12(1):29-39.

Chapin, Bradley. (1983). *Criminal Justice in Colonial America, 1606–1660.* Athens: University of Georgia Press.

Clark, Stephen. (1977). *The Moral Status of Animals.* Oxford: Clarendon.

Clarke, Aidan. (1976). "The Government of Wentworth, 1632–40." Pp. 243–69 in T. W. Moody, F. X. Martin, and F. J. Byrne (eds.), *A New History of Ireland.* Oxford: Clarendon.

————. (1966). *The Old English in Ireland, 1603–1660.* 8 vols. London: MacGibbon & Kee.

Clinard, Marshall B. (1952). *The Black Market: A Study of White Collar Crime.* New York: Rinehart.

Code of Nesilim. [ca. 3500 B.C.] (1901). Pp. 9–11 in Oliver J. Thatcher (ed.), *The Library of Original Resources.* Milwaukee, WI: University Research Extension Co.

Cohen, Stanley. (1980). *Folk Devils and Moral Panics.* New York: St. Martin's.

Coke, Edward. [1628] (1681). *The Third Part of the Institutes of the Laws of England.* London: Thomas Basset.

Coleman, Jon T. (2004). *Vicious: Wolves and Men in America.* New Haven, CT: Yale University Press.

Collard, Andrée, with Joyce Contrucci. (1989). *Rape of the Wild.* Bloomington: Indiana University Press.

Collins, Anne-Marie. (1991). "Woman or Beast? Bestiality in Queensland, 1870–1949." *Hecate* 17(1):36–42.

Cooper, Alvin, Coralie R. Scherer, Sylvain C. Boies, and Barry L. Gordon. (1999). "Sexuality on the Internet: From Sexual Exploration to Pathological Expression." *Professional Psychology: Research and Practice* 30(22):155–64.

Coughlan, P. (1990). "'Cheap and Common Animals': The English Anatomy of Ireland in the Seventeenth Century." Pp. 205–23 in T. Healy and J. Sawday (eds.), *Literature and the English Civil War.* Cambridge: Cambridge University Press.

Croall, Hazel. (2007). "Food Crime." Pp. 206–29 in Piers Beirne and Nigel South (eds.), *Issues in Green Criminology.* Cullompton: Willan.

Cronon, William. (1983). *Changes in the Land: Indians, Colonists, and the Ecology of New England.* New York: Hill and Wang.

Cunningham, Bernadette. (1986), "Native Culture and Political Change in Ireland, 1580–1640." Pp. 148–70 in Ciaran Brady and Raymond Gillespie (eds.), *Natives and Newcomers: Essays on the Making of Irish Colonial Society 1534–1641.* Dublin: Irish Academic Press.

Dadds, Mark R., Cynthia M. Turner, and John McAloon. (2002). "Developmental Links between Cruelty to Animals and Human Violence." *Australian and New Zealand Journal of Criminology* 35(3):363–82.

Dahmer, Lionel. (1994). *A Father's Story.* New York: W. Morrow.

Darnton, Robert. (1999). *The Great Cat Massacre and Other Episodes in French Cultural History.* New York: Basic Books/Perseus Group.

Davidson, Arnold J. (1991). "The Horror of Monsters." Pp. 36–67 in James J. Sheehan and Morton Sosna (eds.), *The Boundaries of Humanity: Humans, Animals, Machines.* Berkeley: University of California Press.

Davies, Christine. (1998). "They Save Horses, Don't They?" *The Big Issue, Cymru,* p. 9.

Dekkers, Midas. (1994). *Dearest Pet.* Translated by Paul Vincent. London: Verso.

Desiderata Curiosa Hibernica. (1772). 2 vols. Dublin: David Hay.

Deviney, Elizabeth, Jeffery Dickert, and Randall Lockwood. (1983). "The Care of Pets within Child Abusing Families." *International Journal for the Study of Animal Problems* 4(4):321–29.

Dillard, Jennifer. (forthcoming). "A Slaughterhouse Nightmare: Psychological Harm Suffered by Slaughterhouse Employees and the Possibility of Redress through Legal Reform." *Georgetown Journal on Poverty Law and Policy* 15(2).

Dineley, Thomas. [1680] (1893). "Dineley's Journal." Pp. 534–54 in James Frost (ed.), *The History and Topography of the County of Clare from the Earliest Times to the Beginning of the 18th Century.* Dublin: Sealy, Bryers & Walker.

Donley, Lori, Gary J. Patronek, and Carter Luke. (1999). "Animal Abuse in Massachusetts: A Summary of Case Reports at the MSPCA and Attitudes of Massachusetts Veterinarians." *Journal of Applied Animal Welfare Science* 2(1):59–73.

Donovan, Josephine. (1990). "Animal Rights and Feminist Theory." *Signs* 15(2):350–75.

———. (2006). "Feminism and the Treatment of Animals: From Care to Dialogue." *Signs* 31(2):305–29.

Donovan, Josephine, and Carol J. Adams. (1996). *Beyond Animal Rights: A Feminist Caring Ethic for the Treatment of Animals.* New York: Continuum.

Douglas, Mary. (1984). *Purity and Danger: An Analysis of the Concepts of Pollution and Taboo.* London: ARK Paperbacks.

Drape, Joe. (2006). "Now Is a Time for Healing, for Barbaro and for Matz." *New York Times*, May 25, p. C16.

Dubois-Desaulle, Gaston. (1933). *Bestiality: An Historical, Medical, Legal and Literary Study.* Translated by "A.F.N." New York: Panurge.

Dunayer, Joan. (2004). *Speciesism.* Derwood, MD: Ryce Publishing.

Durkheim, Èmile. (1894). *The Rules of Sociological Method.* Edited and introduced by Steven Lukes. Translated by W. D. Halls. London: Macmillan.

Dvorchak, Robert. (1991). "Dahmer's Troubled Childhood Offers Clues but No Simple Answers." *Dallas Times Herald*, August 11, pp. A6 and A8.

Eisnitz, Gail A. (2007). *Slaughterhouse: The Shocking Story of Greed, Neglect, and Inhumane Treatment inside the U.S. Meat Industry.* Amherst, NY: Prometheus Books.

Elander, James, Michael Rutter, Emily Siminoff, and Andrew Pickles. (2000). "Explanations for Apparent Late Onset Criminality in a High-Risk Sample of Children Followed Up in Adult Life." *British Journal of Criminology* 40(3):497–509.

Elias, Norbert. (2000). *The Civilizing Process.* Translated by Edmund Jephcott. New York: Wiley.

Elias, Norbert, and Eric Dunning (1985). *The Quest for Excitement: Sport and Leisure in the Civilizing Process.* Oxford: Basil Blackwell.

Erikson, Kai T. (1986). *Wayward Puritans: A Study in the Sociology of Deviance.* New York: Wiley.

Evans, E. E. 1976. "Some Problems of Irish Ethnography: the Example of Ploughing by the Tail." Pp. 30–39 in Caoimhín Ó Danachair (ed.), *Folk & Farm: Essays in Honour of A. T. Lucas.* Dublin: Royal Society of Antiquaries.

Evans, E. P. (1906). *The Criminal Prosecution and Capital Punishment of Animals.* New York: E.P. Dutton and Company.

Faber, Eli. (1978). "Puritan Criminals: The Economic, Social, and Intellectual Background to Crime in Seventeenth-Century Massachusetts." *Perspectives in American History*, vol. 9. Cambridge, MA: Harvard University Crimson Printing Co.

Faller, Kathleen Coulborn. (1990). *Understanding Child Sexual Maltreatment.* Newbury Park, CA: Sage.

Favre, David, and Vivien Tsang. (1993). The Development of Anti-Cruelty Laws during the 1800s. *Detroit College of Law Review* 1:1–35.

Fenton, Alexander. (1976). "The Light and Improved Scots Plough." Pp. 40–53 in Caoimhín Ó Danachair (ed.), *Folk and Farm: Essays in Honour of A. T. Lucas.* Dublin: Royal Society of Antiquaries.

———. (1978). *The Northern Isles: Orkney and Shetland.* Edinburgh: John Donald.

Ferguson, Moira. (1998). *Animal Advocacy and Englishwomen, 1780–1900: Patriots, Nation, and Empire.* Ann Arbor: University of Michigan Press.

Ferraro, Kathleen J. (2006). *Neither Angels nor Demons: Women, Crime and Victimization.* Boston: Northeastern University Press.

Finkelhor, David, and Linda Meyer Williams with Nanci Burns. (1988). *Nursery Crimes: Sexual Abuse in Day Care.* Newbury Park, CA: Sage.

Fischer, David. (1989). *Albion's Seed: Four British Folkways in America.* Oxford: Oxford University Press.

Fitzgerald, Amy J. (2006). "Spillover from 'The Jungle' into the Larger Community: Slaughterhouses and Increased Crime Rates." PhD diss., Michigan State University.

Fleismann, Sigmund. (1968). *Bestiality: Sexual Intercourse between Men and Women and Animals.* Translated by Robert Harris. Baltimore: Medical Knowledge Press.

Flynn, Clifton P. (1999). "Animal Abuse in Childhood and Later Support for Interpersonal Violence in Families." *Society & Animals* 7(2):161–72.

———. (2000a). "Battered Women and Their Animal Companions: Symbolic Interaction Between Human and Nonhuman Animals." *Society & Animals* 8(2):100–127.

———. (2000b). "Woman's Best Friend: Pet Abuse and the Role of Companion Animals in the Lives of Battered Women." *Violence Against Women* 6(2):162–77.

Forbes, Thomas R. (1973). "London-Coroner's Inquests for 1590." *Journal of the History of Medicine and Allied Sciences* 28(4):376–86.

Foster, Stephen. (1971). *Their Solitary Way: The Puritan Social Ethic in the First Century of Settlement in New England*. New Haven, CT: Yale University Press.

Foucault, Michel, ed. (1975). *I, Pierre Rivière, Having slaughtered my mother, my sister, and my brother . . .* Translated by Frank Jellinek. Lincoln: University of Nebraska Press.

Fowler, P. J. (1969). "Early Prehistoric Agriculture in Western Europe: Some Archaeological Evidence." Pp. 153–82 in D. D. A. Simpson (ed.), *Economy and Settlement in Neolithic and Early Bronze Age Britain and Europe*. Leicester: Leicester University Press.

Francione, Gary L. (1996). *Rain without Thunder: The Ideology of the Animal Rights Movement*. Philadelphia: Temple University Press.

———. (2004). *Animals, Property and the Law*. Philadelphia: Temple University Press.

———. (2008). *Animals as Persons: Essays on the Abolition of Animal Exploitation*. New York: Columbia University Press.

Franklin, Adrian. (1999). *Animals and Modern Cultures: A Sociology of Human-Animal Relations in Modernity*. London: Sage.

Friedman, Lawrence. (1993). *Crime and Punishment in American History*. New York: Basic Books.

Friedrich, William N., Anthony J. Urquiza, and Robert L. Beilke. (1986). "Behavior Problems in Sexually Abused Young Children." *Journal of Pediatric Psychology* 11(1):47–57.

Fudge, Erica. (2002). *Perceiving Animals: Humans and Beasts in Early Modern English Culture*. Carbondale: University of Illinois Press.

———. (2006). *Brutal Reasoning: Animals, Rationality, and Humanity in Early Modern England*. Ithaca, NY: Cornell University Press.

Fumerton, Patricia. (1999). "Introduction: A New New Historicism." Pp. 1–17 in Patricia Fumerton and Simon Hunt (eds.), *Renaissance Culture and the Everyday*. Philadelphia: University of Pennsylvania Press.

Garner, Robert. (2005). "Feminism and Animals." Pp. 147–56 in *The Political Theory of Animal Rights*. Manchester: Manchester University Press.

Gerbasi, Kathleen C. (2004). "Gender and Nonhuman Animal Cruelty Convictions: Data from Pet-Abuse.com." *Society & Animals* 12(4):359–65.

Gibson, Owen. (2007). "Interview with Christopher." *Guardian*, October 8, p. 5.

Gillespie, Raymond. (1985). *Colonial Ulster: The Settlement of East Ulster 1600–1641*. Cork: Cork University Press.

———. (1995). "Dissenters and Conformists, 1661–1700." Pp. 11–28 in Kevin Herlihy (ed.), *The Irish Dissenting Tradition*. Dublin: Four Courts Press.

———. (2006). *Seventeenth-Century Ireland*. Dublin: Gill and Macmillan.

Gilligan, Carol. (1982). "In a Different Voice." *Psychological Theory and Women's Development*. Cambridge, MA: Harvard University Press.

Godlovich, Stanley, Roslind Godlovitch, and John Harris, eds. (1974). *Animals, Men and Morals*. New York: Grove Press.

Gold, M. (1993). "Straight from the Horse's Mouth." *Animal Aid Report*, August.

———. (1995). *Animal Rights: Extending the Circle of Compassion*. Oxford: Carpenter.

———. (1996). "Racing's Dead End." *Outrage, the Magazine of Animal Aid*, December/January.

Goleman, Daniel. (1991). "Clues to a Dark Nurturing Ground for One Serial Killer." *New York Times*, August 7, p. A8.

Goodich, Michael. (1979). *The Unmentionable Vice: Homosexuality in the Later Medieval Period*. Santa Barbara, CA: Clio.

Government of Canada. (1972). *Commission of Inquiry into the Non-Medical Use of Drugs*. Ottawa: Canadian Government Information.

Graham, Elspeth. (2004). "Reading, Writing, and Riding Horses in Early Modern England." Pp. 116–37 in Erica Fudge (ed.), *Renaissance Beasts: Of Animals, Humans and Other Wonderful Creatures*. Urbana: University of Illinois Press.

Gregor, Walter. (1883). "Some Old Farming Customs and Notions in Aberdeenshire." *Folk-Lore Journal* 2(11):329–32.

Griffin, Emma. (2005). *England's Revelry: A History of Popular Sports and Pastimes 1660–1830*. Oxford: Oxford University Press.

Guymer, E. C., D. Mellor, E. S. L. Luk, and V. Pearse. (2001). "The Development of a Screening Questionnaire for Childhood Cruelty to Animals." *Journal of Childhood Psychology and Psychiatry* 42:1057–63.

Haraway, Donna. (2004). *The Haraway Reader*. New York: Routledge.

Haskins, George L., and Samuel E. Ewing. (1969). "The Spread of Massachusetts Law in the Seventeenth Century." Pp. 186–91 in David H. Flaherty (ed.), *Essays in the History of Early American Law*. Chapel Hill: University of North Carolina Press.

Hay, Douglas. (1975). "Poaching and the Game Laws on Cannock Chase." Pp. 189–253 in Douglas Hay, Peter Linebaugh, John G. Rule, E. P. Thompson, and Cal Winslow (eds.), *Albion's Fatal Tree*. New York: Pantheon.

Heller, Bill. (2005). *After the Finish Line: The Race to End Horse Slaughter in America*. Irvine, CA: Bow Tie Press.

Hensley, Christopher, Suzanne E. Tallichet, and Stephen D. Singer. (2006). "Exploring the Possible Link between Childhood and Adolescent Bestiality and Interpersonal Violence." *Journal of Interpersonal Violence* 21(7):910–23.

Hill, George. (1877). *An Historical Account of the Plantation in Ulster at the Commencement of the Seventeenth Century, 1608–1620*. Belfast: McCaw, Stevenson and Orr.

Hindle, Steve. (2000). *The State and Social Change in Early Modern England, 1550–1640*. New York: St. Martin's Press.

Hindley, Myra. (1995). "The Moors Murderess." *The Guardian*, December 18.

Hittite Laws. [ca. 3500 B.P.] (1951). Translated by E. Neufeld. London: Luzac & Co.

Hollander, Xaviera. (1972). *The Happy Hooker*. New York: Dell.

Holmes, Ronald M. (1991). *Sex Crimes*. Newbury Park, CA: Sage.

Horowitz, Roger. (2008). "That Was a Dirty Job! Technology and Workplace Hazards in Meatpacking over the Long Twentieth Century." *Labor* 5(2):13–25.

Hunter, Mic. (1990). *Abused Boys: The Neglected Victims of Sexual Abuse*. New York: Lexington.

Innes, Stephen. (1983). *Labor in a New Land: Economy and Society in Seventeenth-Century Springfield*. Princeton, NJ: Princeton University Press.

———. (1995). *Creating the Commonwealth: The Economic Culture of Puritan New England*. New York: Norton.

International Association of Chiefs of Police. (1989). "Cruelty to Animals and Human Violence." Training Key No. 392: IACP.

Itzin, Catherine. (1997). "Pornography and the Organization of Intra- and Extra-Familial Child Sexual Abuse." Pp. 58–79 in Glenda Kaufman Kantor and Jana L. Jasinski (eds.), *Out of the Darkness: Contemporary Perspectives on Family Violence*. Thousand Oaks, CA: Sage.

Jackson, Clare. (2003). *Restoration Scotland, 1660–1690: Royalist Politics, Religion and Ideas*. Woodbridge: Boydell Press.

Jasper, James M., and Dorothy Nelkin. (1992). *The Animal Rights Crusade*. New York: Free Press.

Kamensky, Jane. (1992). "Words, Witches and Woman Trouble: Witchcraft, Disorderly Speech, and Gender Boundaries in Puritan New England." *Essex Institute Historical Collections* 128(4):286–306.

Kearney, Hugh F. [1959] (1989). *Strafford in Ireland 1633–41*. Manchester: Manchester University Press.

Kelley, Susan J. (1989). "Stress Responses of Children to Sexual Abuse and Ritualistic Abuse in Day Care Centers." *Journal of Interpersonal Violence* 4(4):502–13.

Kelly, Fergus. (2000). *Early Irish Farming*. Dundalk: Dublin Institute for Advanced Studies/Dundalgan Press.

Kinsey, Alfred C., Wardell B. Pomeroy, and Clyde E. Martin. (1948). *Sexual Behavior in the Human Male*. Philadelphia: W. B. Saunders.

Kinsey, Alfred C., Wardell B. Pomeroy, Clyde E. Martin, and Paul H. Gebhard. (1953). *Sexual Behavior in the Human Female*. Philadelphia: Saunders.

Knowles, James. (2004). "Can Ye Not Tell a Man from a Marmoset?" Pp.138-163 in Erica Fudge (ed.), *Renaissance Beasts: Of Animals, Humans, and Other Wonderful Creatures*. Urbana: University of Illinois Press.

Konig, David Thomas. (1979). *Law and Society in Puritan Massachusetts: Essex County, 1629–1692*. Chapel Hill: University of North Carolina Press.

Krafft-Ebing, Richard von. [1886] (1978). *Psychopathia Sexualis*. Translated by Franklin S. Klaf. New York: Stein and Day.

Langevin, R., D. Paitich, B. Orchard, L. Handy, and A. Russon. (1983). "Childhood and Family Background of Killers Seen for Psychiatric Assessment." *Bulletin of the American Academy of Psychiatry and the Law* 11(4):331–41.

Larkin, James F., and Paul L. Hughes (eds.). (1973). *Stuart Royal Proclamations*. Oxford: Clarendon Press.

Larson, Laurence M., ed. (1935). *The Earliest Norwegian Laws*. New York: Columbia University Press.

Lasik, Aleksander. (1998). "Rudolf Höss: Manager of Crime." Pp. 288–300 in Yisrael Gutman and Michael Berenbaum (eds.), *Anatomy of the Auschwitz Death Camp*. Bloomington: Indiana University Press.

Lea, Suzanne R. Goodney. (2007). *Delinquency and Animal Cruelty*. New York: LFB Scholarly Publishing.

Leavitt, Emily Stewart, and Diane Halverson. (1990). "The Evolution of Anti-Cruelty Laws in the United States." Pp. 1–47 in *Animals and Their Legal Rights*. Washington, DC: Animal Welfare Institute.

Levin, Eve. (1989). *Sex and Society in the World of the Orthodox Slavs, 900–1700*. Ithaca, NY: Cornell University Press.

Levin, Jack, and James Alan Fox. (2001). *Dead Lines: Essays in Murder and Mayhem*. Needham Heights, MA: Allyn and Bacon.

Levy, Neil. (2003). "What (if Anything) Is Wrong with Bestiality?" *Journal of Social Philosophy* 34(3):444–456.

Liliequist, Jonas. (1991). "Peasants against Nature: Crossing the Boundaries between Man and Animal in Seventeenth- and Eighteenth-Century Sweden." *Journal of the History of Sexuality* 1(3):393–423.

Linebaugh, Kate. (2005). "On a Hong Kong Trail, a Serial Dog Slayer Terrorizes Pet Owners." *Wall Street Journal* (Eastern ed.), October 27, p. A1.

Lithgow, William. [1632] (1906). *The Totall Discourse of the Rare Adventures and Painefull Peregrinations*. London: James MacLehose & Sons.

Lovelace, Linda, with Mike McGrady. (1980). *Ordeal*. New York: Bell.

Lucas, A. T. (1973). "Irish Ploughing Practices." *Tools and Tillage* 2(1):67–83.

Lund, Thomas A. (1975). "British Wildlife Law before the American Revolution: Lessons from the Past." *Michigan Law Review* 74(1):49–74.

Lynch, Michael J., and Paul Stretesky. (2007). "Green Criminology in the United States." Pp. 248–69 in Piers Beirne and Nigel South (eds.), *Issues in Green Criminology*. Cullompton: Willan.

Macaulay, T. B. [1848] (1899). *History of England*. 10 vols. Boston: Houghton Mifflin.

MacLysaght, Edward. (1979). *Irish Life in the Seventeenth Century*. Dublin: Irish Academic Press.

Malcolmson, Robert W. (1973). *Popular Recreations in English Society 1700–1850*. Cambridge: Cambridge University Press.

Markham, Gervase. (1607). *Cavelarice, or the English Horseman: Contayning All the Arte of Horse-manship, As Much As Is Necessary for Any Man to Understand*. London: Edward Allde and W. Jaggard (bk. 1) and Edward White (bks. 2–7), in 1 vol.

———. [1613] (1982). *The English Husbandman*. New York: Garland.

———. [1625] (1974). *The Souldiers Exercise: In Three Bookes*. Amsterdam: Walter J. Johnson.

———. [1625] (1973) *The Inrichment of the Weald of Kent: Or, A Direction to the Husbandman*. Amsterdam: Theatrum Orbis Terrarum.

Mascal, Leonard. (1590). *A Book of Engines. A Booke of Engines and Traps to take Polcats, Buzardes, Rattes, Mice and all other kindes of Vermin and Beasts Whatsoever, most profitable for all Warriners, and such as delight in this kind of sport and pastime.* London: John Wolfe.

———. (1620). *The Government of Cattel.* London: "T.S."

Mason, Jim. (1993). *An Unnatural Order: Uncovering the Roots of Our Domination of Nature and Each Other.* New York: Simon and Schuster.

Mather, Cotton. (1708). "Tribute to Ezekiel Cheever." Pp. 21–31 in *Old South Leaflets,* vol. 8. Boston: Old South Meeting House.

Matthews, Mark. (1994). *The Horseman: Obsessions of a Zoophile.* Amherst, NY: Prometheus.

Maxwell-Stuart, P. G. (2002). "'Wild, Filthie, Execrabill, Detestabill, and Unnatural Sin': Bestiality in Early Modern Scotland." Pp. 82–93 in Tom Betteridge (ed.), *Sodomy in Early Modern Europe.* Manchester: Manchester University Press.

May, Robert. (1685). *The Accomplisht Cook, or the Art and Mystery of Cooking.* London: Obadiah Blagrave.

McAuliffe, J. J. (1943). "Ploughing by Horses' Tails." *The Irish Book Lover* 29(1):9–11.

McCavitt, John. (1998). *Sir Arthur Chichester: Lord Deputy of Ireland 1605–1616.* Belfast: Institute of Irish Studies.

McFarlane, J., J. Campbell, S. Wilt, C. Sachs, Y. Ulrich, and X. Xu. (1999). "Stalking and Intimate Partner Femicide." *Homicide Studies* 3(4):300–316.

McManus, Edgar J. (1993). *Laws and Liberty in Early New England: Criminal Justice and Due Process, 1620–1692.* Amherst: University of Massachusetts Press.

McNeill, John T., and Helena M. Gamer. (1938). *Medieval Handbooks of Penance.* New York: Columbia University Press.

McRae, Andrew. (1996). *God Speed the Plough: The Representation of Agrarian England, 1500–1660.* Cambridge: Cambridge University Press.

Menard, Scott, and Delbert Elliott. (1990). "Longitudinal and Cross-Sectional Data Collection in the Study of Crime and Delinquency." *Justice Quarterly* 7(1):11–55.

Merritt, J. F. (1996). "Power and Communication: Thomas Wentworth and Government at a Distance during the Personal Rule, 1629–1635." Pp. 109–32 in J. F. Merritt (ed.), *The Political World of Thomas Wentworth Earl of Strafford 1621–1641.* Cambridge: Cambridge University Press.

Merz-Perez, Linda, and Kathleen M. Heide. (2004). *Animal Cruelty: Pathway to Violence against People.* Walnut Creek, CA: AltaMira Press.

Merz-Perez, Linda, Kathleen M. Heide, and Ira J. Silverman. (2001). "Childhood Cruelty to Animals and Subsequent Violence against Humans." *International Journal of Offender Therapy and Comparative Criminology* 45(5):556–73.

Messerschmidt, James W. (1993). *Masculinities and Crime: Critique and Reconceptualization of Theory.* Lanham, MD: Rowman & Littlefield.

Miletski, H. (2001). "Zoophilia—Implications for Therapy." *Journal of Sex Education and Therapy* 26(2):85–89.

Milgrom, Jacob. (2000). *Leviticus 17–22*. New York: Doubleday.

Mill, John Stuart. [1825] (1925). "A Hitherto Unprinted Speech on the Influence of Lawyers." *Economica* 13(1):1–6.

Miller, Hugh. (1850). *Scenes and Legends of North Scotland*. Edinburgh: T. Constable.

Miller, Karla S., and John F. Knutson. (1997). "Reports of Severe Physical Punishment and Exposure to Animal Cruelty by Inmates Convicted of Felonies and by University Students." *Child Abuse and Neglect* 21(1):59–82.

Mills, David. (1998). *Recycling the Cycle: The City of Chester and Its Whitsun Plays*. Toronto: University of Toronto Press.

Milton, John. (1649). "Observations on the Articles of Peace, 1649." Pp. 1049–73 in Merritt Hughes (ed.), *The Complete Prose Works of John Milton*, vol. 3. New Haven. CT: Yale University Press.

———. [1667] (1935). *Paradise Lost*. New York: The Odyssey Press.

Montaigne, Michel de. [1580] (1910). "Cruelty." Pp. 162–93 in Charles Cotton (trans.), *Essays of Montaigne*, vol. 4. New York: Edwin C. Hill.

———. [1576] (1967). *Apology for Raymond Sebond*. Paris: Gallimard.

Monter, E. William. (1980). "Sodomy and Heresy in Early Modern Switzerland." *Journal of Homosexuality* 6(1/2):41–55.

———. (1990). *Frontiers of Heresy: the Spanish Inquisition from the Basque Lands to Sicily*. Cambridge: Cambridge University Press.

Moody, T. W. (1939). *The Londonderry Plantation 1609–41*. Belfast: William Mullen and Son.

Morison, Samuel Eliot. [1930] (1958). *Builders of the Bay Colony*. Boston: Houghton Mifflin.

———. (1933). "Introduction." Pp. xvii–xciv in *Records of the Suffolk County Court 1671–1680*. Boston: Colonial Society of Massachusetts.

Morris, Polly. (1989). "Sodomy and Male Honor: The Case of Somerset, 1740–1850." *Journal of Homosexuality* 16(1):383–406.

Moryson, Fynes. [1617] (1998). *Itinerary*. Reprinted (bk. 2, chap. 5) as *The Irish Sections of Fynes Moryson's Unpublished Itinerary*. Edited by Graham Kew. Dublin: Irish Manuscripts Commission.

Munro, Helen, and M. V. Thrusfield. (2001). "Battered Pets: Features That Raise Suspicion of Non-Accidental Injury." *Journal of Small Animal Practice* 42:218–26.

———. (2005). "'Battered Pets': Sexual Abuse." Pp. 23–45 in Andrea M. Beetz and Anthony L. Podberscek (eds.), *Bestiality and Zoophilia*. West Lafayette, IN: Purdue University Press.

Munro, Lyle. (2005). *Confronting Cruelty*. Leiden: Brill Academic Publishers.

Murrin, John M. (2002). "Things Fearful to Name: Bestiality in Early America." Pp. 115–56 in Angela N. H. Creager and William Chester Jordan (eds.), *The Animal/Human Boundary*. Rochester, NY: Rochester University Press.

Nagaraja, J. (1983). "Sexual Problems in Adolescence." *Child Psychiatry Quarterly* 16:9–18.

Nibert, David. (2002). *Animal Rights/Human Rights: Entanglements of Oppression and Liberation.* Lanham, MD: Rowman & Littlefield.

Noske, Barbara. (1997). *Beyond Boundaries: Humans and Other Animals.* Montreal: Black Rose Books.

Oates, Caroline. (1989). "Metamorphosis and Lycanthropy in Franche-Comté, 1521–1643." Pp. 304–63 in Michel Feher (ed)., *Fragments for a History of the Human Body,* pt. 1. New York: Urzone.

O'Brien, George. (1919). *The Economic History of Ireland in the Seventeenth Century.* Dublin: Maunsel.

O'Donovan, John. (1858). "Notes." *Ulster Journal of Archaeology* 6:133–35.

O'Hearn, Denis. (2005). "Ireland in the Atlantic Economy." Pp. 3–26 in Terrence McDonough (ed.), *Was Ireland a Colony?* Dublin: Irish Academic Press.

Ó Siechrú, Micheál. (1999). *Confederate Ireland 1642–1649.* Dublin: Four Courts Press.

Osborough, W. N. (1995). "Introduction." Pp. A–U in *The Irish Statutes, 3 Edward II to the Union AD 1310–1800.* Dublin: Round Hall Press.

Parker, Graham. (1986). "Is a Duck an Animal? An Exploration of Bestiality as a Crime." *Criminal Justice History* 7:95–109.

Paul, Elizabeth S. (2000). "Empathy with Animals and with Humans: Are They Linked?" *Anthrozoös* 13(4):194–202.

Petersen, Marie Louise, and David P. Farrington (2007). "Cruelty to Animals and Violence to People." *Victims and Offenders* 2(1):21–43.

Philp, Robert Kemp. (1859). *The History of Progress in Great Britain.* London: Houlston and Wright.

Pierson, Melissa Holbrook. (2000). *Dark Horses and Black Beauties.* New York: Norton.

Pinkerton, W. (1858). "Ploughing by the Horse's Tail." *Ulster Journal of Archaeology* 6:212–21.

Quilligan, Maureen. (1983). *Milton's Spenser: The Politics of Reading.* Ithaca, NY: Cornell University Press.

Radford, M. (2005). *Animal Welfare Law in Britain: Regulation and Responsibility.* Oxford: Oxford University Press.

Randal, Jonathan, and Nora Boustany. (1990). "Children of War in Lebanon." Pp. 59–82 in Caroline Moorehead (ed.), *Betrayal: A Report on Violence toward Children in Today's World.* Garden City, NY: Doubleday.

Rarick, Gina. (2007). "I'm Not Barbaro, for Lots of Reasons." *Boston Globe,* February 4.

Rawlinson, John. (1612). *Mercy to a Beast: Sermon Preached at Saint Maries Spittle in London.* Oxford: Joseph Barnes.

Raymond, Joad. (2004). "Complications of Interest: Milton, Scotland, Ireland, and National Identity in 1649." *Review of English Studies* 55(220):315–45.

Record Commissioners of the City of Boston. (1877). *Second Report, 1634–1661.* Boston: Rockwell and Churchill.

Records of the Colony and Plantation of New Haven. [1641] (1857). Edited by Charles J. Hoadly. Hartford, CT: Case, Tiffany.

"Records of the Court of Assistants, 1641–1644." (1890). Pp. xxv–xliii in William H. Whitmore (ed.), *Laws of the Massachusetts Colony, from 1630 to 1686: A Bibliographical Sketch.* Boston: Rockwell and Churchill.

Records of the Court of Assistants. Colony of the Massachusetts Bay. 1630–1692. (1901). Vol. 1. Boston: County of Suffolk.

Records and Files of the Quarterly Courts of Essex County Massachusetts (1911–1913). 8 vols. Edited by George Dow. Salem, MA: Essex Institute.

Records of the Governor and Company of the Massachusetts Bay in New England. (1853). Edited by Nathaniel B. Shurtleff. 5 vols. Boston: William White Press.

Regan, Tom. (1983). *The Case for Animal Rights.* Berkeley: University of California Press.

———. (2007). "Vivisection: The Case for Abolition." Pp. 114–39 in Piers Beirne and Nigel South (eds.), *Issues in Green Criminology.* Cullompton: Willan.

Renzetti, Claire. (1992). *Violent Betrayal: Partner Abuse in Lesbian Relationships.* Newbury Park, CA: Sage.

Rhoden, William C. (2006). "Witnessing an Unknown Filly's Death." *New York Times,* May 25, p. C16.

Rich, Barnabe. (1610). *A New Description of Ireland.* London: Thomas Adams.

Rivière, Pierre. [1835] (1975). "The Memoir." Pp. 53–121 in Michel Foucault (ed.), *I, Pierre Rivière, having slaughtered my mother, my sister, and my brother . . .* Translated by Frank Jellinek. Lincoln: University of Nebraska Press.

Robertson, Roger. (1792). "Observations and Facts concerning the Breed of Horses in Scotland in Ancient Times." *Archaeoolgia Scotica: Transactions of the Society of Antiquaries of Scotland* 1:272–81.

Robinson, Philip. (2000). *The Plantation of Ulster: British Settlement in an Irish Landscape 1600–1670.* Belfast: Ulster Historical Foundation.

Russell, Jeffrey Burton. (1982). *A History of Witchcraft.* New York: Thames and Hudson.

Ryder, Richard D. (1979). "The Struggle against Speciesism." Pp. 3–14 in David Paterson and Richard D. Ryder (eds.), *Animals' Rights—A Symposium.* Fontwell: Centaur Press.

———. (1989). *Animal Revolution: Changing Attitudes towards Speciesism.* Oxford: Basil Blackwell.

Rydström, Jens. (2003). *Sinners and Citizens: Bestiality and Homosexuality in Sweden, 1880–1950.* Chicago: University of Chicago Press.

Sack, Kevin. (1997). "Grim Details Emerge in Teen-Age Slaying Case." *New York Times,* October 15, p. A10.

Salisbury, Joyce. (1994). *The Beast Within: Animals in the Middle Ages.* New York: Routledge.

Santillo, Pekka, and Jaana Haapasalo. (2001). "Neurological and Psychological Risk Factors among Young Homicidal, Violent and Nonviolent Offenders in Finland." *Homicide Studies* 1(3):234–53.

Sauder, Joseph. (2000). "Enacting and Enforcing Felony Animal Cruelty Laws to Prevent Violence against Humans." *Animal Law* 6:1–21.

Saunders, K. (1996). "What's So Grand about the National?" *Wildlife Guardian* 34(summer):8.

Schofield, Michael. (1971). *The Strange Case of Pot*. Harmondsworth: Pelican.

Schurman-Kauflin, Deborah. (2000). *The New Predator: Women Who Kill*. New York: Algora.

Schweber, Howard. (1998). "Ordering Principles: The Adjudication of Criminal Cases in Puritan Massachusetts, 1629–1650." *Law & Society Review* 32(2):367–408.

Semonin, Paul. (1996) "Monsters in the Marketplace: The Exhibition of Human Oddities in Early Modern England." Pp. 69–81 in Rosemarie Garland Thomson (ed.), *Freakery: Cultural Spectacles of the Extraordinary Body*. New York: New York University Press.

Serpell, J. A., and E. S. Paul. (1994). "Pets and the Development of Positive Attitudes to Animals." Pp. 127–44 in A. Manning and J. Serpell (eds.), *Animals and Human Society: Changing Perspectives*. London: Routledge.

Shaffer, Jennifer N., and R. Barry Ruback. (2002). *Violent Victimization as a Risk Factor for Violent Offending among Juveniles* (NCJ no. 195737). Washington, DC: U.S. Department of Justice.

Shaffer, Peter. (1973). *Equus*. London: Samuel French.

Sharpe, Andrew N. (2007). "Structured Like a Monster: Understanding Human Difference through a Legal Category." *Law and Critique* 18(2):207-228.

Sharpe, J. A. (1983). *Crime in Seventeenth-Century England*. Cambridge: Cambridge University Press.

Shea, William R., and Mariano Artigas. (2003). *Galileo in Rome: The Rise and Fall of a Troublesome Genius*. New York: Oxford University Press.

Simon, David R. (2006). *Elite Deviance*. Boston: Pearson.

Singer, Peter. [1975] (1990a). *Animal Liberation*. New York: Avon.

———. (1990b). "The Significance of Animal Suffering." *Behavioral and Brain Sciences* 13(1):9–12.

———. (2001a). "Clarification [of] the Circumstances and Intent of [My] Review of Midas Dekkers' Book *Dearest Pet*." Princeton University press release, April 14.

———. (2001b). "Heavy Petting." *Nerve*, March/April, available at http://www.nerve.com/Opinions/Singer/heavyPetting.

Smith, Joseph H. (1961). "Introduction: Criminal Jurisdiction." Pp. 103–28 in *Colonial Justice in Western Massachusetts, 1639–1702: The Pynchon Court Record*. Cambridge, MA: Harvard University Press.

Solot, Dorian. (1997). "Untangling the Animal Abuse Web." *Society & Animals* 5(3):257–65.

South, Nigel, and Piers Beirne. (2007). "Introduction to Green Criminology." Pp. xiii–xxvii in Piers Beirne and Nigel South (eds.), *Green Criminology*. Aldershot: Ashgate.

Spenser, Edmund. [1633] (1997). *A View of the Present State of Ireland*. Edited by W. L. Renwick. Oxford: Clarendon.

Story, M. D. (1982). "A Comparison of University Student Experience with Various Sexual Outlets in 1974 and 1980." *Adolescence* 17:737–47.

Tannenbaum, Jerrold. (1995). "Animals and the Law: Property, Cruelty, Rights." *Social Research* 62(3):539–607.

Tester, Keith. (1991). *Animals and Society: The Humanity of Animal Rights*. London: Routledge.

Thomas, Keith. (1983). *Man and the Natural World: Changing Attitudes in England 1500–1800*. Oxford: Oxford University Press.

Thompson, Kelly L., and Eleonora Gullone. (2006). "An Investigation into the Association between the Witnessing of Animal Abuse and Adolescents' Behavior toward Animals." *Society & Animals* 14(3):221–43.

Thompson, Roger. (1986). *Sex in Middlesex: Popular Mores in a Massachusetts County, 1649–1699*. Amherst: University of Massachusetts Press.

Tingle, David, George W. Barnard, Lynn Robbins, Gustave Newman, and David Hutchinson. (1986). "Childhood and Adolescent Characteristics of Pedophiles and Rapists." *International Journal of Law and Psychiatry* 9:103–16.

Treadwell, Victor. (1998). *Buckingham and Ireland, 1616–1628: A Study in Anglo-Irish Politics*. Dublin: Four Courts Press.

———, ed. (2006). *Irish Commission of 1622: An Investigation of the Irish Administration, 1615–1622, and Its Consequences, 1623–1624*. Dublin: Irish Manuscripts Commission.

U.S. Department of Agriculture. (2006a). "Livestock Slaughter: 2005 Summary." National Agricultural Statistics Service (USDA data for "red meat" slaughtered are available at http://usda.mannlib.cornell.edu/usda/current/LiveSlauSu/LiveSlau).

———. (2006b). "Poultry Slaughter: 2005 Annual Summary." National Agricultural Statistics Service (USDA data for slaughtered poultry are available at http://usda.mannlib.cornell.edu/usda/current/PoulSlauSu).

Vecsey, George. (2006). "The Psychic Pull of an Injured Racehorse." *New York Times*, May, 24, p. C16.

Watson, Katherine D. (2006). "Medical and Chemical Expertise in English Trials for Criminal Poisoning, 1750–1914." *Medical History* 50(3):373–90.

Wedgwood, C. V. (1961). *Thomas Wentworth, First Earl of Strafford, 1593–1641: A Revaluation*. London: Jonathan Cape.

Westen, Peter K. (2004). *The Logic of Consent: The Diversity and Deceptiveness of Consent as a Defense to Criminal Conduct*. Burlington, VT: Ashgate.

White, Kenneth. (1992). "The Shape of Cruelty." *The Latham Letter* 13(3):9-10.

White, Rob. (2007). "Green Criminology and the Pursuit of Social and Ecological Justice." Pp. 32–54 in Piers Beirne and Nigel South (eds.), *Issues in Green Criminology*. Cullompton: Willan.

Wiehe, Vernon R. (1990). *Sibling Abuse*. Lexington, MA: Lexington Books.

Williams, Colin J., and Martin S. Weinberg. (2003). "Zoophilia in Men: A Study of Sexual Interest in Animals." *Archives of Sexual Behavior* 32(6):523–35.

Winthrop, John. (1629). "Reasons to be Considered, and Objections with Answers." *Winthrop Papers* 2:138–145.

———. [1650] (1790). *A Journal, 1630–1644*. Hartford, CT: Elisha Babcock.

Wise, Steven M. (2000). *Rattling the Cage: Toward Legal Rights for Animals*. Cambridge, MA: Perseus Books.

Wolfe, Jason. (2000). "Suspect's Death Holds Promise of Closure."

Wood, G. (1995). "Flogging a Live Horse: The Hidden Trade in Neglect." *Independent*, February 15.

Wright, Jeremy, and Christopher Hanley. (2003). "From Animal Cruelty to Serial Murder: Applying the Graduation Hypothesis."

Wrightson, Keith. (1982). *English Society 1580–1680*. London: Hutchinson.

Yates, Roger. (2003). "Developing the Sociology of Animal Abuse." PhD diss., University of Wales.

Yates, Roger, Chris Powell, and Piers Beirne (2001). "Horse Maiming in the English Countryside: Moral Panic, Human Deviance, and the Social Construction of Victimhood." *Society & Animals* 9(1):1–23.

Young, Arthur. [1780] (1892). *Tour in Ireland*. London: George Bell and Sons.

Zilney, Lisa Anne. (2007). *Linking Animal Cruelty and Animal Violence*. Youngstown, NY: Cambria Press.

Index

About the Author

Piers Beirne is professor of sociology and legal studies at the University of Southern Maine. He has pioneered scholarship in the developing field of criminology and animal rights.